THE HUMAN RIGHTS CRISIS IN KASHMIR

PREVIOUSLY PUBLISHED REPORTS ON INDIA AVAILABLE
FROM HUMAN RIGHTS WATCH

Rape in Kashmir: A Crime of War
No End in Sight: Human Rights Violations in Assam
The Crackdown in Kashmir: Torture of Detainees and Assaults on the Medical Community
Police Killings and Rural Violence in Andhra Pradesh
Before the Deluge: Human Rights Abuses at India's Narmada Dam
Encounter in Pilibhit: Summary Executions of Sikhs
Punjab in Crisis
Kashmir under Siege
Prison Conditions in India

THE HUMAN RIGHTS CRISIS IN KASHMIR

A Pattern of Impunity

Asia Watch
A Division of Human Rights Watch

Physicians for Human Rights

Human Rights Watch
New York • Washington • Los Angeles • London

Copyright © June 1993 by Human Rights Watch and Physicians for Human Rights
All rights reserved.
Printed in the United States of America.

ISBN 1-56432-104-5
Library of Congress Catalogue Number 93-78901

Cover design by Robert Kimzey.

Cover photo: Masroof Sultan, a 19-year-old college student, who was taken into custody on April 8, 1993, by Border Security Force troops, beaten and tortured with electric shock and then taken to a field where he was shot and left for dead. Photo copyright © Klaus Holsting, April 1993.

Asia Watch was founded in 1985 to monitor and promote internationally recognized human rights in Asia. The Chair is Jack Greenberg and the Vice Chair is Orville Schell. Sidney Jones is Executive Director. Mike Jendrzejczyk is Washington Representative. Therese Caouette, Patricia Gossman, Jeannine Guthrie and Robin Munro are Research Associates. Grace Oboma-Layat and Vicki Shu are Associates, and Mickey Spiegel is Research Consultant.

Asia Watch is a division of Human Rights Watch, which also includes Africa Watch, Americas Watch Helsinki Watch, Middle East Watch and the Fund for Free Expression. The Chair of Human Rights Watch is Robert L. Bernstein and the Vice Chair is Adrian DeWind. Kenneth Roth is the Acting Executive Director

Physicians for Human Rights (PHR) is an organization of physicians and other health professionals that brings the knowledge and skills of the medical sciences to the investigation and prevention of violations of international human rights and humanitarian laws. Since its founding in 1989, it has conducted over forty missions concerning over twenty-five countries.

Physicians for Human Rights works to apply the special skills of health professionals to stop torture, "disappearances" and political killings by governments and opposition groups; to report on conditions and protection of detainees in prisons and refugee camps; to investigate the physical and psychological consequences of violations of humanitarian law and medical ethics in internal and international conflicts; to defend the right of civilians and combatants to receive medical care during times of war; to protect health professionals who are victims of human rights abuses and to prevent physician complicity in torture and other human rights abuses.

Physicians for Human Rights adheres to a policy of strict impartiality and is concerned with the medical abuses regardless of the ideology of the offending government or group. The President of the Board of Directors is H. Jack Geiger, M.D.; the Vice President is Carola Eisenberg, M.D.; Eric Stover is the Executive Director; Susannah is Deputy Director; Shana Swiss, M.D. is Director of the Women's Program; Barbara Ayotte is Senior Program Associate; and Gina VanderLoop is Development Director. Physicians for Human Rights is located at 100 Boylston Street, #702, Boston, MA 02116, USA; Tel: (617) 695-0041; Fax: (617) 695-0307.

HUMAN RIGHTS WATCH

Human Rights Watch conducts regular, systematic investigations of human rights abuses in some sixty countries around the world. It addresses the human rights practices of governments of all political stripes, of all geopolitical alignments, and of all ethnic and religious persuasions. In internal wars it documents violations by both governments and rebel groups. Human Rights Watch defends freedom of thought and expression, due process of law and equal protection of the law; it documents and denounces murders, disappearances, torture, arbitrary imprisonment, exile, censorship and other abuses of internationally recognized human rights.

Human Rights Watch began in 1978 with the founding of Helsinki Watch by a group of publishers, lawyers and other activists and now maintains offices in New York, Washington, D.C., Los Angeles, London, Moscow, Belgrade, Zagreb and Hong Kong. Today, it includes Africa Watch, Americas Watch, Asia Watch, Helsinki Watch, Middle East Watch, the Fund for Free Expression and three collaborative projects, the Arms Project, Prison Project and Women's Rights Project. Human Rights Watch is an independent, nongovernmental organization, supported by contributions from private individuals and foundations. It accepts no government funds, directly or indirectly.

The executive committee includes Robert L. Bernstein, chair; Adrian W. DeWind, vice chair; Roland Algrant, Lisa Anderson, Peter D. Bell, Alice Brown, William Carmichael, Dorothy Cullman, Irene Diamond, Jonathan Fanton, Jack Greenberg, Alice H. Henkin, Stephen L. Kass, Marina Pinto Kaufman, Alexander MacGregor, Bruce Rabb, Orville Schell, Gary Sick, Malcolm Smith and Robert Wedgeworth.

The staff includes Kenneth Roth, acting executive director; Holly J. Burkhalter, Washington director; Gara LaMarche, associate director; Susan Osnos, press director; Ellen Lutz, California director; Jemera Rone, counsel; Stephanie Steele, operations director; Michal Longfelder, development director; Allyson Collins, research associate; Joanna Weschler, Prison Project director; Kenneth Anderson, Arms Project director; and Dorothy Q. Thomas, Women's Rights Project director.

The executive directors of the divisions of Human Rights Watch are Abdullahi An-Na'im, Africa Watch; Juan E. Méndez, Americas Watch; Sidney Jones, Asia Watch; Jeri Laber, Helsinki Watch; Andrew Whitley, Middle East Watch; and Gara LaMarche, the Fund for Free Expression.

Addresses for Human Rights Watch
485 Fifth Avenue
New York, NY 10017-6104
Tel: (212) 972-8400
Fax: (212) 972-0905
email: hrwatchnyu@igc.org

1522 K Street, N.W., #910
Washington, DC 20005
Tel: (202) 371-6592
Fax: (202) 371-0124
email: hrwatchdc@igc.org

10951 West Pico Blvd., #203
Los Angeles, CA 90064
Tel: (310) 475-3070
Fax: (310) 475-5613
email: hrwatchla@igc.org

90 Borough High Street
London, UK SE1 1LL
Tel: (071) 378-8008
Fax: (071) 378-8029
email: africawatch@gn.org

Torture 86
   Torture Victims with Acute Renal Failure [Rhabdomyolysis] 91
   Additional Torture Cases 92
Rape by Indian Government Forces in Kashmir 95
   A Pattern of Impunity 97
      Rape in Shopian 101
      Rape in Haran 107
      Rape in Gurihakhar 108
Indiscriminate Attacks and Assaults on Civilians 109
   Assaults on Journalists 111
Violations of Medical Neutrality by Government Forces 112
   Preventing Medical Personnel from Transporting the Wounded 113
   Refusal by Security Forces to Provide or Permit Medical Care for Wounded 116
   Raids on Hospitals 118
   Detentions, Harassment and Assaults on Health Care Workers 120
Other Medical Consequences of the Conflict 125
The Government's Comments and Asia Watch/PHR's Response 129

V. THE MURDER OF H.N. WANCHOO 137

VI. THE KILLING OF DR. ABDUL AHAD GURU 141

VII. VIOLATIONS BY MILITANT ORGANIZATIONS 147
Militant Operations 149
The Pakistan Conduit 150
Executions of Civilians and Other Non-Combatants 153
   Summary Executions and Other Abuses Against Accused Informers 155
Summary Executions of Captured Security Force Personnel .. 159
Rape by Militant Groups 160
Kidnapping 163
Indiscriminate Attacks 164
Threats 166
   Threats and Assaults on Journalists 166
   Threats Against the Hindu Minority 168
Violations of Medical Neutrality by Militant Groups 171

VIII. CONCLUSIONS AND RECOMMENDATIONS 174

APPENDIX A: Disappearances 178

APPENDIX B: The Code of Medical Neutrality 189

APPENDIX C: The Comments of the Government of India 190

ACKNOWLEDGMENTS

This report was written by Patricia Gossman, research associate for Asia Watch. It is based on research undertaken in Kashmir in October 1992 by Ms. Gossman and Vincent Iacopino, M.D., a consultant to Physicians for Human Rights and Medical Director of Survivors International of Northern California, and on further research by James A. Goldston, an attorney, in April and May 1993. This second mission was carried out in coordination with Jens Noerbaek of Physicians for Human Rights-Denmark. The report was edited by Sidney Jones, Executive Director of Asia Watch, and Holly Burkhalter, Washington Director of Human Rights Watch. It was reviewed by Dr. Iacopino and Mr. Goldston, and by Susannah Sirkin, Barbara Ayotte, Richard Claude, Robert Cook-Deegan M.D. and Hurst Hannum of Physicians for Human Rights. Dorothy Q. Thomas, Director of Human Rights Watch's Women's Rights Project, and Shana Swiss, M.D., Director of the Women's Program for Physicians for Human Rights, provided expert advice. Ken Anderson, Director of Human Rights Watch's Arms Project, contributed to Chapter III. Vicki Shu, Asia Watch Associate, assisted in preparing the final manuscript.

Asia Watch and Physicians for Human Rights are grateful to the many people in Kashmir who assisted them in interviewing individuals and families and gathering crucial medical and legal documentation for this report. We would especially like to thank members of the human rights and medical communities who generously provided us with access to their records, documents, patients and facilities. We would also like to thank members of the press and legal community who helped us understand the violence that has devastated Kashmir. To those who undertook great risk in speaking to us in confidence, we are especially grateful.

I. INTRODUCTION

Since early 1990, the valley of Kashmir[1] in the north Indian state of Jammu and Kashmir has been the site of a vicious conflict between Indian security forces and Muslim insurgents demanding independence or accession to Pakistan. In their efforts to crush the insurgency, Indian forces in Kashmir have engaged in massive human rights violations, including extrajudicial executions, rape, torture and deliberate assaults on health care workers. Armed insurgent groups have murdered Hindu and Muslim civilians, summarily executed persons in their custody and have commited rape, assault, kidnapping and indiscriminate attacks which have injured and killed civilians. In late 1992 and early 1993, human rights conditions further deteriorated as Indian troops embarked on a "catch and kill" campaign against suspected militants. Since then, summary executions of detainees by security forces have sharply increased. In October 1992, Asia Watch and Physicians for Human Rights (PHR) sent a delegation to Kashmir to document human rights abuses and violations of the laws of war by Indian security forces and by militant forces. Following the upsurge in violent reprisals against civilians and attacks on human rights activists in late 1992 and early 1993, Asia Watch sent a second mission to Kashmir in April and May 1993, in cooperation with Physicians for Human Rights-Denmark.

The conflict in Kashmir, which has its origins in the state's disputed accession to India in 1947, erupted in December 1989 when Indian government troops launched a brutal crackdown on rising violence by armed militant groups in the predominantly Muslim Kashmir valley. From the outset, that crackdown was marked by brutality against civilians, including the shooting of unarmed demonstrators, civilian massacres and summary executions of detainees. At the same time, militant groups -- who received arms and training from Pakistan -- stepped up their attacks, murdering and threatening Hindu residents, carrying out kidnappings and assassinations of government officials, civil servants and suspected informers and engaging in sabotage and bombings. In the three and a

---

[1] The valley of Kashmir lies between the Pir Panjal and Karakoram mountain ranges. The term refers to the area that includes the towns and villages along the Jhelum river, from Handwara in the northwest to Anantnag in the southeast.

half years since the conflict began, at least 6,000, and possibly twice that number, have been killed by all sides and well over 100,000, mainly Hindus, have fled the valley. In 1992 alone, at least 2,000 were reported to have been killed -- most of them civilians.[2] Despite the escalation of violence, militant groups continue to command popular support throughout the valley, not necessarily for ideological reasons but because they are seen to represent the only alternative to the government's repressive policies and widespread abuses by the security forces.

In August 1992, Indian government forces launched a new offensive against the militants, called Operation Tiger, a campaign of surprise raids designed to capture and kill suspected militants and terrorize civilian sympathizers. Summary executions of detainees and indiscriminate attacks on civilians escalated during the operation, and during another which followed, called Operation Shiva. Over the next several months, the security forces also engaged in frequent arson attacks, burning houses, shops and entire neighborhoods.

In early 1993, following the massacre of at least 43 civilians by Border Security Force (BSF) troops in the western city of Sopore, the Indian government launched a new initiative, spearheaded by Union Minister of State for Internal Security Rajesh Pilot, to open negotiations toward a political settlement to the conflict and restore the civil administration to the state. Ironically, these efforts met with an upsurge in violence, provoked by hard-line elements in both the government and

---

[2] No precise figure of the number killed is available. The U.S. State Department Country Report for 1990 cites press figures of 1,214 civilians, 189 security forces and 890 militants killed. For 1991, the figures were 900 civilians, 1,305 alleged militants and 155 security forces. For 1992, the figures were 1,106 civilians and 982 militants. However, the figures cannot be considered accurate because official sources cited in such press accounts often describe civilians killed by the security forces as militants. As the Country Report for 1992 notes, many of the alleged militants "died in encounters with security forces or under other suspicious circumstances." See U.S. Department of State, *Country Reports on Human Rights Practices for 1992*, February 1993, p. 1134. In early 1993, press reports citing records maintained by local hospitals, journalists and lawyers reported that more than 12,000 people may have been killed since 1989. See, for example, Molly Moore and John Ward Anderson, "Kashmir's Brutal and Unpublicized War,"*Washington Post*, June 7, 1993.

intelligence agencies and by extremist militant factions. As Prime Minister Rao's administration appeared increasingly divided over its Kashmir policy, human rights conditions in the state worsened dramatically. By mid-1993, human rights groups and journalists in Kashmir reported figures of several hundred executions of detainees since Operation Tiger began.[3] Among those killed was Constable Riaz Ahmed, a Jammu and Kashmir police officer who had been taken into army custody on April 21, 1993, and died apparently as a result of torture that same day. The killing sparked a revolt by almost the entire Jammu and Kashmir police force.[4] State security officials responded by disarming the police and calling in army reinforcements to assume control of security operations in the state. By June 1993, several key political figures had returned to the civil administration. The army, under the command of General Zaki, was reportedly given overall command of all security operations and forces, including the BSF, whose controversial head, Ashok Patel, was transferred out of Kashmir. Whether any of these changes would result in a change in the human rights situation remained to be seen.

The Asia Watch/PHR team which visited Kashmir in October 1992 traveled throughout the Kashmir valley from Srinagar to Handwara and Sopore in the northwest, and Anantnag and Shopian in the southeast. They directly investigated 44 extrajudicial killings, eight cases of torture, and fifteen rapes committed by Indian security forces. In the second

---

[3] For details on these killings, see Chapter IV.

[4] Other Jammu and Kashmir policemen had appealed to Senior Superintendent of Police (SSP) K. Rajendra Kumar to intercede on behalf of Riaz Ahmed, but he refused. According to a press report, Ahmed had been arrested by the Border Security Force and "died in their custody after Kumar had reportedly told them to 'teach Ahmed a lesson.'" See "Kashmiri Police Demand Chief's Dismissal," Agence France Press, April 23, 1993, as cited in the Foreign Broadcast Information Service (FBIS), NES-93-078, April 26, 1993, p. 52. After Ahmed's body was found, officials claimed he had been killed in "cross-fire." See Qaiser Mirza, "Soldiers Disarm Striking Policemen in Srinagar," Associated Press, April 28, 1993. Among the demands of the striking police was that a criminal case be registered against SSP Kumar. The authorities ordered a joint inquiry by the army and police, and Kumar was transferred to Jammu." See "Screening of J-K Policemen Begins," *Times of India*, April 29, 1993.

mission conducted in April and May, 1993, Asia Watch and PHR-Denmark, documented an additional 22 extrajudicial killings and a case of torture and attempted summary execution by the security forces. During both research missions, Asia Watch and PHR interviewed local health professionals, journalists, teachers, human rights activists and lawyers, and reviewed *habeas corpus* petitions, High Court judgments, and medical documents on hundreds of incidents of abuse by the security forces. PHR inspected six health facilities. During visits to three of the major hospitals in Srinagar, the PHR researcher interviewed and examined patients who had been tortured or had suffered injuries as a result of indiscriminate shootings or assaults by government forces. Asia Watch and PHR also interviewed witnesses about incidents of abuse by militant groups. Information about 14 cases of murder, three cases of rape, seven cases of kidnapping, 16 cases of threats and seven incidents of indiscriminate attacks by militant groups are included in this report. In all, Asia Watch and PHR conducted more than 130 interviews with witnesses and other informed sources, including government officials. In most of the cases investigated, testimony was corroborated by multiple witnesses and physical evidence. While many of those interviewed had sympathies with one side or the other in the conflict, the findings contained in this report are based on Asia Watch and PHR's independent selection of cases and witnesses and analysis of eyewitness testimony, medical examinations and other documentation of the incidents described.

This report is the final of a series of three published by Asia Watch and Physicians for Human Rights in 1993. This last incorporates the previous two in their totality,[5] and focuses particularly on the sharp escalation in human rights abuses, particularly summary executions -- "custodial deaths" -- and reprisal killings by Indian paramilitary and military forces in Kashmir during the twelve month period ending June 1993.

Before this report was published, Asia Watch and PHR provided the government of India with details on all of the cases we investigated and requested an official response. The full text of all the comments received as of June 1993 is included in Appendix C. Information that relates to

---

[5] The first report, *The Crackdown in Kashmir: Torture of Detainees and Assaults on the Medical Community*, was released on February 28, 1993. The second, *Rape in Kashmir: A Crime of War*, was released on May 9, 1993.

individual cases and issues is also included in the relevant sections of Chapter IV. Many of the government's comments relate to issues of impunity and access for international organizations. Because these issues are fundamental to any efforts to provide basic human rights protections in Kashmir, we have chosen to highlight them here. The report concludes with a set of specific recommendations for all parties and the international community.

The Pattern of Impunity

In its comments on the Asia Watch/PHR reports, the government has stated that, "*Wherever there is transgression, action has been taken. By now, over the last two years, action has been taken against over 100 personnel of the security forces, and this has involved punishments including imprisonment ranging from less than a month to seven years and various forms of departmental action including suspension pending enquiry in a number of cases.*" Again, in a statement issued after publication of the first Asia Watch/PHR report was published, the government claimed that, "*[W]e do not hesitate to take action against security force personnel where deliberate acts of excesses and cases of gross negligence and over-reaction etc., come to notice. The swift and firm response in the recent unfortunate incident in Sopore would bring this out clearly.*"

While such punishments would be a sign of progress, the Indian government has never responded to queries from Asia Watch and PHR as to the specifics regarding the nature of the abuses, the identity and rank of those responsible for abuses, and what punishments have been ordered in any cases. More important, the government has not made information about these punishments public, a measure absolutely critical if the victims and their families, and the people of Kashmir as a whole are to believe that justice has been done. Local human rights groups in Kashmir have also requested information about any measures taken against security personnel responsible for abuses, but have had no response. Moreover, by not communicating information about such punishments to police and security personnel, the authorities have failed to insure that these measures function as a deterrent against future abuses.

In the case of the Sopore massacre, the investigation into which the government holds up as an example of "swift and firm action", Border Security Force troops went on a rampage and killed at least 43 persons, some of whom died of gunshot wounds, others of whom were burned alive when the troops set fire to their shops and homes. Independent investigations into the incident by human rights groups and international and Indian journalists corroborated eyewitness accounts that BSF forces deliberately opened fire on civilians and set fire to buildings.[6] In its report, the BSF claimed the victims died in "cross-fire." The government ordered a judicial inquiry and the BSF commandant and other officers and constables suspended pending completion of that inquiry. No details of the proceedings or findings have been made public. The significance of the need to prosecute those responsible for the massacre and inform the public of the truth about what happened in Sopore is clear from the fact that, after the incident, the BSF troops responsible for the massacre -- the 94th Battalion -- were transferred to the town of Pulwama where, according to government sources, they threatened the local population with similar abuse.[7] As is clear from the government's record on this case, "swift and firm action" means nothing if the investigation is not completed and those responsible not held to account.

Even when the authorities have ordered inquiries into incidents of abuse, the investigations are frequently never conducted or the findings not made public. Director General of Police (DGP) B. S. Bedi, when he was first appointed to Srinagar, had promised to make public the findings of all such inquiries. When questioned in a press interview in October 1992 about his failure to do so, he responded,

> We have done so deliberately -- it would lower the morale of the forces. Why should we tell everyone? They will talk about it right and left.[8]

Although an inquiry was ordered into the killing of 25 civilians in Handwara on October 12, 1990, the findings have never been made public. An inquiry ordered into the killings of 33 civilians in Srinagar on June 12, 1991, has never commenced. An investigation was ordered in the case of five women reportedly raped near Anantnag on December 5,

---

[6] For more on this case, see p.70.

[7] Several months later, the troops were reportedly sent out of Kashmir altogether.

[8] Sukhmani Singh, "'I Have Already Restrained My Men'," *Illustrated Weekly*, October 10-16, 1992, p. 9.

1991, but the magistrate's report has never been submitted. According to the *Kashmir Times*, inquiries have been ordered into 87 incidents of killings, rape and arson. None has resulted in criminal prosecutions. In seven courts-martial held between April 1990 and July 1991 involving incidents of rape, deaths in custody, illegal detention and indiscriminate firing on civilians by army soldiers, only one officer has been dismissed. The most severe punishment for the remaining officers was either a suspended promotion, or marks of "severe displeasure" in their files.[9]

According to the 1993 U.S.Department of State *Country Reports on Human Rights Practices for 1992,* only 33 army and paramilitary personnel have been imprisoned for unexplained abuses in Kashmir, 27 of these for terms of one month or less. Eighteen were dismissed and 45 were demoted or reprimanded.[10] The only conviction that has been made public is that of two army soldiers convicted for the rape of a Canadian tourist in October 1990. To Asia Watch and PHR's knowledge, both soldiers have yet to begin their prison terms and remain in barracks in Kashmir while an appeal is pending.

One of the most striking aspects of the government of India's response to the Asia Watch/PHR reports has been the conspicuous omission of any attempt to counter the charge that the security forces in Kashmir have systematically tortured persons in their custody. As is noted in some of the cases documented in this report, the security forces themselves admit that they torture detainees on the orders of their officers. From these statements, and the irrefutable physical evidence of torture obtained by medical examinations and documented in this report, it is clear that torture by security forces is condoned.

In its comments to Asia Watch/PHR, the government has stated that "*Asia Watch regularly calls for investigations to enquire into human rights abuses while simultaneously displaying an unwillingness, indeed an intolerance in accepting results of such investigations if they do not correspond to its a priori views.*" Asia Watch and PHR regularly call for independent, judicial investigations into incidents of human rights abuse for the obvious reason that the party accused of the abuse cannot be given the responsibility of

---

[9] From South Asia Human Rights Documentation Centre, "Massacre in Sopore," p. 12.

[10] See U.S. Department of State, *Country Reports on Human Rights Practices for 1992*, February 1993, p. 1140.

investigating itself. For that reason, we have been critical of investigations which have been conducted exclusively by the security forces, army or police. Moreover, Asia Watch and PHR are particularly troubled by the government of India's failure to hold to account high-ranking officers of the security forces who have directly ordered or condoned abuses by forces under their command. Asia Watch and PHR believe that the need for full accountability does not end with the transfer of such officials from the state. In this regard, the government of India is obligated to insure full accountability for grievous human rights abuses commited by forces operating under the command of former Inspector General of the Border Security Force (BSF), Ashok Patel, and former Senior Superintendent of Police K. Rajendra Kumar.

In the cases Asia Watch and PHR have documented in this report, the government has not made public the status of investigations, charges, prosecutions or other actions taken to punish members of the security forces responsible for torture, rape or murder. These cases include:

- The burning of Lal Chowk, Srinagar, on April 10, 1993, during which BSF troops set fire to buildings and shot civilians trying to flee the flames.
- The torture and attempted summary execution of a young man, Masroof Sultan, taken into custody by the BSF on April 8, 1993, severely beaten and tortured with electric shock, and then taken to a field where he was shot four times and left for dead.
- The killing of four young men, Sajad Ahmed Chaudhury, Ishtaq Ahmed Khan, Tahar Mughal and Darzi, all shot dead after being taken into custody on April 9, 1993, despite the fact that the Deputy Commissioner, Abdul Salam Bhatt, acknowledged that the young men were in custody and repeatedly told relatives that they would be released.
- The killing of ten civilians and the rape of four women in Batekote and Gurhihaker on October 1, 1992, after an attack by militants on an army convoy on the road between Bhaki Haker and Batekote.
- The killing of Imtiazuddin Farooqi, a boy of 14, who was shot dead by BSF forces when he answered their knock on the door of his home in Srinagar on the evening of July 13, 1992, and his brother, Tajuddin Farooqi, who was dragged out of the house and shot dead seconds later.
- The killing of a shopkeeper, Ghulam Qadir, and a woman named Sajida who were burned to death when BSF forces of the

53rd Battalion stationed at Kokernag locked them in a shop and set it on fire in Badasgam on October 15, 1992.
- The killing of Ghulam Nabi Mahajan, who was shot in the back after he witnessed BSF troops drag his son, Aijaz, out of the house and shoot him dead in the street in Srinagar on September 29, 1992.
- The torture of a schoolteacher, Muzaffar Ahmed Mirza, from Tral, who died after being taken into custody on October 4, 1991, tortured with electric shock and by having an iron rod inserted in his rectum which was pushed through to his chest, rupturing his lung.

Security legislation has encouraged these abuses by authorizing security personnel to use lethal force even against unarmed demonstrators and destroy property, and has insured that these forces cannot be prosecuted for any abuses committed under these laws unless such proceedings receive the prior sanction of the government. In response to concerns raised by Asia Watch/PHR about the sweeping powers granted to the security forces under these laws, and the provision giving them immunity from prosecution, the government has stated, "*[T]he security forces in Kashmir or elsewhere are not a law unto themselves and none of the Acts [the Disturbed Areas Act and the Armed Forces Special Powers Act] provide any immunity to them. What they require is prior sanction for prosecution as is also provided under India's Criminal Procedure Code (Section 197). ... The suggestion that Government policy condones excesses is totally baseless.*"

Asia Watch and PHR are concerned about all such immunity provisions. According to the U.S. State Department *Country Reports*,

> Extrajudicial killing by police received increased public attention in 1992, but there was little evidence that those responsible were punished. Moreover, a September 1991 amendment to the Code of Criminal Procedure granted broad protection to all public servants, including the security forces, from prosecution for acts committed while discharging their official duties in states under President's rule; any such prosecution may now be pursued only after the central Government's permission has been received.[11]

---

[11] See U.S. Department of State, *Country Reports on Human Rights Practices for 1992*, February 1993, p. 1134.

In addition, the Indian government's response to Asia Watch and PHR fails to adequately address the fact that the central problem with the Disturbed Areas Act and the Armed Forces Special Powers Act is that these laws give the security forces increased powers to use lethal force and to suspend legal safeguards against abuse in situations that are vaguely defined and even authorize the shooting of unarmed persons who have merely violated laws "prohibiting the assembly of five or more persons." It is with regard to these broad provisions for the use of lethal force that the immunity clause is particularly troubling. In addition, the security forces are not required to provide any report of deaths caused by the resort to force, or explanation of the decision that lethal force was necessary, even though Section 176 of the Criminal Procedure Code requires inquest and autopsy into all cases of death by "extraordinary circumstances." The significance of the immunity clause can be understood from the comment of one senior official in Kashmir, who admitted privately to a journalist that the Disturbed Areas Act was needed,

> [O]therwise every soldier would be hauled up in court. Now we can just say that we had suspicion that there were militants around.[12]

Access for International Organizations

In its comments on the Asia Watch/PHR report on rape in Kashmir, the government stated that, "*[T]he team did not, by choice, meet any government official during its visit which further limits the objectivity of its findings. It did not give any indication of its intention to visit Kashmir and to that extent the visit was conducted in a clandestine manner.*" Five days after issuing this statement, the government issued another statement which appears to contradict the first by using the Asia Watch\PHR mission as an example of the government's openness. In a press release titled, "Access to International Human Rights Organisations," the government stated that, "*Kashmir and Punjab are not closed areas ... Some of the reports of international human rights organisations on Kashmir were written after their officials visited Kashmir. The most recent example is the Asia Watch - Physicians for Human Rights Report published February 1993.*" The statement goes on

---

[12] Interview in Srinagar, October 1992.

to say that "*Government of India has shown its openness in receiving representatives of nongovernmental organisations of repute. This clearly reflects the intention to deal with such organisations with transparency and to continue a dialogue with them.*"

Before the October 1992 Asia Watch-PHR mission to Kashmir, the Embassy of India in Washington D.C. was informed by letter about the visit, and, immediately after the visit, the Home Ministry issued a press release stating that it was aware of the visit. In March 1993, Asia Watch held discussions with several government officials in Delhi, including Joint Secretary (Home) Madhukar Gupta, Joint Secretary (Home) C. D. Arha, and Secretary of Defense, N.N. Vohra. Asia Watch also met briefly with Union Minister for Internal Security Rajesh Pilot. On other occasions Asia Watch representatives have held discussions with other officials, including Foreign Secretary J.N. Dixit. It is precisely because this level of dialogue exists that we find it unfortunate that the government of India should attempt to characterize our visits as "clandestine."

In April 1993, Asia Watch informed the government of India in advance about its visit to Kashmir. Regrettably, when an Asia Watch consultant requested a meeting with Governor Krishna Rao in Srinagar, he was informed that it would not be possible. The governor's office also informed him that it had no way of contacting Inspector General of the BSF, Ashok Patel, with whom Asia Watch also wanted to meet. The consultant was able to speak briefly with Director General of Police Bedi, but subsequent efforts to meet were unsuccessful because of the DGP's busy schedule.

The government of India has also stated that requests for visits will be judged on the merits of each request, "*being guided by the security situation on the ground. The need to move cautiously is governed by the scale of terrorism and the sheer quantity and sophistication of weapons available to terrorists.*" Clearly, such concerns have no merit in the case of denial of access for international human rights groups, who seek no guarantees of security, and even more so for the International Committee of the Red Cross (ICRC). The ICRC, despite long-standing requests for access to Kashmir, has not been permitted to provide its humanitarian services in the state. The ICRC is a neutral body with a unique mandate under international law to provide protection to civilians at risk of violence by armed groups of any kind, and to visit detainees and assist local medical personnel. Its mission is to provide services precisely in situations in which there are legitimate security threats and to operate in strict confidence, reporting only to the authorities concerned. The ICRC also works in non-conflict situations to provide medical care and to conduct visits to detainees.

Finally, with respect to the government's criticism of the "*accuracy and impartiality*" of the methodology employed in Asia Watch and PHR's research, and the alleged "*willing gullibility*" of the researchers, the findings contained in this report are based on two research missions and Asia Watch and PHR's independent analysis of the testimony of over 130 witnesses, medical examinations and other physical evidence of the incidents described, and legal documentation. Asia Watch and PHR are aware that many witnesses to abuse by either security forces or militants may have had a motive to fabricate or exaggerate reports of abuse. Many witnesses were also afraid of reprisals by either the security forces or the militants. For this reason, the investigators took a variety of steps to insure the reliability and honesty of the accounts we have included in this report. The investigators on their own selected which cases to investigate, sought out eyewitnesses to events, interviewed them individually, and probed them for details they were unlikely to have planned or coordinated in advance. In most cases, that testimony was corroborated separately by other witnesses. Whenever possible, the Asia Watch and PHR researchers also visited the sites of the incidents and asked witnesses to re-enact the events they had described, again with the goal of probing their accounts and clarifying details. On the strength and consistency of multiple eyewitness testimony, and the irrefutable corroborating medical and other physical evidence gathered, Asia Watch and PHR have determined that the Indian security forces have committed and continue to commit widespread and systematic human rights violations in Kashmir. Asia Watch and PHR have also determined that many of the militant groups in Kashmir have committed grave abuses against civilians and other non-combatants, and that the weaponry they obtained from Pakistan has contributed to these violations.

Summary of Conclusions

• In their efforts to crush the militant separatist movement in Kashmir, Indian government forces have systematically violated international human rights and humanitarian law. Among the worst of these violations have been the summary executions of hundreds of detainees in the custody of the security forces in Kashmir. Such killings are carried out as a matter of policy. More than any other phenomenon, these deliberate killings reveal the magnitude of the human rights crisis in Kashmir. In the first four months of 1993, more than 130 persons are reported to have died in custody in Kashmir.[13] Asia Watch and PHR directly investigated 19 custodial executions and 47 other extrajudicial killings by government forces that occurred between July 1992 and April 1993. We also obtained information from human rights groups documenting hundreds of other extrajudicial killings which occurred in this period. Detainees have also disappeared in the custody of the security forces. A list of 99 disappearances appears in Appendix A. In most cases, the detainees were taken into custody during crackdowns, cordon-and-search operations during which the security forces have surrounded an area and ordered all the men to assemble for an identification parade in front of hooded informants. Those pointed out are detained for interrogation; routinely, a number of the detainees are murdered in custody within hours of their arrest.

• Indian army soldiers and federal paramilitary troops of the Central Reserve Police Force (CRPF) and the Border Security Force (BSF) have also engaged in frequent reprisal attacks against civilians, opening fire in crowded markets and residential areas, and burning down entire neighborhoods. During search operations, the security forces have routinely assaulted civilians. The security forces have also used lethal force against peaceful demonstrators, shooting unarmed civilians. Security legislation has increased the likelihood of such abuses by authorizing the security forces to shoot to kill and to destroy civilian property. Under these laws, the security forces are protected from prosecution for human rights violations.

• The government of India's failure to institute an independent judicial inquiry into the assassination of human rights advocate H.N.

---

[13] See Chapter IV.

Wanchoo raises serious questions about the possibility of government complicity in the murder.

• Most detainees taken into custody by the security forces in Kashmir are tortured. Torture is practiced to coerce detainees to reveal information about suspected militants or to confess to militant activity. It is also used to punish detainees who are believed to support or sympathize with the militants and to create a climate of political repression. The practice of torture is facilitated by the fact that detainees are generally held in temporary detention centers, controlled by the various security forces, without access to the courts, relatives or medical care.

• Methods of torture include severe beatings, electric shock, suspension by the feet or hands, stretching the legs apart, burning with heated objects, sexual molestation and psychological deprivation and humiliation. One common form of torture involves crushing the leg muscles with a heavy wooden roller.[14] This practice results in the release of toxins from the damaged muscles that may cause acute renal (kidney) failure. This report documents a number of such cases which required dialysis. Since 1990, doctors in Kashmir have documented 37 cases of torture-related acute renal failure; in three cases the victims died.

• Since the government crackdown against militants in Kashmir began in earnest in January 1990, reports of rape by security personnel have become more frequent. Rape most often occurs during crackdowns, cordon-and-search operations during which men are held for identification in parks or schoolyards while security forces search their homes. In these situations, the security forces frequently engage in collective punishment against civilians by assaulting residents and burning their homes. Rape is used as a means of targetting women whom the security forces accuse of being militant sympathizers; in raping them, the security forces are attempting to punish and humiliate the entire community.[15] Rape has also occurred frequently during reprisal attacks

---

[14] These techniques, in particular the stretching of the legs and the roller treatment, are used by police and security forces throughout India, and have been widely documented in Punjab. See Asia Watch, *Punjab in Crisis* (August 1991).

[15] Male detainees have been subjected to sexual molestation. For more on this see Asia Watch, *Kashmir Under Siege*, (May 1991), p. 73.

on civilians following militant ambushes. In many of these attacks, the selection of victims is seemingly arbitrary and the women, like other civilians assaulted or killed, are targeted simply because they happen to be in the wrong place at the wrong time. The significance of rape as a gender-specific form of abuse in Kashmir must be understood in the context of the subordinate status of women generally in South Asia, as in much of the rest of the world. Women who are the victims of rape are often stigmatized, and their testimony and integrity impugned. Social attitudes which cast the woman, and not her attacker, as the guilty party pervade the judiciary, making rape cases difficult to prosecute and leaving women unwilling to press charges.

- Health professionals in Kashmir have frequently been detained, assaulted and harassed while attempting to perform their duties. In some of the worst incidents of abuse, the security forces have deliberately prevented ambulance drivers from transporting injured persons to hospitals for emergency care. In several cases investigated by PHR and Asia Watch, security forces beat, shot or strafed ambulance drivers who were attempting to provide care to the wounded, and shot dead one driver while he was on duty.[16] Doctors and other medical staff frequently have been threatened, beaten and detained. Several have been shot dead while on duty; others have been tortured. A prominent victim of extrajudicial execution by the security forces was Dr. Farooq Ahmed Ashai, who was shot by CRPF troops as he passed a security force bunker near the Rambagh bridge in Srinagar on February 18, 1993.

- Security forces have also repeatedly raided hospitals and other medical facilities, even pediatric and obstetric hospitals. During these raids, the security personnel have forced doctors at gunpoint to identify recent trauma patients. Because of their injuries, the security forces have suspected these patients of militant activity. Injured patients have been arrested from hospitals, in some cases after being disconnected from intravenous medications or other treatments. The security forces have also discharged their weapons within hospital grounds and inside hospitals, and have entered operating theaters and destroyed or damaged medical supplies, transports and equipment.

- The strict night curfew imposed on the towns and villages of the Kashmir valley has also seriously impaired health services. Because the

---

[16] See Chapter III for applicable international law.

neutrality of medical transport[17] is not respected by government security forces, ambulances cannot travel at night. Thus, physicians cannot attend to medical emergencies that occur after dark, including cases unrelated to the conflict, and individuals cases may undergo life-threatening delays before receiving medical care. During raids, hospitals are not accessible to patients in need of emergency care. Since the escalation of the conflict in 1990, many ordinary health services have ceased to operate or have been severely curtailed. Attrition of health professionals, particularly in rural areas, has left many primary health care centers, clinics and district hospitals virtually unable to perform ordinary health services. Their loss, together with the increase in traumatic injuries resulting from the conflict, has seriously overburdened hospitals in Srinagar, which are also short-staffed, overcrowded and experiencing serious shortages of essential supplies.

• While there is no question that the conflict in Kashmir constitutes a serious security threat, the steps the Indian government has taken to confront that threat have resulted in grave violations of international human rights and humanitarian law. Moreover, the Indian authorities have done little to curb these abuses. Members of the Indian army and security forces are seldom prosecuted for human rights violations in Kashmir. In the rare cases in which investigations have taken place, the most severe punishments for abuses have generally been limited to dismissals or suspensions from duty. The Indian central government may not have explicitly sanctioned all of the abuses that have taken place in Kashmir; it has, however, abdicated its responsibility to enforce the law and has given the security forces free rein to engage in gross abuses in the name of fighting armed militants. The Indian government's failure to account for these abuses and take rigorous action against those members of its forces responsible for murder, rape and torture amounts to a policy of condoning human rights violations by the security forces.

• While it is not possible to say for certain who was responsible for the assassination of the JKLF leader, Dr. Abdul Ahad Guru, on March 31, 1993, there is substantial circumstantial evidence implicating militant groups in the killing. Questions remain about the government's actions before and after the murder.

---

[17] For a definition of medical neutrality, see Chapter III.

- Armed militant organizations[18] in Kashmir have committed many grave violations of international human rights and humanitarian law. Particularly in early 1990, militant groups threatened, assaulted and murdered Hindus residing in the Kashmir valley -- driving more than 100,000 to flee to refugee camps in Jammu and Delhi, where most remain in increasingly desperate conditions. Asia Watch directly investigated many such incidents of threats, a number of which are included in this report.[19]

- Armed with sophisticated weaponry mostly procured in Pakistan, militant groups have continued to attack civilians. In some cases, those who have been attacked have been civil servants, or members of political organizations opposed by the militants. In other cases, the victims have been accused of being informers or of not supporting the militants' political views. Militant groups have also tortured persons in their custody, and have carried out summary executions of such persons and of captured security personnel as a matter of policy. Fourteen such cases are included in this report.

- Various armed militant groups in Kashmir have also committed rape. In some cases, militants have raped women whose family members were believed to be informers or supporters of rival groups. In other cases, women have been raped and killed after being held as hostages for their male relatives. Three cases of rape by militant groups are included in this report. Extremist militant groups seeking to enforce an "Islamic" code of behavior have launched other violent attacks on women, thereby

---

[18] There are several dominant groups fighting Indian troops in Kashmir, and perhaps as many as one hundred smaller ones. The two most prominent are the Jammu and Kashmir Liberation Front (JKLF), which is considered the most popular and which supports independence, and the Hezb-ul Mujahidin, which is reportedly the best armed and which supports accession to Pakistan.

[19] For centuries, the Kashmiri Hindu community, often called Pandits, shared the Kashmir valley and its distinct culture with the majority Muslim population. The exodus of more than 100,000 in early 1990 was provoked by violent attacks by armed militant groups. Most remain in refugee camps in Delhi and Jammu. For more on this, see Chapter VII and Asia Watch, *Kashmir Under Siege* (May 1991), pp.147-151.

creating a climate of fear for women in Kashmir in which violent abuses are committed with impunity.

• Militants have also thrown grenades at buses and government buildings and have detonated car bombs, killing and wounding civilians. These attacks have occurred not only in the Kashmir valley but have also been reported in Jammu. Seven incidents are included in this report.

• The attacks by armed militant groups on members of the Hindu community in Kashmir since 1990 and attacks on those Muslims who were seen as opponents of the militants, drove many professionals, including medical personnel, to flee Kashmir. Their departure has had a devastating effect on medical services in the state. Militants have also assassinated and threatened health professionals suspected of giving information on injured militants to officials. Not only do these abuses jeopardize the health of the entire population, they also constitute grave violations of international law.

In this report, Asia Watch and Physicians for Human Rights hope to draw the attention of the international community to the urgency of the human rights disaster in Kashmir. The report concludes with our recommendations for action to be taken by the government of Prime Minister Rao, the militant forces in Kashmir, the government of Pakistan and the international community to address this crisis. The most important of these is for the government of India to grant access to the ICRC to assist in providing medical care, protection from abuse for detainees and other humanitarian services in Kashmir.

Other crucial steps include the following:

• The government of India should support swift investigations of extrajudicial executions, deaths in custody, torture and rape by security forces and paramilitary forces in Kashmir. Security personnel, including police, army and paramilitary, responsible for these abuses should be prosecuted in civilian courts. Only with such trials and appropriate punishments will these forces receive the clear, unequivocal message that human rights violations are not condoned by their superiors. Those found guilty of abuse should be punished regardless of rank. The punishments should be at least as severe as those specified under civilian law. The results of these investigations and the punishments should be made public as a means of giving the people of Kashmir a reason to believe in the government's commitment to justice and the rule of law.

• A centralized register of detainees accessible to lawyers and family members should be established in the state. In addition, the security agencies should require that arresting officers provide signed receipts for all detainees to family members, village elders or persons of similar status. The receipt would be retrieved when the person is released.

• To insure adequate protection against rape, the government of India should provide police training, perhaps after consultation with international experts, on gathering adequate evidence for rape prosecutions. Explicit prohibitions against rape should be included in training for all enlisted men and officers in the police, paramilitary and military as a way of sending a clear signal that rape is not tolerated by the state. Medical workers who have examined and treated rape victims should be protected from abuse. Medical facilities, including private licensed physicians, should be encouraged to give testimony and introduce physical evidence in court with regard to rape and other forms of sexual and physical abuse.

• State authorities and the headquarters of the army and paramilitary operations in Kashmir should issue public statements affirming the security of medical personnel and institutions. The statement should include explicit guarantees for the security of ambulances traveling at night and during curfews, and for neutrality of hospital premises. Removal of patients from hospital premises should be prohibited until the patient's treatment is completed. Security personnel should be trained in the principles of medical neutrality and those violating those principles should be prosecuted.

• The international community should condemn abuses such as murder, rape and assault by and threats to civilians by militant groups as grave violations of international human rights and humanitarian law. Militant groups should abide by human rights norms and the provisions of Common Article 3 of the Geneva Conventions which prohibits cruel, inhumane and degrading treatment and executions.

• Militant organizations should immediately desist from actions that interfere with or impede the delivery of health services, including attacks on or threats against health professionals, violating the medical neutrality of hospitals by committing abuses within hospital premises.

• The government of Pakistan should end all support for abusive militant organizations in Kashmir. The international community should condemn Pakistan's efforts to support any of these groups.

II. HISTORICAL BACKGROUND

The origins of the conflict in Kashmir lie in the subcontinent's partition in 1947 which created the independent states of India and Pakistan. As a result of the partition, hundreds of nominally independent "princely states"[20] were absorbed into the two new nations. However, Kashmir's ruler, Maharaja Hari Singh, refused to accede to either nation, apparently in the hope that the state might be permitted to remain independent. An invasion by Pakistani tribesmen[21] in August and September 1947 and an uprising among Kashmiri Muslims in the state's western regions ultimately compelled the maharaja to seek the assistance of Prime Minister Nehru of India, who agreed to send troops only if Kashmir formally acceded to India. On October 27, 1947, the maharaja agreed to Kashmir's accession to India, on the condition that Kashmir be permitted to retain its own constitution.[22] Indian troops succeeded in halting the Pakistani forces, driving them back to the western third of the state, which then acceded to Pakistan as "Azad" (free) Kashmir.

At the time, British authorities stated that the question of Kashmir's accession should be settled by a plebiscite as soon as law and order was re-instated and the invading forces had left. But the plebiscite was never held. The Indian government argued first that the essential precondition to a plebiscite, the exit of Pakistani troops from "Azad Kashmir," had not

---

[20] These nominally independent states were ruled by Indian princes under the suzerainty of the British government. At the time of partition, they were officially free to accede to either Pakistan or India or remain independent.

[21] According to most reports, the forces included Pakistan army soldiers and irregulars in civil dress.

[22] Instrument of Accession, clause 7. Thus Kashmir retained autonomy in all areas except defence, currency and foreign affairs. As a consequence of Kashmir's conditional accession, article 370 was incorporated in 1949 into the Indian constitution which provided *inter alia* that other articles of the constitution "may be extended to Kashmir ... only in 'consultation' with the state government if it pertains to matters regarding legislative power of Parliament, and with the 'concurrence' of the state government if it pertains to other matters."

been met, and later that the Kashmiri people had effectively ratified accession by voting in local elections and adopting a state constitution. United Nations intervention achieved a cease-fire on January 1, 1949.

Through the 1950s and 1960s, political discontent with the central government's attempts to control politics in the state grew. Pro-independence and pro-plebiscite activists were repeatedly jailed. In 1964 the first militant group, the Jammu and Kashmir Liberation Front (JKLF), was formed to fight for independence. On July 2, 1972, India and Pakistan signed the Simla Accord, under which both countries agreed to respect the cease-fire line and to resolve differences over Kashmir "by peaceful means" through negotiation and meetings to discuss "a final settlement." Since then, the Simla Accord has been the cornerstone of all bilateral discussions of the Kashmir issue.

In 1986, then Indian Prime Minister Rajiv Gandhi and Farooq Abdullah, Chief Minister of Jammu and Kashmir, forged a new accord, which was widely criticized in the state as a betrayal of Kashmiri interests. Charges of widespread corruption soon discredited Farooq Abdullah's National Conference party. A new opposition party, the Muslim United Front (MUF), which had the support of pro-independence activists, Islamic fundamentalists and many frustrated Kashmiri youth, was launched and contested the March 1987 polls for seats in the state assembly. Widespread irregularities in the vote count and mass arrests of MUF candidates in the election's aftermath caused a watershed in popular disillusionment with state politics and drove many to support emerging militant groups.

After the elections, militants of the JKLF and other groups -- many of whom openly admitted that they received arms and training in Pakistan -- grew bolder, detonating bombs at government buildings, buses and the houses of present and former state government officials, and enforcing a state-wide boycott of the November 1989 national parliamentary elections. One month later, JKLF militants abducted the daughter of Home Minister Mufti Mohammad Sayeed, then freed her when the government gave in to demands for the release of five detained militants. That event, together with a surge in popular protest against the state and central governments, led New Delhi to launch a massive crackdown on the militants. In response, the state government resigned in protest and governor's rule was declared on January 19, 1990.[23] In the weeks that followed, security forces opened fire on crowds of unarmed demonstrators, killing hundreds, and militants[24] intensified their attacks on the security forces. As protests, attacks and reprisals intensified over the next few months, Kashmir's civil war began in earnest. In May 1990, rising tension between Pakistan and India following the escalation of the conflict in Kashmir raised fears of another war between the two countries.[25]

By mid-1992, political negotiations for resolving the crisis in Kashmir remained deadlocked. In March 1992, five prominent political leaders were released from prison, apparently as part of a government effort to pave the way for elections in the state. since then, government officials have stated that they were willing to negotiate with militant leaders as long as such talks remained "within the framework of the Indian constitution." Taking advantage of the crisis, Pakistani leaders have sought out international forums to call for a plebiscite along the lines of the 1948 settlement, excluding the option of independence from the parameters of that plebiscite. Militant leaders continued to reject limitations from both Pakistan and India. Independent observers and the

---

[23] Under the Jammu and Kashmir Constitution, governor's rule may be imposed for six months, after which, pursuant to the Constitution of India, president's rule, which permits New Delhi to suspend state government and rule directly, may be enacted for six-month periods. Article 370 of the constitution allows president's rule in Kashmir for only one year at a stretch and only after six months of governor's rule. President's rule was imposed in July 1990. Jammu and Kashmir's legislative assembly was formally dissolved in February 1990.

[24] By 1990, there were already more than 50 armed militant groups, some of which were loosely aligned with the JKLF, the Hezb-ul Mujahidin, or other groups.

[25] That concern prompted the U.S. and the then Soviet Union to warn both governments against provoking a confrontation.

international press reported that independence continued to be favored by the most popular of the militant groups in the valley of Kashmir.[26]

In August 1992, the Indian government launched a brutal new offensive in the Kashmir valley called "Operation Tiger," which was characterized by surprise raids and search operations designed to capture and kill militant leaders. Summary executions of detainees increased during this period. A second security operation, code named Operation Shiva, followed. In early October 1992, the central transmitting station for telecommunications between Kashmir and the rest of India was all but destroyed in a bomb blast. It was not known who was responsible for the sabotage, which virtually shut down telephone connections to the Kashmir valley.

On January 6,1993, in the single largest civilian massacre of the conflict, at least 43 people were shot dead or burned to death when Indian paramilitary forces rampaged through a neighborhood in the city of Sopore, reportedly in retaliation for a militant attack that killed two soldiers. A local police official at the scene stated that the security forces "ran amok"[27] and prevented police and fire fighters from intervening. Army officials claimed that those who died were killed in "cross-fire." Central government authorities suspended the BSF commandant and several other officers and ordered an inquiry. At the time this report went to press, the results of that inquiry were not available.

In early 1993, Union Minister of State for Internal Security Rajesh Pilot spearheaded a new government initiative to negotiate a political settlement to the conflict. In March, Governor Saxena was replaced with Governor Krishna Rao, and in the weeks that followed, several senior Kashmiri civil authorities returned to the state administration. Telecommunication links with the rest of India were restored.[28] These

---

[26] In addition to the Muslim-majority valley of Kashmir, where the actual armed conflict is located, the disputed state includes the Hindu majority area of Jammu and the Buddhist majority area of Ladakh with histories and political interests distinct from those of the valley.

[27] See discussion on p.70. See also "India Says Troops 'Went Amok' in Kashmir", New York Times, January 8, 1993.

[28] Government sources told Asia Watch that state authorities had resisted repairing telephone services, apparently in order to bring greater

efforts were almost immediately undermined, however, by an upsurge in violence which included the burning of a large section of downtown Srinagar by security forces and a sharp increase in summary executions which provoked demonstrations in cities throughout the valley. Hard-line elements in the government and intelligence agencies seeking to impose a military solution on Kashmir were blamed for sabotaging efforts by those in the government advocating a political settlement to the crisis. The efforts at negotiation also provoked internecine conflict among and within some militant groups.

The rising tensions culminated in April 1993 in an unprecedented revolt by the Jammu and Kashmir police force following the death of one of their colleagues in army custody. The standoff ended when security forces stormed the headquarters and disarmed the police force. As a result, in May 1993, the army was ordered to assume unified command of all security operations in Kashmir. In May, the controversial BSF Inspector General Ashok Patel was transferred out of Kashmir, apparently as part of the government's efforts to pursue a political settlement. However, Governor Krishna Rao rejected appeals from human rights groups to transfer another source of controversy, Amar Kapoor, the Deputy Director General of Intelligence. At the same time, the Indian press reported that militant groups were claiming to have taken control of pockets of the valley, notably in the town of Sopore.[29] By June 1993, members of the civil adminstration had returned to the state, but there were few indications that there would be an end to the abuses and the violence anytime soon.

---

pressure militant groups in the state.

[29] See Harinder Baweja, "Losing Contol," *India Today*, May 31, 1993.

III. THE SCOPE OF THE CONFLICT AND THE APPLICABLE INTERNATIONAL LAW

Government forces operating in Kashmir include the Indian Army and India's federal paramilitary forces, the Central Reserve Police Force (CRPF) and the Border Security Force (BSF). As of mid-1993, at least 300,000 paramilitary troops were deployed in the valley, together with at least 100,000 Indian Army troops. According to defense analysts, as of April 1991 the Jammu and Kashmir garrison force consisted of army eight divisions, including the 57th division with long experience in counter-insurgency operations in Sri Lanka, Mizoram and Punjab.[30] The paramilitary forces included at least 27 battalions of the BSF, 24 battalions of the CRPF, 14 battalions of Indo-Tibetan Border Police and two battalions of the Assam Rifles.[31] In May 1993, a reporter observed, "The escalation is self-evident. While in 1990 there were only 36 paramilitary companies, today there are 300, and two more army divisions will be moving in this month."[32] The local Jammu and Kashmir policemen are generally not involved in counter-insurgency operations, largely because they are believed to be sympathetic to the insurgency.[33]

At least eleven major militant organizations, and perhaps dozens of smaller ones, operate in Kashmir. Their forces are variously estimated at between 5,000 and 10,000 armed men. They are roughly divided between those who support independence and those who support accession to Pakistan. The oldest and most widely known militant organization, the Jammu and Kashmir Liberation Front (JKLF), has spearheaded the

---

[30] Ibid.

[31] R.A. Davis, "Kashmir in the Balance," *International Defence Review*, Vol. 24, No. 4., April 1993, p. 301.

[32] Harinder Baweja, "Losing Control," *India Today*, May 31, 1993, p. 25.

[33] In fact, in April 1993 most of the force went on strike to protest the death in custody of a constable, Riaz Ahmed. After security forces stormed the police headquarters, some 1,000 of the police were disarmed and interrogated.

movement for an independent Kashmir. Its student wing is the Jammu and Kashmir Students Liberation front (JKSLF). A large number of other militant organizations have emerged since 1989, some of which also support independence, others of which support Kashmir's accession to Pakistan. Although all groups reportedly receive arms and training from Pakistan, the pro-Pakistani groups are reputed to be favored by Pakistan's military intelligence, the Directorate of Inter-Services Intelligence (ISI).[34] The most powerful of these is the Hezb-ul-Mujahidin. The other major groups are Al-Jehad, Al-Barq, Hizbollah, Ikhwan-ul-Muslimin, Jamait-ul Mujahidin, Tekriq-ul Mujahidin, Allah Tigers, Al-Umar Mujahidin and Al-Umar Commandos. According to press reports, several hundred fighters from Afghanistan and Sudan have also joined some of the militant groups.[35]

Intense rivalries among the militant groups, and particularly between the dominant groups, has sparked frequent clashes and has often prevented the militants from coordinating military operations.[36] As of mid-1993, a Coordination Committee comprised of representatives of the leaders from the JKLF, Hezb-ul Mujahidin, Iqwan Muslim, Harkat-ul-Mujaheedin, Jamait-ul-Mujaheedin, Tahreek-ul-Mujaheedin, Hizbollah and Muslim Mujahidin had assumed some judicial oversight for the various groups, under the authority of recognized legal and religious advisors. The committee reportedly has no written laws or regulations.

---

[34] Under Pakistan's late president Zia ul-Haq, the ISI gained increased powers over domestic and foreign intelligence operations. The ISI was the conduit for outside covert assistance to the Afghan resistance and has reportedly provided some of that weaponry to a number of militant groups in Kashmir. *See* Selig S. Harrison, "Showdown in Kashmir," *Peace and Security*, Vol. 5, Number 3, Autumn 1990, pp. 8-9. *See also*, Steve Coll, "India, Pakistan Wage Covert 'Proxy Wars'," *Washington Post*, December 8, 1990.

[35] See for example, Harinder Baweja, "Losing Control," *India Today*, May 31, 1993.

[36] See Sumit Ganguly, "Avoiding War in Kashmir," *Foreign Affairs*, Winter 1990/91 (1990) p. 65, and Steve Coll, "Kashmiris Describe India Resorting to Arson in Rebel War," *Washington Post*, November 16, 1990.

It is not known whether the Committee has coordinated any military operations.

The militant forces do not control territory in Kashmir, but certain parts of the valley have gained a reputation as strongholds of particular militant groups, particularly towns near the Line of Control which separates the Indian state of Jammu and Kashmir from the territory controlled by Pakistan. Many of these towns, notably Kupwara, are along the supply lines for weaponry from Pakistan. The Hezb-ul Mujahidin, for example, is reported to have a dominant presence in the town of Sopore where, according to some press reports, the group has claimed to have established pockets of control from which they have launched attacks on Indian government troops trying to conduct search operations in the vicinity.

> [H]eavily armed insurgents have for the first time established "liberated zones" in pockets of Baramulla, Srinagar and Anantnag districts which resemble fortified garrisons that even the Indian armed forces cannot enter. ... The Indian army, which tried to enter the town [of Sopore] last month for a cordon and search operation, was forced to withdraw, for as soon as a column entered the city, it came under heavy firing that left one officer and two *jawans* [soldiers] dead.[37]

The militants' military operations are generally characterized by ambushes of security force patrols and convoys and hit-and-run attacks on security force bunkers and pickets, for which they generally use grenades, rocket-propelled grenade launchers and anti-personnel and anti-tank mines. Some militant groups have organized commando units responsible for attacking specific targets, such as security force bunkers. The militants also engage army troops and other security forces in gun battles. For these operations they rely on weapons such as AK-47 and AK-56 assault rifles, light machine guns, revolvers and other light weapons. The militants are also reported to have sophisticated night vision and wireless communication equipment. The availability of this sophistcated weaponry has had a measurable impact on the effectiveness of the militants' military operations. As one press report noted,

---

[37] See Harinder Baweja, "Losing Control," *India Today*, p. 27.

Improved weaponry has led to a significant increase in the frequency of insurgent-initiated contacts, as well as a growing boldness in the choice of targets. In Srinagar, one visitor recently counted 10 to 15 incidents involving RPGs [rocket-propelled grenades] each night over several nights. Firefights and ambushes have become a daily routine.[38]

State authorities claim that nearly 8,000 AK series assault rifles, 455 rocket launchers and 8,030 grenades have been recovered since 1988. Much of this weaponry reportedly reaches Kashmir from Pakistan, and militant leaders freely acknowledge that they receive support from Pakistan's ISI. Officially, the Pakistani government has denied involvement in arming and training Kashmiri militants, but the claim is generally not considered credible.[39]

The Applicable International Law

International Human Rights Law and Standards

International human rights law prohibits the arbitrary deprivation of life under any circumstances. The Government of India is a signatory to the International Covenant on Civil and Political Rights (ICCPR). Article 6 of the the ICCPR expressly prohibits derogation from the right to life. Thus, even during time of emergency, "[n]o one shall be arbitrarily deprived of his life."[40]

The International Covenant on Civil and Political Rights (ICCPR) also prohibits torture and other forms of cruel, inhuman and degrading treatment. Articles 4 and 7 of the ICCPR explicitly ban torture, even in

---

[38] R.A. Davis, "Kashmir in the Balance," *International Defense Review*, Vol. 24, No. 4, April 1991, p. 301.

[39] See Chapter VII. Pakistan's support for pro-independence groups like the JKLF has reportedly waned in favor of pro-Pakistani groups like the Hezb-ul Mujahidin.

[40] Article 4, Article 6, International Covenant on Civil and Political Rights.

times of national emergency or when the security of the state is threatened.[41]

The evidence gathered by Asia Watch and PHR indicates that the Indian army, the Central Reserve Police Force and the Border Security Force -- the principal government forces operating in Jammu and Kashmir[42] -- have systematically violated these fundamental norms of international human rights law.

International Humanitarian Law

In addition to internationally recognized human rights, Asia Watch and PHR believe that both the government of India and armed groups fighting against it in Kashmir are bound in this situation by international humanitarian law (the law of armed conflict) applicable in non-international (internal) armed conflict. The applicable law is found in Article 3 common to the four Geneva Conventions of August 12, 1949 ("Common Article 3"); additional authoritative standards are found in Protocol II (1977) Additional to the Geneva Conventions of 1949 ("Protocol II"). Common Article 3 and Protocol II each provide international law and standards governing the conduct of parties in an internal armed conflict, including government forces and insurgents. India has ratified the four Geneva Conventions of 1949, and is thus obliged to uphold Common Article 3.[43]

---

[41] Article 4 states "In time of public emergency which threatens the life of the nation and the existence of which is officially proclaimed... no derogation from articles 6, 7, 8 (paragraphs 1 and 2), 11, 15, 16 and 18 may be made under this provision." Article 7 states "No one shall be subjected to torture or to cruel, inhuman or degrading treatment or punishment." International Covenant on Civil and Political Rights, U.N. General Assembly Resolution 2200 A (XXI) of 16 December 1966. India became a signatory on April 10, 1979.

[42] The paramilitary forces deployed in Kashmir, the CRPF and the BSF have combat duties and sometimes conduct operations jointly with Indian army forces.

[43] India has not ratified Protocol II. Moreover, Asia Watch and PHR do not believe that the conflict in Kashmir currently reaches the threshold

Asia Watch and PHR believe that the extent of armed conflict as described in the preceding "Scope of the Conflict" section establishes that the conflict rises to the level of application of Common Article 3.[44] The factors that Asia Watch and PHR have relied on in reaching this conclusion include the widespread and frequent fighting throughout the disputed territory, recourse by the government to its regular armed forces, the organization of insurgents into armed forces with military commanders responsible for the actions of those forces and capable of adhering to law of war obligations, the military nature of operations conducted on both sides (including the general targetting of military targets by insurgent forces), the size of the insurgent forces and size of the government's military forces, and other such factors. It is essential to acknowledge, however, that Common Article 3 carries no implications for the legitimacy of insurgent forces; the government is entitled to prosecute those captured in internal insurgency for the violation of domestic law.[45]

---

necessary for Protocol II to apply, that is, an armed conflict that takes place "in the territory of a High Contracting Party between its armed forces and dissident armed forces or other organized armed groups which, under responsible command, exercise such control over a part of its territory as to enable them to carry out sustained and concerted military operations and to implement this Protocol." Nevertheless, India and the insurgents are obligated to uphold Common Article 3, and Protocol II provides authoritative guidance for the interpretation of the provisions of Common Article 3.

[44] See generally Heather A. Wilson, *International Law and the Use of Force by National Liberation Movements* (Clarendon-Oxford, 1988), at 45-48, for a review of generally debated criteria and state practice; see also G.I.A.D. Draper, *The Red Cross Conventions* (Stevens and Sons, 1958), at 15-16.

[45] "The application of [Common Article 3] shall not affect the legal status of the Parties to the conflict." Common Article 3 to the Geneva Conventions of 1949; current state practice is best reflected in *Public Prosecutor* v. *Oie Hee Koi* (Federal Court of Malaysia, 1968) (nationals of the Detaining Power are not entitled to protection as prisoners of war and may be tried under municipal law); see also Wilson at 46-48.

On the assumption that Common Article 3 applies to the conflict in Kashmir, each Party is absolutely bound to apply the following provisions, irrespective of the behavior of other Parties:

(1) Persons taking no active part in the hostilities, including members of armed forces who have laid down their arms and those placed *hors de combat* by sickness, wounds, detention, or any other cause, shall in all circumstances be treated humanely, without any adverse distinction founded on race, color, religion or faith, sex, birth or wealth, or any other similar criteria.

To this end, the following acts are and shall remain prohibited at any time and in any place whatsoever with respect to the above-mentioned persons:

(a) violence to life and person, in particular murder of all kinds, mutilation, cruel treatment and torture;

(b) taking of hostages;

(c) outrages upon personal dignity, in particular humiliating and degrading treatment;

(d) the passing of sentences and the carrying out of executions without previous judgment pronounced by a regularly constituted court, affording all the judicial guarantees which are recognized as indispensable by civilized peoples.

(2) The wounded and sick shall be collected and cared for.[46]

These principles apply to all parties to the conflict, both government and guerrillas. The obligation to comply with Common Article 3 is absolute and independent of the obligation of the other parties.[47] Thus, the government of India, like other governments, is obliged to abide by these provisions and is responsible for violations committed by and attributable to its armed forces and paramilitary forces.[48] It cannot

---

[46] Common Article 3, subsections 1 and 2.

[47] Common Article 2, The Geneva Conventions of 1949, "Although one of the Powers in conflict may not be a party to the present Convention, the Powers who are parties thereto shall remain bound by it in their mutual relations."

[48] The principal government forces operating in Jammu and Kashmir -- the Indian army, the Central Reserve Police Force and the Border Security Force -- are all entities of the central government in New Delhi.

excuse itself from complying with Common Article 3 on the grounds that the militants are violating Common Article 3, and vice versa. However, Common Article 3 in no way precludes the government of India from punishing persons for crimes under its domestic laws. Indeed, Asia Watch and PHR believe that it is the Indian government's duty to do so. Thus, Kashmiri militants may be tried for murder, kidnapping or other crimes, so long as they are afforded the rights of due process.

Persons protected by Common Article 3 of the Geneva Conventions include all noncombatants, even if they have provided food, shelter or other partisan support to one side or the other, and members of the armed forces of either side who are in custody, are wounded or are otherwise *hors de combat*. If under these circumstances, such persons are summarily executed or die as a result of torture, their deaths are tantamount to murder.

Torture, hostage-taking, and rape have all been prominent abuses in the Kashmir conflict, and it is evident that Common Article 3 forbids each of them.[49] Rape is clearly prohibited by Common Article 3; it is customarily understood to constitute both cruel treatment and an outrage on personal dignity.[50] Although the line between cruel and inhuman

---

Army soldiers report, ultimately, to the Minister of Defense; the CRPF, BSF and other national paramilitary police forces report to the Home Minister. As such, the actions of these troops are governed by the international laws of war and international human rights law which bind the government of India. In addition, since January 19, 1990, the central government has ruled the state directly.

[49] See Chapter VII.

[50] Protocol II provides authoritative guidance for interpreting Common Article 3's prohibition on "outrages upon personal dignity." Protocol II outlaws "humiliating treatment, rape, enforced prostitution and any form of indecent assault." The commentary of the International Committee of the Red Cross explains that this article "reaffirms and supplements Common Article 3 ... [because] it became clear that it was necessary to strengthen ... the protection of women ... who may also be victims of rape, enforced prostitution or indecent assault." Protocol II, article 4(2)(e). For a discussion of the status of rape in international humanitarian law, see Helsinki Watch, division of Human Rights Watch,

treatment and torture is not well defined in either humanitarian or human rights law, rape also violates the ICCPR and Common Article 3 prohibitions on torture. The Convention Against Torture and other Cruel, Inhuman or Degrading Treatment or Punishment defines torture as

> any act by which severe pain or suffering, whether physical or mental, is intentionally inflicted on a person for such purposes as obtaining from him or a third person information or a confession, punishing him for an act he or a third person has committed or is suspected of having committed, or intimidating or coercing him or a third person for any reason based on discrimination of any kind, when such pain or suffering is inflicted by or at the instigation of or with the acquiescence of a public official or other person acting in an official capacity.[51]

When any party to an armed conflict, internal or international, uses rape, or acquiesces in the use of rape by its combatants, with the intention of inflicting severe pain or suffering and for the purposes of coercing, punishing, or intimidating, or to obtain information or a confession, it constitutes torture.

Allowing medical personnel to care for the sick and wounded is also a key principle of international humanitarian law. Common Article 3 of the Geneva Conventions states, "The wounded and sick shall be collected and cared for."[52]

War Crimes in Bosnia-Hercegovina, vol. II (April 1993), at 20.

[51] The Convention Against Torture and other Cruel, Inhuman or Degrading Treatment or Punishment, Article 1. Although India has not ratified the convention, this definition is considered authoritative under international law.

[52] Standards for the protection of medical neutrality have been incorporated into the Code of Medical Neutrality in Armed Conflict, (see Appendix A), which provides, in Article 1, that sick and wounded combatants and civilians be protected and provided with medical care without delay; in Article 2, that medical workers be respected, protected and assisted in the performance of their medical duties and that, under

In addition to Common Article 3, Asia Watch and PHR also find that the Code of Medical Neutrality in Armed Conflict applies to the Kashmir conflict. This code provides standards for the protection of medical workers and their humanitarian work during armed conflict.[53]

Article 3, the sick and wounded shall be treated regardless of their affiliations and with no distinctions on any grounds other than medical ones. Article 5 of the Code prohibits attacks on defenseless sick or wounded combatants or civilians. Moreover, even if the Kashmir conflict were not judged to be an "armed conflict" by the standards of international humanitarian law, the principle of protecting civilians and adhering to norms of medical neutrality is increasingly recognized as being equally valid in situations of "internal strife."

[53] The Code of Medical Neutrality in Armed Conflict is reproduced in full as Appendix B.

IV. VIOLATIONS BY GOVERNMENT FORCES

Indian army and security forces operating in Kashmir have systematically violated international human rights and humanitarian law by summarily executing detainees and killing civilians in reprisal attacks. Extrajudicial executions and disappearances in Kashmir number at least in the hundreds. Government forces have also violated international human rights law by using lethal force against peaceful demonstrators. Security legislation authorizing the security forces to shoot to kill and protecting them from prosecution has encouraged such abuses.

Most detainees taken into custody by the security forces in Kashmir are tortured. Torture is practiced not only to coerce detainees to reveal information but also to punish detainees who are believed to support or sympathize with the militants and to create a climate of political repression. Methods of torture include prolonged beatings, electric shock, burning with heated objects and crushing the muscles with a wooden roller. Detainees are generally held in temporary detention centers, controlled by the various security forces, without access to the courts, relatives or medical care.

Rape often occurs during reprisal attacks on civilians. In such attacks, security forces engage in collective punishment against the civilian population by assaulting residents. Rape is also used as a means of targetting women whom the security forces accuse of being militant sympathizers. The security forces have also engaged in the wanton destruction of civilian property, primarily by burning down residential neighborhoods.

The security forces have violated international humanitarian law protecting medical neutrality by obstructing the provision of care to the sick and wounded. Health professionals have been detained, assaulted and harassed while attempting to perform their duties. Security forces have also raided hospitals and have forced doctors at gunpoint to identify recent trauma patients, who, because of their injuries, are then accused of militant activity. Injured patients have been arrested from hospitals, in some cases after being disconnected from intravenous medications or other treatments.

Extrajudicial Executions and Reprisal Killings

In a pattern that is repeated every day in Kashmir, the security forces detain young men during "crackdowns" -- cordon and search operations during which all the men of a neighborhood or village are called to assemble for an identification parade in front of hooded informers. According to journalists and human rights activists in Kashmir, the informers are often detainees themselves who have been threatened with death unless they identify a quota of militants.[54] Those whom the informers point out are taken away for torture and interrogation. A number of the detainees are simply taken out and shot. Human rights groups in Kashmir have documented several hundred of these killings since July 1992. Asia Watch and PHR directly investigated 19 such killings during two research missions to Kashmir in 1992 and 1993.

Officials in Kashmir admit privately that the government is pursuing a "catch and kill" campaign. One official told a reporter, "Yes, they're killing them. Maybe it's because the jails are full -- or they want to frighten the people. We try going by the rules, but nobody else is."[55] In April 1993, a senior security official in Srinagar told the *New York Times*, "We don't have custodial deaths here, we have alley deaths. ... If we have word of a hard-core militant, we will pick him up, take him to another lane and kill him."[56]

Lawyers in Kashmir told Asia Watch that the number of deaths in custody had increased since the launching of "Operation Walla" in September 1991, and escalated further with the launching of Operations "Tiger" and "Shiva" in late 1992. The increase has been reported in the Indian press.

> The charges of custody deaths have increased in the three months since 'Operation Tiger' was launched. ... [I]n September, when Mohammad Iqbal Zargar, the deputy chief of the Al-Umar

---

[54] For example, see the case of Mohammad Yaqub Mir, p. 57.

[55] See Tim McGirk, "Kashmiri Student Tells of Torture," *Independent*, May 25, 1993.

[56] See Edward Gargan, "Indian Troops Are Blamed as Kashmir Violence Rises," *New York Times*, April 18, 1993.

Mujahedin, was arrested during a search, an official spokesman confirmed his arrest to the press. The next morning, however, the authorities claimed Zargar had been killed in an encounter soon after his arrest. How he could have been killed 'after his arrest' is a question no one has any answer to. ... Officials in the Raj Bhavan concede that the charges against custody deaths are the most serious crisis the administration has faced in the past couple of years.[57]

While it is impossible to confirm a precise number of deaths in custody during this period, human rights groups and others monitoring detentions and deaths since the conflict began have also reported the increase. In an article published on January 15, 1993, *India Today* reported that human rights activists in the state claimed to have documented some 300 deaths in custody since the conflict began.[58] One local human rights groups reported figures of up to 127 deaths in custody in the first three months of 1993.[59] According to a report in the *Kashmir Times*, there were 132 alleged deaths in custody between March 22 and April 26, 1993.[60] Asia Watch and PHR obtained lists of deaths in custody compiled by human rights monitors and lawyers, documenting fifteen deaths in custody in July, 1992; 19 in August, 1992; 37 in September, 1992; and 36 in the first two weeks of October, 1992. Writ petitions urging a judicial inquiry into the deaths were filed in the Jammu and Kashmir High Court each month during this period. Asia Watch and PHR also obtained incomplete lists for the period from December 1992 through March 1993 which detail an additional 128 deaths in custody.

---

[57] See Harinder Baweja, "Severe Setback," *India Today*, January 15, 1993, pp. 81-82.

[58] See Harinder Baweja, "Severe Setback," *India Today*, January 15, 1993, p. 81.

[59] See "Kashmir Rebels Say 13 Killed in Ambush," Reuter, April 17, 1993.

[60] See Noor-ul Qamrain, "Issues that Rock Kashmir Now," *Kashmir Times*, April 26, 1993.

Detainees have also disappeared in the custody of the security forces. A list of 99 disappearances appears in Appendix A.

Government security forces have also engaged in reprisal killings against civilians. In most cases, these attacks follow militant ambushes in which security personnel are injured or killed. The security forces then retaliate against civilians in the area of the attack by shooting indiscriminately into crowded market places and residential areas.[61] In other cases, the security forces cordon off the neighborhood from which they believe the attack was launched and conduct house-to-house searches. Residents are routinely beaten, and in many cases detained and tortured or shot dead. As with other summary executions, the authorities generally claim that civilian casualties during such operations result from "cross-fire." Asia Watch and PHR obtained documents on more than 200 reprisal killings that took place between July and September 1992. We directly investigated 47 such killings which occurred between July 1992 and April 1993. The evidence gathered by Asia Watch and PHR indicates that in many of these cases, the killings are deliberate.

Additionally, Indian security forces have used lethal force against peaceful demonstrators, shooting unarmed civilians. The use of lethal force in such circumstances violates the 1979 United Nations Code of Conduct for Law Enforcement Officials. Article 3 of the Code provides: "Law enforcement officials may use force only when strictly necessary to the extent required for the performance of their duty." The official commentary to the Code adds:

> This provision emphasizes that the use of force by law enforcement officials should be exceptional.... The use of firearms is considered an extreme measure.... In general, firearms should not be used except when a suspected offender offers armed resistance or otherwise jeopardizes the lives of others and less extreme measures are not sufficient to restrain or apprehend the suspected offender.

Thus, the use of lethal force should be proportional to the threat. The evidence Asia Watch and PHR gathered indicates that on a number of

---

[61] In these cases, the security forces responded to militant attacks by attacking targets which do not constitute military objectives. Such attacks are strictly prohibited under the laws of war. See Protocol I, Article 51.

occasions, the Indian security forces opened fire on civilians in non-life-threatening situations where other means of control could and should have been used.

Security legislation has increased the likelihood of such abuses by authorizing the security forces to shoot to kill and to destroy civilian property. Under these laws, the security forces are protected from prosecution for human rights violations. On July 5, 1990, the governor of Jammu and Kashmir, Girish Saxena, promulgated the Armed Forces (Jammu and Kashmir) Special Powers Ordinance, 1990, which in September was passed by the Indian Parliament as the Armed Forces (Jammu and Kashmir) Special Powers Act. The act authorizes the governor or the central government to declare the whole or any part of the state to be a "disturbed area" if it is found that disturbances in the area are such that "the use of the armed forces in aid of the civil power" is necessary to prevent "terrorist acts" or activities directed towards bringing about secession. In a "disturbed area," the act empowers "any commissioned officer, warrant officer, non-commissioned officer or any other person of equivalent rank in the armed forces" to,

> after giving such due warning as he may consider necessary, fire upon or otherwise use force, even to the causing of death, against any person who is acting in contravention of any law or order for the time being in force in the disturbed area prohibiting the assembly of five or more persons or the carrying of weapons or of things capable of being used as weapons or of fire-arms, ammunition or explosive substances....

The legislation also authorizes such personnel to "enter and search, without warrant, any premises" to make an arrest where "reasonable suspicion exists that [a person] has committed or is about to commit a cognizable offence." It also states that a magistrate or police officer not below the rank of sub-inspector may

> destroy any arms dump, prepared or fortified position or shelter from which armed attacks are made or are likely to be made or are attempted to be made, or any structure used as a training camp for armed volunteers or utilised as a hide-out by armed gangs or absconders wanted for any offence.

Such a provision makes it possible for security forces to engage in arson with impunity.

Also on July 5, 1990, the state government promulgated the Jammu and Kashmir Disturbed Areas Act and declared as "disturbed areas" all six districts of the Kashmir valley and a 20-kilometer belt in the border districts of Poonch and Rajouri in Jammu region.[62] The Jammu and Kashmir Disturbed Areas Act, 1990, also empowers a magistrate or a police officer to use lethal force "against any person who is indulging in any act which may result in serious breach of the public order or is acting in contravention of any law or order for the time being in force prohibiting the assembly of five or more persons or the carrying of weapons."[63] Both acts provide, "No suit, prosecution, or other legal proceedings shall be instituted except with the previous sanction of the State Government against any person in respect of anything done or purporting to be done in exercise of the powers conferred [by the Acts]."[64] The provisions in both of these acts on the use of lethal force directly violate the U.N. Code for Law Enforcement (Article 3).

Thus, while it is clear that the conflict in Kashmir constitutes a serious threat to civil order, the steps the government has taken in its efforts to stem the insurgency violate international human rights laws which prohibit the arbitrary deprivation of life and other human rights abuses. Security legislation in force in Kashmir grants extraordinary power to officers in the security forces to shoot and kill peaceful demonstrators and unarmed civilians. By encouraging the use of lethal force and protecting the police from accountability for their actions, these laws effectively grant the security forces a license to kill.

---

[62] Yusuf Jameel, "Armed Forces in J & K Get Special Powers," *Telegraph*, July 7, 1990.

[63] The Jammu and Kashmir Disturbed Areas Act, 1990, Section 4.

[64] Ibid, Section 6; and Armed Forces (Jammu and Kashmir) Special Powers Act, Section 7.

Summary Executions and Deaths in Custody

Attempted Execution of Masroof Sultan

Masroof Sultan, 19, told Asia Watch that on April 8, 1993, he was traveling by municipal bus from his residence in Batmaloo to Siri Partap College in Lal Chowk, Srinagar, where he was a first year student in chemistry -- a trip he made every day. He boarded the bus at Rambagh Bridge at 11:00 a.m. Just after it crossed the bridge, the bus was stopped by BSF security forces. Masroof told Asia Watch:

> The BSF came to me, pointed their rifles and ordered me to get off the bus. They said, "If you don't get down we will shoot you. We will let you go after 10 minutes." When I got down I could see that other buses had also been stopped there. I was told to sit by the side of the road together with about 50 other people. The security forces surrounded us.

The BSF had launched a crackdown in the area, and had stopped dozens of vehicles on the road. Masroof was the only person taken from his bus. After about an hour, Masroof was told to go to Rambagh park on the right side of the bridge. There were several hundred people assembled there, mostly young men, surrounded by dozens of security forces. After some time, the detainees were divided into groups. As Masroof sat there he saw other young men taken in front of twelve security vehicles for identification. As each young man was brought forward, he was ordered to close his eyes as a soldier turned him to face the vehicles. Masroof was kept there for about an hour, and then ordered to move back to the side of the road. He was ordered to show his college identification card. He did so, telling the security forces that he had to take his examinations at college. Again he was told he would be released in ten minutes. He was ordered to sit by the side of the road again, together with three other detainees. After an hour, four BSF came up to Masroof and kicked and punched him until his nose and lips were bleeding. An officer whom Masroof described as having three stars on the shoulder of his uniform told Masroof, "We will kill you." The soldiers also kicked and punched the other three men who were detained with Masroof. One of the BSF soldiers then told Masroof to come with them. The BSF blindfolded Masroof and made him walk for about five minutes. When the blindfold was removed, Masroof saw that he was in a small room. The three other young men were also in the room, along with about twelve security forces.

The security forces took down the names and addresses of Masroof and the other three men. They said to them, "You are our brothers. Tell us that you are militants and we can't hit you. One of them said, "If you don't admit you are a militant, we will beat you. This is your last chance."" Then the other three men were taken out of the room. The remaining four or five security forces told Masroof to take off his clothes and sit on the floor. They told him, "Admit you are a militant. Admit you are a member of Hezb-ul Mujahidin." When he replied that he was a student, they said:

> Everyone in Kashmir is a militant. Even a child is a militant. You are also a militant. We don't care about you or your examinations. Our work is to hit you. Our officers tell us to hit you if you don't admit to being a militant and
> tell us about your weapons.

They told him they would release him if he admitted to being a militant and gave up his guns. They told him,

> If you admit to being a militant, we will release you. If you don't want to be released, we will take you in custody. If you don't want to be in custody, we will make you an officer and we will take you with us.

Then the security forces put a wooden stick under Masroof's knees and tied his feet and hands together with rope. Then they took a two-foot long wooden stick and struck him in the legs, hips, arms, chest, stomach and neck, aiming particularly for the joints. While they were beating him they continued to accuse him of being a militant. Masroof stated that at one point, the uniformed man with three stars on his shoulder came in and asked the other security forces if Masroof had admitted to being a militant. When they told him no, the officer told the others to continue the beating. After some time Masroof fell unconscious.

Masroof awakened when cold water was thrown on his face and his hands were loosened. The BSF told him that if he did not admit to being a militant they would give him electric shocks. Then the officer returned and told the soldiers to take Masroof to "Papa 2" -- the name for the interrogation center at Hari Niwas -- and to give him electric shocks there. Masroof said that when they told him that, he believed he was going to die.

> I was paining in my heart. They told me they would release me after ten minutes. I am a student, a college student, I am nothing. What are they doing? What is Indian government doing? This is the rule of the Indian government? A person is going to college and they catch him and interrogate him and kill him?

The security forces untied him, dressed him in his clothes and put him in a jeep. At that time his parents, who had come to the interrogation center, tried to come over to the jeep but the security forces pushed them away. One of the BSF told Masroof, "Look at your mother. This is the last time in your life -- look at your mother's face. After that you have to die now." Then Masroof was told to put his head down, and the jeep drove off for about thirty minutes. When the jeep stopped, the blindfold was removed and Masroof could see the same three men who had been with him on the side of the road getting out of three other jeeps, and all three appeared to be limping. At Papa II, the BSF captain who had kicked him said to him "Why are you limping? Now we will do with you." One soldier took down his name and then he was put in a dimly-lit room with two BSF soldiers but no officers. His clothes were again removed. They soldiers told Masroof, "We don't want to kill you. Admit you are a militant and give up your gun and we will release you." When he replied that he had been told he would be released in ten minutes, the BSF threw cold water on him. Then the BSF took two copper wires which were attached to an electric socket in the wall, rubbed them together and said, "If you don't admit, you can die." Then they touched the wires to his feet and genitals, holding it each time for several seconds. They moved the wire from one foot to the other and to his genitals repeatedly for half an hour. While they were doing this, they kept asking Masroof if he was a militant and telling him to give up his gun. When they removed the wires, Masroof saw that he had blood on his genitals. Then the BSF touched the wires to Masroof's chest and arms and back until he lost consciousness. After a while, the three-starred officer returned and told the other soldiers to take Masroof back to Rambagh.

Masroof was blindfolded with his sweater, then dressed in his own clothes and carried out to a jeep. When he told them he could not breathe, the soldiers loosened the blindfold and Masroof could see a little bit underneath it. Inside the jeep were four or five BSF who punched and kicked him, and jabbed him with the barrels of their guns as they drove. They parked beside a building near Rambagh bridge and the officer went inside the interrogation center. Then he came out with four or five others. They drove for ten or fifteen minutes. Masroof stated:

> Then they took me out of the jeep and stood me up against a tree. I said to them again, "What are you doing? You told me you would release me." And they told me, "We know you are innocent. But last night, in Batmaloo there was a blast and four of our men were killed. We know you are nothing, you are a student. Four of our men were killed, so now we take four persons from that area and kill them. Then we equalize for our persons killed. Now we will release you forever. Take your mind to god." I was still blindfolded. I heard the security forces walk away from me and then I heard them cock their guns. Someone said, "one, two, three" then they fired and I flew up into the air. I had been shot in both legs. I fell on the ground. I tore off the sweater they blindfolded me with and saw I was lying on a hill next to the river. There was a full moon. I heard someone say, "Make sure he's dead." One of them came up to me and kicked me in the head and said, "He's still alive." The officer said, "Shoot him in the heart." Then the soldier shot me in the chest and arm. Someone again shouted, "Check if he is dead or alive." Someone kicked me again and said, "He's still alive." Then someone said, "Shoot close." I heard a shot but nothing hit me. Then a voice said, "What are you doing you bloody bastard? Shoot him in the head." Then I heard a shot and a bullet grazed the back of my neck, causing a lot of blood. I held my breath. Someone kicked me again, then shouted, "He's dead." The soldier took my sweater and left. I heard other gunshots after that. I was bleeding badly and in great pain. It was hard to breathe. After about an hour and a half, I saw a jeep coming and men looking around with a flashlight. They were speaking Kashmiri. I asked for water and saw that they were Jammu and Kashmir policemen. They took me to the hospital.

When Masroof was examined[65] on April 27, 1993, he had a circular encrusted wound measuring 1.5 centimeters on the left side of his thorax; an irregularly-shaped wound 8 x 5 centimeters on the right side of his thorax; an irregularly shaped black mark measuring 3 x 4 centimeters above the nipple of his left breast; a circular, encrusted wound measuring 2.5 centimeters on his right upper arm; a wound 5x2 centimeters on his right hip; a circular wound measuring 1 centimeter on his right buttock; and a reddened area measuring 20 x 10 centimeters on his left lower leg which was extremely sensitive when touched. The X-rays showed a partial fracture of the upper right thigh bone which may have been caused by severe beating. There were also open wounds on each leg and under the right arm which appeared to be gunshot wounds. PHR-Denmark examined Masroof's X-rays, which showed bullet injuries in both thighs, the left armpit, the left side of the neck and the right elbow. At the time of his arrival at the hospital, the left cavity of Masroof's chest was partially filled with blood. According to the medical report prepared by PHR-Denmark, the physical examination showed wounds and scars consistent with the beating and electric shock torture Masroof described.

The doctor who was treating Masroof stated that before Masroof was arrested, a grenade had killed a number of soldiers in Batmaloo. Afterwards, the security forces launched a crackdown in the area and stopped all the buses at Rambagh. Masroof may have been singled out because he was from Batmaloo.[66]

The Killing of Gowhar Amin Bahadur and Javed Bakshir

Gowhar Amin Bahadur, 21, a resident of Batmaloo, Srinagar, was killed after being taken into custody by the BSF, also on April 8, 1993.

---

[65] Masroof was examined by Jens Norbaek, M.D., a member of Physicians for Human Rights--Denmark on April 27, 1993. The results of the examination were documented in photographs, some of which appear in this report. The interview was recorded on video.

[66] Masroof was also interviewed by foreign journalists. See Tim McGirk, "Kashmiri Student Tells of Torture," *Independent*, May 25, 1993, and Molly Moore and John Anderson, "Kashmir's Brutal and Unpublicized War," *Washington Post*, May 31, 1993.

His father stated that on that morning, Gowhar had gone to his in-laws' house. At about 10:30 a.m., BSF forces entered Batmaloo.[67]

B.,[68] a resident of Batmaloo, stated that he was at home on the morning of April 8. At about 7:10 a.m., BSF forces knocked on his door and told him that a crackdown was underway and that he and all the male members of his family were to come outside and report to the park. B. told Asia Watch:

> I left the house and saw the main road was filled with BSF. When I reached Batmaloo Colony Park, I saw Gowhar there. I asked him why he was there. He said he was not worried since he had the release order from the court. There were many people in the park. At 8:30 a.m. the BSF told everyone to go to the general bus stand. Gowhar and I went to the bus stand. At about 10:30 a.m. the BSF told a crowd of maybe 100 people at the bus stand to walk in front of five security vehicles. All day I and others were paraded in front of the security vehicles.[69] Gowhar was in the first row of persons made to walk in front of the vehicles. As he was walking, he was pulled out of the line by a BSF officer and his *pheran* [a cape-like coat traditionally worn by Kashmiri men] was pulled off and wrapped around his head. He was then taken behind the vehicles. Shortly afterwards, Javed Bakshir was taken from the line and put behind one of the vehicles. Only Gowhar and Javed were taken. After a few minutes, a military van pulled up and the two of them were put into it and the van drove off. An hour later the same van returned to the general bus stand. All the rest of us were still there. The van came down a road that leads to Balpora, a neighborhood in Batmaloo. At about 2:30 p.m. I was still at the bus stand, I saw a Jammu and Kashmir police flatbed

---

The crackdown reportedly followed a grenade attack on a BSF bunker in which a number of security personnel were killed.

[68] PHR and Asia Watch have chosen to use initials to protect the identity of witnesses. In some cases of death, or where the incident has previously been publicized, the victim's full name appears.

[69] Informers who sit inside the vehicles are either hooded or are obscured by tinted glass.

truck coming from Balpora and saw two pairs of feet sticking out of the back as it drove by. I was released at 5:30 p.m.

A., Gowhar's father, was permitted to go to his office after he showed the BSF his government identity card. When he reached his office at 11:10 a.m., A. received a phone call saying that Gowhar had been arrested. A. could not identify who called him. He went home to collect the court papers showing Gowhar's release from jail in June 1992 to show to the BSF,[70] but as he walked out of the house, the troops told him an operation was underway and he could not go to the BSF office. At 3:30 p.m. Gowhar's father-in-law called A. to tell him that Gowhar's body was lying in a truck outside the police control room. A. told Asia Watch:

> I went there and saw the body. There was blood on the back of his head which had been smashed open. He had bullet wounds in his back, the right side of his abdomen and the right side of his neck.

The body of Javed 'Tanga' Bakshir, which was lying in the same truck, also had bullet wounds.

A witness, L., who resides in Bolpora stated that she was at home between 2:30 p.m. and 3:00 p.m. on April 8 when she saw a van and two security vehicles stop fifteen yards from her house. She saw uniformed security forces make two people, whose heads were covered with their *pheran*s, come down from the van. She stated that she had known Gowhar for many years and recognized him by his *pheran* because it was black, an unusual color. The men were made to enter a lane, accompanied by about thirty security forces.

Two witnesses, J. and S., who live next door to L., stated that they were in their house at the time. Two soldiers came to J. at the window and told her not to look or they would kill her. She went up to the second floor and looked again and saw the security forces carry a wooden log, which had been propped up against a house. Other soldiers were in the compound watching. J. told Asia Watch:

---

[70] Gowhar had previously been arrested May 17, 1990 under the Terrorist and Disruptive Activities Act. He was held in the Jammu jail. He was released on June 24, 1992, after the charges were dismissed.

Then the soldiers tied the boys' hands behind their backs and forced them both to lie face down with their heads on the logs. One soldier was carrying a white bag out of which he took a stick of some kind. Then he struck both of the boys on the head with the stick four or five times. Then several of the soldiers went into the street and fired two bursts of machine gunfire. Several soldiers shouted into their wirelesses, "We have killed two militants. They had been hidden and we killed them." Shortly after that a Jammu and Kashmir police truck came and the police removed the two bodies.

Then J. and S. went out and saw that there was blood and flesh on the log. J., L. and S. all stated that they recognized Gowhar's height and general physical appearance and his *pheran*.

The Killings in Srabala

Sajad Ahmed Chaudhury, Ishtaq Ahmed Khan, Tahar Mughal and a man known as Darzi were killed after being taken into custody by the BSF in Srabala on April 9, 1993. From the time the men were taken into custody until their bodies were handed over to their families, the Deputy Commissioner (D.C.), Abdul Salam Bhatt -- the senior civilian authority in Srinagar -- repeatedly told the families that the four were in custody and maintained that they would be released.

At about 5:30 a.m. on April 9, 1993, the BSF launched a crackdown in Srabala, Srinagar. All of the men from the area were ordered to assemble at Iqbal Park. The forces conducted three identification parades, during which the men were made to form a line and march past rows of security vehicles. G., a 60-year-old shopkeeper, told Asia Watch that the younger men were paraded twice before two separate rows of security vehicles. Inside the vehicles sat a driver and an informer whose head was covered. Nine men were taken into custody in the first round, and five in the second. As each of the fourteen young men were paraded in front of the vehicles, a hooded man inside would indicate something to the driver, who would then signal to one of the soldiers outside to send the young man to the vehicle. Among the fourteen who were detained, G. recognized Sajad Ahmed Chaudhury, Ishtaq Ahmed Khan, Tahar Mughal, and a man he knew only as Darzi. Afterwards, the vehicles drove off.

On April 9, at 5:00 p.m. the Jammu and Kashmir police brought the dead body of Darzi to his residence in Srabala. G. stated that there was blood on the chest.

M., a retired civil servant who witnessed the detention of the four men, told Asia Watch:

> I saw the fourteen young men taken, four of whom I knew: Sajad, Ishtaq, Tahar and Darzi. Afterwards, I went with Sajad Chaudhury's father to speak with a BSF officer on behalf of Sajad and Tahar Mughal. The officer said the two would be screened and after screening they would be let go.

Sajad's father, Ghulam Nabi, stated that after the crackdown had ended, at about 4:30 p.m., he and some others went to Deputy Commissioner Abdul Salam Bhatt to find out what happened to the young men that had been taken. Ghulam Nabi told Asia Watch that the D.C. had assured them that the detainees would be set free. Afterwards, several detainees were released after being beaten by the security forces. Then Ghulam Nabi and the other parents went back to the D.C. at about 6:00 p.m. and asked for the release of their sons. The D.C. showed them a list of all the men who had been taken. The list included Sajad, Ishtaq, Tahar and Darzi. The D.C. assured the families that all the men on the list would be released by 9:30 p.m. Shortly thereafter, when Ghulam Nabi and the others returned home, the body of Darzi was brought by the police. Ghulam Nabi called the D.C. again and was again told that that all would be released by 9:30 p.m. The D.C. told him that Sajad Chaudhury had taken his meals in the D.C.'s presence. Early on the morning of April 10, Ghulam Nabi and the others went to the D.C.'s residence, and he again told them that when he got to his office he would bring back all the detained men, including Sajad.

On April 10 at 12:30 p.m., a Jammu and Kashmir police truck parked near the Mahaboobia Press, a printing press in Srabala, and local residents took the bodies of Sajad Ahmed Chaudhury, Ishtaq Ahmed Khan and Tahar Mughal out of the truck.

A government press statement issued on April 11, 1993, stated that the bodies of Tahir, Sajad and Ishtaq had been found in Malabagh, Lal Bazaar and that another body of an unidentified male killed by militants was found in Laweypora.

The Killing of Ashiq Hussain Masoodi

On December 16, 1992, at about 11:30 a.m., four BSF battalions launched a crackdown in the Narwara area of Srinagar. At 2:00 p.m., all the men in the neighborhood were ordered to assemble at the Idgah.[71] The BSF troops came to the house of M. and his brother, Ashiq Hussain Masoodi, 19, a weaver, and told them to come outside. The security forces then searched the house. M. told Asia Watch that all the men were paraded in a line one by one in front of five BSF vehicles. Five men were selected in the first line-up. In the second identification parade, Ashiq was taken at 9:00 p.m. M. told Asia Watch:

> I was sitting in the Idgah. I saw Ashiq walk in front of the vehicles, then he was brought back in front of one of them and his *pheran* was pulled over his head and he was placed in a green truck and taken away. At 10:00 p.m. we were allowed to leave.

G., a resident of Narwara, stated that on December 17, 1992, at about 3:00 p.m. he was looking out of the window of his house when he saw five BSF vehicles pull up in front of a shed housing a sawmill about 25 feet away. He told Asia Watch:

> The soldiers went into the shed and made the workers get out. Eight to ten soldiers then pulled the boy with his head still covered by his *pheran* and took him into the shed. I could see the saw running and heard cries. After a few minutes all was quiet. This was about 3:30 p.m. At about 5:00 p.m., the security forces withdrew. The workers went back into the shed. Then I left the house and went into the shed and saw Ashiq's body lying there in the sawdust and bits of wood. His right arm was nearly severed; he had a deep gash to the neck, and blood was collecting in the corner of his mouth.

---

[71] An idgah is an open area used for community prayers on the holy days of Id'ul Fitr and Id'ul Azha.

The Killings at Tengpora

At about 12:00 noon on October 18, 1992, the BSF launched a crackdown in the Tengpora neighborhood of Srinagar. All of the men in the area were ordered to assemble on the roadside. At about 3:00 p.m., a large number of security forces entered the house of M. where a number of women and children from the neighborhood had gathered. The women stated that the security forces insulted them, took Rs. 4,000 [U.S.$ 130] and some gold chains, and then left.

At about 5:00 p.m., the security forces returned to the house, bringing with them three men taken into custody in the crackdown: Abdul Rashid Dar, 28, a shopkeeper; Maulvi Mohammad Dar, 31; and Abdul Rahman Dar, 40. The BSF accused the women of sheltering the men. They told the men to put their hands up and then opened fire, shooting two of the men in the chest. Maulvi Mohammad Dar was shot in the yard as he tried to run away. As they left, the BSF took the other two bodies and left them out on the road.

The body of a fourth man taken into custody that day, Farooq Ahmed, who was described by local residents as a member of the Hezb-ul Mujahidin militant group, was brought back at about 10:00 p.m.

On October 18, the authorities in Srinagar released a press statement about the incident. In it, the government claimed that, "The security forces conducted an operation at Tengpora, Srinagar, when they were fired upon by militants. The fire was returned and in exchange of fire, four militants were killed. One security official also lost his life, and another one was injured. Eight subversive elements were apprehended and ... arms and ammunition recovered."

The Dal Gate Killings

On October 14, 1992, at approximately 6:00 a.m., a unit of the BSF launched a crackdown[72] in a seven kilometer area of Srinagar known as Dal Gate. Using loudspeakers, the BSF ordered all the men in the area to assemble at Tang Bagh, a park near Dal Lake. During the next twelve hours, the security forces ordered the men to parade past a row of BSF vehicles in which hooded informers sat. There were three such

---

[72] Crackdown is the term ordinarily used for cordon and search operations.

identification parades. Those who were identified were put in vans and driven away. In all, some 60 men were detained.

Asia Watch and PHR interviewed many of the men who had been ordered to assemble at Tang Bagh and who had witnessed the detentions. They stated that they heard gunfire between 7:00 - 7:45 p.m. from the Shankar Char Hill area, not far from Dal Gate. One man, H., told Asia Watch/PHR:

> While I was lined up for the identification parade, I asked one BSF, "What are you doing with those men you have taken?" He told me, "We will give you the answer in half an hour." Half an hour later we heard gunfire.

The crackdown ended at about 9:30 p.m. At about 6:00 a.m. the next morning, the Jammu and Kashmir police called the families of four of the men who had been detained to inform them that the bodies of their relatives were in the police control room. The dead men were identified as Mohammad Hussain, about 25, an employee in a government shop; Shabir Ahmed Mir, about 20, a student; Musadiq Ahmed, also in his early 20s, a student; and Zahid Hussain, 24, a student. Zahid walked with a cane because he had broken his leg while playing soccer some ten weeks earlier. Witnesses told Asia Watch and PHR that they feared that the BSF might have detained him on the suspicion that the injury had resulted from militant activity. Family members showed Asia Watch/PHR a copy of the doctor's report, dated August 2, 1992, corroborating the report that the fracture had occurred during the game.

A former Jammu and Kashmir police officer living near the site where the bodies were found told Asia Watch/PHR that at about 7:30 p.m. he heard approximately six intermittent bursts of gunfire about 200 meters from his house. He also stated that he saw security vehicles moving in a wooded area behind his house at that time. When PHR and Asia Watch visited the site at about 12:00 noon on October 15, we found fresh tire tracks and blood on the pavement, and detected the distinct odor of blood. Other witnesses who had seen the security vehicles stated that the security vehicles they saw belonged to the 92nd Battalion of the BSF.

The government's statement about the incident, which was published in the Kashmir Times on October 16, claimed that,

> Four people were killed in an exchange of fire between militants and security personnel in the Buchwar area of the city. ... Three AK-47 rifles, one pistol, four magazines and some ammunition and incriminating documents were recovered after the encounter.

In response to a request from Asia Watch/PHR, the government subsequently provided a statement describing the incident as occurring during a "joint operation by the Border Security Force and the Police." The statement claimed that

> [W]hen the party was approaching Dal Gate, militants opened fire which was returned by the security forces. During a search of the area, four bodies of terrorists who had been killed were found along with 3 AK 56 rifles with magazines and ammunition, a pistol with magazine and ammunition, two grenades and some documents and binoculars etc. The bodies of all the four terrorists were handed over to the Police. It would be clear from this that this was a targeted operation based on information and the persons who were killed can by no means be categorized as innocent students.

However, Asia Watch and PHR interviewed numerous eyewitnesses who testified that the four men had been taken into custody before they were killed. Moreover, journalists who subsequently investigated the incident reported that the four had been taken into custody during an identification parade.

> What every Kashmiri knows is that only the other day, on hearing incessant firing, security forces cordoned off the Dal Lake area for an identification parade and detained 60 suspects. The next day security forces claimed that four of them had been killed after they challenged the forces.[73]

The other sixty men detained on the night of October 15 were apparently taken to a BSF interrogation center. Despite requests from Asia Watch and PHR, the government has not provided any information

---

[73] See Harinder Baweja, "Severe Setback," *India Today*, January 15, 1993, p. 81.

about their whereabouts and the charges against them, or whether they have been released. Asia Watch and PHR are concerned that some may have been killed, or may still be held in detention centers in Kashmir. Witnesses provided the names, and in some cases the ages and occupations of some of the detainees, which we have listed here.

Altaf Ahmed Wani, 28; son of Zahoor Wani
Ashaq Hussain, son of Abdul Majid Sheikh
Syed Tanvir, son of Gulzar Ahmed
Zaffar Ahmed, son of Mohammad Azim Jhon
Fida Hussain, son of Ghulam Mohammad Raja
Jahn Mohammad Mir, son of Mir Habibullah
Riaz Ahmed Baba, a student, son of Abdul Gani Baba
Aijaz Ahmed Bhatt, son of Ali Mohammad Bhatt
Sayyad Ahmed Bhatt, a student, son of Abdul Qayyum Bhatt
Mushtaq Ahmed Shiekh, 16, son of Moiuddin Sheikh
Muzzafar Ahmed Bhatt, son of Mohammad Yusuf
Feroz Ahmed Gilkar, son of Ali Mohammad Gilkar
Hilal Ahmed Najar, a student, son of Ali Mohammad Najar
Bashir Ahmed Sofi, son of Ghulam Mohammad Sofi
Javed Ahmed Mir, son of Ghulam Moiuddin Mir
Mohammad Amin Dar, son of Mohammad Yusuf
Muzaffar Sheikh, son of Mahad Sheikh
Anis Ahmed Wani, a student, son of Ghulam Wani
Mohammad Maqbool Sheikh, son of Habibullah Sheikh
Naseer Ahmed Mir, son of Assadullah
Bashir Ahmed Shah, resident of Tral
Mohammad Shaban Gugree, son of Abdul Karim
Bilal Ahmed, son of Abdul Gani
Zaffar Bhatt, son of Ghulam Ahmed Bhatt
Abdul Khaliq, son of Abdul Rehman
Javed Ahmed Mir, son of Ghulam Nabi Mir
Pupa Wali, son of Mohammad Sultan Wali
Abdul Majid Najar, son of Abdul Gani
Javed Ahmed Khan, son of Ghulam Moiuddin

The Killings in Abeguzar

On October 10, 1992, at about 12:00 noon the BSF launched a crackdown in the Lal Chowk area of Srinagar. A witness, M., who was present during the crackdown, told Asia Watch/PHR that the security forces had called the neighborhood men to assemble in Lal Chowk at around noon. Twice they were paraded in front of twelve security vehicles. Shakil was taken aside in the first round and put inside an armored vehicle. During the second round, another eight men were taken. After that, the security forces ordered everyone to turn away while the vehicles drove away.

K., a resident, told Asia Watch/PHR that she was at home at the time. The BSF shouted for all the men to come out for an identification parade. During the crackdown, nine men were detained. Sometime after 4:00 p,m, K. saw that three of the young men who had been detained -- two of which were from Abeguzar, one from Kanyar -- had been brought back to Abeguzar by the BSF. She told Asia Watch/PHR:

> The BSF brought them to a metal gate in front of a yard near my house and shot open the lock. The three men had their heads covered with their own clothes. The security forces pushed them through the gate and beat them with their rifle butts. About a minute later, I heard gunfire from inside the gate. The gunfire lasted about fifteen minutes. At about 6:30 p.m., the crackdown was lifted and the security forces left. About fifteen minutes later, the Jammu and Kashmir police came and carried out three bodies. Then we went inside the yard. There was blood everywhere and bullet holes in the wall.

Mohammad M., the father of Shakil Ahmed, told PHR/Asia Watch that when he returned home after the crackdown was lifted, his neighbors told him that his son had been arrested. He went to the police control room and identified the body of his son.

M., who later saw the bodies in the police control room, stated that there were bullet wounds in the backs of all three men. He identified one of the bodies as Shakil Ahmed, and another as that of Imtiaz Ahmed, 15. The third man was unknown to him.

Official sources stated that all three had been killed in "crossfire."

The Killing of Mohammad Yaqub Mir

Mohammad Yaqub Mir, 17, a student and part-time auto-rickshaw driver and newspaper hawker, was killed after being taken into custody by the BSF on September 18, 1992. Witnesses told Asia Watch that on

September 18, at about 5:30 a.m. a friend of Mohammad Yaqub's named Bilal came to the house and asked Mohammad Yaqub to accompany him to a place called Syed Shahib Shrine. Bilal took him instead to Barbarshah, where a crackdown was going on, and then slipped away.[74] Mohammad Yaqub was arrested by the BSF, and ordered to identify militants in the neighborhood. When he refused to do so, he was killed by the BSF.

At about 8:30 a.m. the BSF came to Lal Chowk in several security vehicles and brought Mohammad Yaqub with them. The troops ordered the young men in the area to line up and Mohammad Yaqub was told to identify militants in the group. When he did not identify anyone, the security forces withdrew from Lal Chowk at about 10:00 a.m., taking Mohammad Yaqub with them. About fifteen minutes later, witnesses heard gunfire from a location about 200 yards away, near the river. Some time later the Jammu and Kashmir police arrived, having been told by the BSF to collect a body. A neighbor, K., who brought Mohammad Yaqub's body to the police, stated that there were bullet wounds in the back of his head, and stab wounds in his upper right arm and right leg.

A witness, Z., who lives near the pump shed where Mohammad Yaqub was shot, stated that at about 9:30 a.m., she saw a large number of security forces bring Yaqub to the pump shed, and Z. heard him cry out, "Oh god," then heard the gunshots and a short time later saw his body being taken out.

Official sources reported that "Militants fired on a security force vehicle this morning at Abeguzar. The fire was returned. During the firing, one militant was killed."[75]

---

[74] Witnesses told Asia Watch that Bilal was an informer. Shortly after Mohammad Yaqub Mir's killing, Bilal was abducted by militants from the Al-Barq group and shot dead near Nursinggarh, Srinagar.

[75] As cited in Sukhmani Singh, "The Men Behind the Masks," *Illustrated Weekly of India*, October 10-16, 1992, p.6.

Reprisal Attacks

The Burning of Lal Chowk

In one of the most devastating incidents of its kind, on April 10, 1993, a large section of downtown Srinagar known as Lal Chowk was burned to the ground by Indian paramilitary troops, apparently in retaliation for the burning of an abandoned BSF building by local residents. The BSF commanding officer refused to heed warnings about the security risks of abandoning the force's headquarters and bunkers, and then ignored pleas for assistance from local police who were trying to protect these sites. The incident, which was one of the largest such arson attack by Indian forces since the beginning of the conflict,[76] left at least four civilians dead in the immediate area and more in attacks in nearby neighborhoods.[77] Although the senior most civilian authority in the city, Deputy Commissioner Abdul Salam Bhatt, witnessed the behavior of the security forces, he did not intervene.

Officer M. of the Jammu and Kashmir police, told Asia Watch that at 8:05 a.m. on April 10, he left the station on duty and walked toward Lal Chowk. Before he reached Lal Chowk, he was told that the BSF had vacated their building, the Sandam Dharam Sabha building, and their bunkers in Lal Chowk, which they had occupied since the beginning of the conflict. He entered the building and saw that no one was there, and that the bunker had been demolished. He told Asia Watch:

> The local people asked me why the forces had left. I went at 8:15 a.m. to see the BSF commander of the 117th division, B.R. Sharma, in the Dashma Akhara building. I saw that the troops, about 100 men, were standing in position, ready to move. I asked where the commander was, and a BSF deputy superintendent told me that the commander was in his office. I went straight to the office but Commanding Officer Sharma was not there; he was sleeping in the room next door and came out in his nightclothes at 8:15 a.m. I saluted him and told him that I was surprised that

---

[76] Arson has been a weapon in India's counter-insurgency strategy in Kashmir since 1990. See Asia Watch, *Kashmir Under Siege* (May 1991).

[77] See discussion of the "Shikara Killings", p.63.

> the BSF had withdrawn its troops without telling us. He said it was the order of a higher authority to withdraw the troops, and that he had started the withdrawal at 11:30 p.m. the night before. I told him the building was not safe because the local people set fire to buildings which have been abandoned by the security forces. I told him the BSF should provide me one platoon to protect the building. He said he had no troops available. I asked him to please give me six or seven men. He said he would see what he could do. I left the building.

Officer M. informed his superiors at the police control room and then returned to Lal Chowk. When he approached the Sandam Dharam Sabha building he was warned by the crowd that had assembled at the building not to go in because it had been mined. Concerned that the building would be set on fire, he returned to C.O. Sharma's office and again asked for troops to send to Lal Chowk. Officer M. told Asia Watch:

> C.O. Sharma then said, "Let us have a cup of tea." He ignored me. I told him it was not a time for tea, but a time to save Lal Chowk. He said he would arrange to send troops to Lal Chowk. I left the building and saw that the Sandam Dharam Sabha building had been set on fire. It was 8:50 a.m.

At that time, the fire was still small enough to be brought under control. Officer M. ordered the police control room to send the fire brigades, and within ten minutes the fire fighters arrived and tried to put out the fire. Officer M., together with his deputy, then went back to C.O. Sharma of BSF, who was taking tea with his Deputy Commander.

> My DSP told C.O. Sharma that it is a great shame for you that your headquarters is burning and you are taking tea. He asked, "Oh? It's burning? Really?"

The officers returned to Lal Chowk with fire fighters. After a few minutes, C.O. Sharma and a contingent of BSF troops arrived and began firing intermittently in all directions. This was about 9:20 a.m.

Then C.O. Sharma and Senior Superintendent of Police (SSP) Rajendra Kumar arrived and told the Jammu and Kashmir police that the area was under curfew. The curfew order was announced by megaphone. C.O. Sharma and SSP Kumar then proceeded toward Lal Chowk. The

BSF troops contined to shoot in all directions. One officer told Asia Watch that as some of the bullets struck the road, pebbles were knocked up to his head and drew blood. The officer saw BSF soldiers taking aim at civilians and firing. The BSF troops took over the entire Lal Chowk area, and after positioning themselves all around, continued to fire. The Deputy Commissioner, Abdul Salam Bhatt -- the senior civil authority in Srinagar -- hid under the seat of his car and would not come out.

By this time, the Sandam Dharam Sabha building was burning out of control. A Jammu and Kashmir police officer told Asia Watch that he was standing behind a telephone pole just outside of the Bombay and Gujarat hotels, when BSF troops came by and told him not to step out from behind the pole or he would be killed.

At about 9:50 a.m., a fire started at the Kokar Bazar, which is separated from the Sandam Dharam Sabha building by several buildings which were not burning. About five to ten minutes later, a fire started at the Standard Hotel and at residences at either side of the Dashma Akhara building. Witnesses stated that they could hear people in the buildings screaming for help. A police officer told Asia Watch that a waiter at the Standard Hotel screamed from a window to save him, and when the waiters tried to open the windows, the BSF fired at them and one waiter was injured. As the police went to the hotel, the BSF fired at them too, but did not hit any of the police. When the police reached the hotel, they discovered that the doors had been bolted shut from the outside. The police opened the doors and five or six waiters came out. The BSF troops told the police to "let them be burned." The police then went to other houses and rescued people from the fire which by then was consuming the buildings.

The gunfire continued for an hour and a half. Finally, after the fire was out of control, but the gunfire had stopped, the Inspector General of the BSF, Ashok Patel, the Additional Chief Secretary (Home), Mahmood ul-Rahman, the Additional Director General of the Crime Investigation Department (CID), Amar Kapoor, and the Advisor to Governor on Law and Order (Home) D.D. Saklani, arrived and asked what had happened. One of the Jammu and Kashmir police officers told them:

> I requested BSF to save Lal Chowk, but C.O. Sharma showed me a coldness and ignored my request.

The officer asked IG Patel to send army fire fighters. Patel responded that he had already requested them. An hour later Governor Krishna Rao and Director General of Police Bedi arrived. The fire was still raging out of control. At 2:30 p.m., a single army fire truck arrived with enough water to last ten or fifteen minutes.

M., a waiter at one of the hotels, told Asia Watch that on the morning of April 10, 1993, he came to work at the hotel at 8:00 a.m. Everything was quiet at that time and the bunkers near the hotel were still occupied by the security forces, as they had been for many months. Then at about 8:30 a.m. he heard people shouting slogans of "Azadi" (Freedom) and "We want freedom." He said that when he looked out of the first floor kitchen and dining room windows he saw Jammu and Kashmir police and civilians running in Lal Chowk in front of the hotel. Just after 8:30 a.m. he saw smoke and flames rising from the Sandam Dharam Sabha building. He told Asia Watch that at about that time a security vehicle arrived on the scene. The vehicle went towards the fire and then returned. He saw SSP Rajendra Kumar come out of the vehicle, walk toward the Sandam Dharam Sabha building and then walk back to the vehicle and put on a bullet-proof jacket and helmet. SSP Kumar then went inside the Akhara building. After half an hour, he and other security forces came out and, as M. watched from the dining room windows, about 100 security forces surrounded Lal Chowk and started firing indiscriminately.

After the fire started, people who were trapped inside the buildings tried to push open the doors only to discover that they had been bolted from the outside and could not be opened from the inside.[78] The soldiers moved down the street, one of them carrying a green plastic bucket into which another soldier dipped a small can and then threw liquid from the bucket onto wooden portions of the buildings. Within a few minutes, the buildings erupted in flames. The other soldiers continued to shoot all around Lal Chowk. M. saw a waiter from the hotel come to the second floor window and scream, "Spare us!", and then he saw at least two soldiers fire at the man. The man fell backward. Then the soldiers threw liquid from the bucket on the gate of the hotel. Fire erupted. Another soldier pointed some kind of weapon at the top of the Standard Hotel and fired and the roof burst into flames. Then the Jammu and Kashmir police came and opened the bolt on the door from the outside and five persons came out of the hotel. M. said that at about

---

[78] These bolts are normally used when the buildings are locked up for the night.

10:30 a.m., he broke open a window at the back of the hotel and escaped down the staircase of the mosque next door. As he went he saw that the doors of two buildings adjacent to the new Standard Hotel were bolted from the outside and people were pushing on them from the inside. He ran to Barbarshar along the by-ways and two others from the hotel escaped with him.

T., a resident, stated that as he was returning from home from Maisuma Bazaar, he heard bursts from light machine guns. He took refuge with friends in a house on Red Cross Road from where they could see the BSF putting liquid on the Standard Hotel and other buildings which then erupted in flames. When T. learned that his own house was on fire, he ran out on to Red Cross Road. He saw five BSF soldiers on the street, some of whom were gathered around a light machine gun outside the burning Standard Hotel. When T. reached home, he found the front door bolted from outside, as were other houses in the lane. He and his mother and sister then fled to a relative's house in another part of Srinagar.

M., another resident of Lal Chowk, stated that he heard shots at about 10:00 a.m. The security forces banged on the door of his house saying, "Come out, we will kill you." After that, he saw smoke coming from the right side of the house. M. and his family escaped through the back door. Since the burning of their house, the family has lived in a hotel.

In all, 59 houses, 190 shops, 53 stores where inventory was kept, two office buildings, five commercial buildings, two schools and a shrine inside the building were gutted by the fire. Four people were killed: a woman, Shishi Chouralsy; a man, Rahool Chouralsy, about 20; a boy, Mudasir, 14, who died of bullet injuries; and Bashid Ahmed Tantri, 30, a waiter, who was burned to death. One hundred and twenty-seven families lost their homes.

The Shikara Killings

Shortly after the fire began in Lal Chowk, BSF forces shot several people as they tried to cross the Jhelum river to safety. A., a resident of a houseboat on the Jhelum river told Asia Watch that at about 9:30 a.m. on April 10, 1993, while he was on the deck of his houseboat, having tea, he saw smoke rising from the Lal Chowk area behind the river bank. At about 9:30 a.m. he saw ten or eleven young men walk down from the bank in the area of Abeguzar and get into a shikara.[79] A. told Asia Watch that as the shikara started across the river, first one and then ten soldiers appeared on the bank. One soldier leaned on his knee and took aim at the shikara, firing 20-30 times. After the first soldier emptied his magazine, a second soldier began to fire and then a third, all emptying their magazines. A. said that he saw many bullets hitting the water. When the firing started, all the people in the shikara (10-14) crouched down, ducking their heads. One man, Mehraj Pakhtoon, jumped into the river, but he could not swim so he drowned. Then A.'s brother, Ghulam, and another young man, and the driver of the shikara jumped into the river and swam to the opposite bank. Then another boy jumped over the side and caught hold of the shikara and went down the river. At that point, A. went inside his houseboat and continued to watch from the window. He saw soldiers continuing to fire at the shikara while the passengers were jumping into the water. There were 7-8 minutes of continuous firing. A second shikara full of people began to cross the river as the firing started, but then turned back and took shelter under a boat on the river bank.

L., another witness to the shikara shootings, told Asia Watch she was washing clothes in the river along the side of her houseboat when she saw smoke coming from Lal Chowk. She went to a shop to get some bread and the people there told her that there was a fire in Lal Chowk. Then she saw people running from Lal Chowk. She went back to her boat and warned her family that "they" were burning Lal Chowk, and then she continued to wash clothes. After a short time, she heard bursts of gunfire coming from the shore. This continued for about half an hour. She saw many bullets going into the river from the same side.

> Then I saw a shikara crossing the river. It was about 100 meters away. It was full of people. I saw two people jump into the river, and several others fall down into the water. All this time there were bursts of gunfire from the shore. The two who jumped off swam to the other side of the river. After all the others had crouched down, there were more shots fired at the shikara as it floated down the river.

---

[79] A shikara is a small flat boat used to ferry passengers to houseboats, or from one side of the Jhelum river to the other.

At 11:30, after L. saw the shootings at the shikara, her husband saw it finally come aground in Lalmundi. After the gunfire stopped, the husband also saw another shikara with a man in it go across to the far side of the river and pull the shikara back to the near shore. When the husband later asked the man why he had done such a dangerous thing, the man told him that the BSF had threatened to kill him if he did not. There was one dead body in the shikara.

K., 32, a resident of a houseboat, told Asia Watch that she had gone outside to clean rice when her nephew, Farooq Ahmed, went down the bank toward the shikara. The soldiers on the bank called out to him to come to them. When he did so, the soldiers shot him and then threw his body in the river. The body was recovered the next day. There were bullet wounds in the right and left side of his abdomen.

Another witness, S., told Asia Watch that at 9:30 a.m., as he left his house he heard gunshots and saw smoke in the area over Lal Chowk. He told Asia Watch:

> I had been speaking with two friends, Imtiaz and Bilal, for about fifteen minutes when I looked up and saw five or six BSF approach the street firing their guns. People were running to the river, and I ran along with them. I and twelve or thirteen others jumped into a shikara and began to cross the river. When we were three-quarters of the way across, we saw about 20 or 30 BSF on the bank of river we had just left. The BSF opened fire and Ghulam Hassan Malik was the first hit. He fell off the shikara. Nisar and Janna and Miraj Huda jumped into the river. Nisar swam to the other side and took shelter.

A number of bodies were recovered from the river the next day, including that of Mamran Ahmed Katia, which had bullet wounds in chest and back. Imtiaz Ahmed Shah's body was recovered the next day with bullet wounds in the abdomen. The body of Bilal Ahmed Shah, 15, was not recovered for several weeks. Other bodies recovered included those of Mansur Ahmed Kouka, about 16 years old, a taxi driver; Ghulam Hassan Malik, 25; and a boatman's son named Janna.

The day after the incident, a report on All India Radio cited an official spokesman who stated that, "A shikara boat which was on its way from Lal Chowk to Lal Mandi carrying a large number of persons capsized in the river Jhelum."[80] To Asia Watch and PHR's knowledge, this was the only explanation provided by the authorities for the incident. Asia Watch and PHR know of no investigation into the incident.

The April 1993 Sopore Killings

On April 19, 1993, at about 11:00 a.m., between 200 and 300 students, mostly of high school and college age, held a demonstration in the town of Sopore against a television serial "Bible" which was being broadcast on the state-run network. The students were calling for the serial to be banned because of its portrayal of historical figures revered by Muslims. The demonstration was held in Sopore's main *chowk* (square) in the center of the city. In addition to the protesters, some one hundred spectators had gathered to watch the demonstration in the *chowk*, some of whom were chanting slogans demanding independence. BSF troops were stationed inside the State Bank of India building in the *chowk* and also in a bunker in front of the building.

At 11:30 a.m., one of the students stood up on the rubble of buildings burned by the BSF during the January 6, 1993, reprisal attack by the BSF,[81] and began speaking to a crowd of about 100 people, most of whom were seated. The student denounced the television program and led the crowd in shouts for independence.

A witness told Asia Watch:

> As the student was speaking, I heard machine gunfire for a few minutes and I saw many of the crowd lying flat. I saw one young man try to stand up then fall to the ground. The firing stopped for a minute. All the people started running toward the by-lanes away from the *chowk*. Shopkeepers closed their shops. As everyone was running away, I saw two young men lying flat on the ground, including the one who had tried to stand up earlier. At 11:40 a.m. I saw people carrying the two men away -- there was blood on the face of one of them.

---

[80] "Four 'Militants' Killed, 14 Apprehended," All India Radio, April 11, 1993, as cited in FBIS-NES-93-069, p. 40.

[81] See pp. 70.

The witness said that the sound of the gunfire was not that of the AK-47 assault rifle commonly used by the militants, but of the light machine guns (LMG) and self-loading rifles (SLR) carried by the BSF. An arms expert interviewed by Asia Watch confirmed that the sound of the weapons are quite distinct.

Another witness said that the BSF had fired directly at the procession.

> I went into the central *chowk* in Sopore and saw the protest against the screening of the Bible show. They were shouting pro-Islamic slogans. There were some 400 students at the procession, about half boys and half girls. When I returned at about 11:30-12:00 p.m., one of the student leaders was addressing the group. He was saying the government should close down the serial because it is blasphemous. I saw no security forces and no weapons. I walked fifty feet away toward the BSF bunkers. Then I saw 20 BSF troops leave their bunker and walk toward the central square. When the BSF troops reached 20 feet from the protest, an officer at the back of the line of 20 guards shouted at the troops, "Retreat! Retreat!" The troops walked backwards with their guns in a ready position and commenced firing. Three horses, which were attached to carts, were hit and fell to the ground. The BSF fired in the direction of the students for about five minutes. Then as I started to come out of the shop, the BSF troops in nearby bunker signalled to me that I could move. I came out of the shop, and as I walked out I saw students carrying the dead body of a boy who had been shot.

According to a press report, "[S]ome troops fired in the air but many targeted the crowd." Six persons were killed, including three students, and a photographer was threatened at gunpoint by an Indian soldier and forced to hand over most of his film.[82]

A few days later, Amar Kapoor, the Deputy Director General of Intelligence, who was not in Sopore at the time, stated that "a grenade had been thrown at the BSF and that they had been fired on." According to a journalist present at the time, there was no grenade attack. In an

---

[82] "Troops Fire on Student Protestors in Kashmir," Agence France Press, April 19, 1993.

article in *India Today*, Harinder Baweja described the shooting as "retaliatory fire" following an attack on a BSF picket.[83]

The Killing of Dr. Farooq Ahmed Ashai

Dr. Farooq Ahmed Ashai, 54, Chief Orthopedic Surgeon at the Bone and Joint Hospital in Srinagar, was returning home from his brother Nazir Ashai's home in Rambagh, Srinagar, at around 7:30 p.m. on February 18, when he was shot and killed by Indian paramilitary troops. At the time, he was accompanied by his wife, Dr. Farida Ashai, and his daughter, Rehana. The car in which they were traveling was marked by a three-inch cross on the front and rear windows.[84] As they turned off the bridge, they slowed to a crawl and turned on the car's interior light to make themselves visible to the security force post located just past the bridge. They passed that bunker, and as they approached a second CRPF bunker located further down the road, the CRPF opened fire.

Official statements about the incident have maintained that there was a grenade attack on the CRPF headquarters on the other side of the bridge at the time of the shooting, and that Dr. Ashai was killed in "crossfire." But according to Dr. Ashai's wife and daughter, and other witnesses, there was no attack at the time they crossed the bridge. Moreover, there was no sense of urgency in the routine manner in which the first sentry post permitted the car to pass. If the picket were under attack at that time, then it appears highly implausible that the first sentry post would have permitted the car to pass. Other witnesses have stated that a half hour to an hour earlier, a grenade was thrown at the first bunker, killing one soldier and injuring several. Asia Watch and PHR have investigated numerous cases in which security forces have responded to attacks by militants by attacking civilians. The killing of Dr. Ashai, whose car was the first civilian vehicle to appear after the grenade attack, appears to fit that pattern.

---

[83] See Harinder Baweja, "Losing Control," *India Today*, May 31, 1993, p. 27.

[84] Asia Watch examined the car on April 27, 1993 and confirmed that the presence of three-inch square red crosses on the front and rear windows. We were told that at the time of his death, Dr. Ashai had the only white car at the hospital.

Dr. Farida Ashai, the wife of Farooq Ashai, told Asia Watch that, shortly after 7:10 p.m., she and her husband and daughter were returning from Farooq Ashai's brother's home which is about three kilometers away in Rambagh, Srinagar. Dr. Farooq Ashai was driving his car, which was at the time the only white Maruti car at the hospital. When they reached the first security force bunker located on the near side of the Rambagh bridge, Dr. Farooq Ashai slowed the car and turned on the car's inside lights.[85] There was no firing or other militant activity at that time. The security forces said nothing when the car passed, nor did they order the car to stop. Dr. Farida Ashai stated:

> When we passed the second bunker at the far end of the bridge and we were turning onto the road, I heard three shots. One missed, one hit the car's front tire, and the third hit him. I did not realize at first that he had been hit until he collapsed. I asked if he had been shot and he said yes. We went as far as the third bunker where the security forces delayed us for about five minutes, asking who was shot and where we were coming from. After that they permitted me to move Farooq to the back seat, and my daughter drove to the Bone and Joint Hospital. It was a deliberate killing. Instead of reaching home, he reached the graveyard.

In an affadavit Dr. Farida Ashai has filed with the police, she has stated that the security forces were familiar with her husband's car.

Witnesses stated Asia Watch that the three shots were fired from the CRPF bunker at the second bunker. When Asia Watch examined the car we found that the bullet hole in it was 1.5 to 2 feet high on the driver side door, the same height at which it entered Dr. Ashai. The car's very slow progress across the bridge, with its interior lights on, would have provided ample opportunity for the security forces to ask questions, look inside or stop the car if they had any concerns about its occupants. This circumstantial evidence suggests that the shooting was deliberate, rather than a reaction to a sudden attack.

---

[85] Turning on the lights to make oneself visible to the security forces is routine procedure after dark in Kashmir.

Dr Manzoor, an orthopedic surgeon of the Bone and Joint Hospital, told Asia Watch that he was called at his home and reached the hospital's operating theater at about 8:00 p.m. He stated that Dr. Ashai had a bullet wound in the upper left leg and that the bullet had entered Ashai's right hip and had lodged inside the abdomen. By the time he reached the hospital, Dr. Ashai had lost a great deal of blood. Dr. Manzoor operated on Dr. Ashai and Dr. Farida Ashai anesthetized him. Dr. Manzoor manually transfused two units of blood and asked that an ambulance be sent for Dr. T.S. Sethi to bring him to the operating theater. However, the ambulance which carried Dr. Sethi and Dr. Ashai's brother to the Bone and Joint Hospital was stopped by the same CRPF bunker at Rambagh bridge for at least half an hour. Doctors at the Bone and Joint Hospital have stated that had they been permitted to rush medical aid to Dr. Ashai, and had the security forces not prevented the senior surgeon from reaching the hospital promptly, thus delaying the operation, Dr. Ashai might have survived.

Dr. Ashai, who met frequently with foreign journalists and human rights representatives, acted as a spokesman for injured civilians in Kashmir. Because he was an expert in bullet injuries, so he was also frequently sought out by militants. Under international law, medical personnel have a duty to provide such services, regardless of their affiliations.

Under the orders of the former state governor, Girish Saxena, an inquiry into the killing has been ordered, headed by Divisional Magistrate-Commissioner Phonesenge. There is known deadline for the completion of the inquiry. Although Asia Watch and PHR have requested information from the government of India about the status of the inquiry, we have received no response.

The Sopore Massacre

On January 6, 1993, at least 43 persons were killed, and a one-and-a-half-kilometer-long block in central Sopore burned to the ground in the largest reprisal attack by the security forces in the history of the conflict. The incident marked a watershed, forcing state and central government forces to acknowledge for the first time that the BSF forces responsible had retaliated against the town's civilian population after two of their forces were injured and subsequently died in a militant attack.

The BSF unit involved was the 94th Battalion. According to witnesses, the incident occurred after a BSF soldier came under attack by members of the Hezb-ul Mujahidin militant group. Two BSF soldiers were injured, and a light machine gun stolen by the militants. Immediately after the two soldiers were evacuated in a security vehicle at about 10:00 a.m., the BSF troops opened fire on civilians in the main *chowk* (square) and market area at the Sopore-Bandipore Road. According to reports by local human rights organizations, a BSF officer then ordered his troops to, "Kill anyone and everyone you come across." Another witness reported hearing the BSF troops shouting, "*sab ko maro*" (kill them all).[86] BSF troops also boarded a State Transport bus and opened fire indiscriminately, killing and wounding a number of passengers. Witnesses reported seeing BSF soldiers pour gasoline on to rags, set them alight and toss them on to houses and shops. The BSF also prevented fire fighters from putting out the blaze. In addtion to the 43 persons who died as a result of gunshot injuries or burns, 14 persons were injured, and 8 persons remain missing. The fire destroyed or seriously damaged 37 residential buildings, 234 shops, 61 store houses and a cinema.[87]

In his report about the incident, the Commandant of the 94th Battalion stated that the incident began when

> [U]nidentified militants suddenly opened fire from all directions on troops on ROP [routine operation patrol] duty ... Our troops were constrained to return fire in self-defence. Meanwhile one grenade was thrown by the militants on LMG (light machine gun) group consisting of ... Constable Arvind Pandey and ... [Ct.] Jagatpal Singh. ... The grenade exploded near these constables resulting in splinter injuries to them and they collapsed. ...[M]ilitants hiding in the nearby house and who had mingled with the crowds [took] away one light machine gun ... Militants kept up intense fire in the vicinity and were trying to prevent evacuation of these previously injured constables. Our ROP had

---

[86] The incident has been documented by the South Asia Human Rights Documentation Centre in its report, "Massacre in Sopore," (January 31, 1993) and by Justice Bahauddin Farooqi of the Jammu & Kashmir People's Basic Rights (Protection) Committee in a report titled "The Truth About Sopore." The international and Indian press also reported on the massacre.

[87] For a list of those killed, see ibid.

> to resort to cover fire to retrieve the injured constables. In the meantime, some buildings caught fire simultaneously and explosives started exploding in them. ... Due to congested built up area fire started spreading and could be controlled by late evening by which time in spite of best efforts a large number of shops and buildings were gutted by fire. A number of unidentified persons succumbed to bullet injuries in the cross live exchange of fire between the troops and militants.

The official version provided by Police Headquarters is at variance with the BSF report, in that it makes no mention of a grenade attack. Instead, the official report states that the security personnel were killed in an exchange of fire with the militants. Although both reports claim that the civilians who were killed were all killed in "cross-fire", neither report claims that any other security forces or militant forces were killed. If, as the BSF report states, the "militants kept up intense fire in the vicinity " as the security forces were trying to evacuate their wounded men, it is highly unlikely that these forces would escape injury. The fact that only civilians were killed after the initial attack suggests that only the security forces were firing.

On January 8, the government announced that a "thorough" inquiry into the massacre would be conducted, and that the BSF was conducting an internal inquiry. On the basis of that inquiry, the BSF commandant and five constables were suspended. On January 9, the state government instituted a judicial inquiry, and on January 30, Justice Amar Singh Chaudhury was appointed to conduct the inquiry. A BSF subinspector was placed on suspension, along with two assistant subinspectors, and the troops transferred to Pulwama, where, according to government sources, they threatened local residents that they would do the same to them. After that, the troops were reportedly transferred to Rajasthan. Asia Watch and PHR have requested further details from the government of India about the status of the inquiry, but received no response by the time this report went to print.

The Killing of Three Civilians in Sopore

At about 8:30 a.m. on October 18, 1992, BSF troops opened fire on a boat carrying five men, reported to be militants, on the Jhelum river in Sopore, in northwestern Kashmir. According to witnesses, the men were returning from Wular Lake where they had hid during the night.

There were five of them in the boat, together with a boatman. When they reached the bank, about 30 BSF called out for them to come to shore. Two of the men jumped off the boat and swam to shore and escaped. As the boat headed toward the river bank, the BSF opened fire. Two of the men were killed, and the boatman was injured. The third man was believed to have drowned. Immediately after the shootings, when all of the suspected militants had either been killed or had escaped, the BSF troops retaliated against local civilians. Asia Watch and PHR took testimony from local residents a few hours after the killings.

According to F., a local resident,

> The BSF ordered five local men to bring back the bodies and guns. They threatened them, saying, "If you do not, we'll rape your women." The men went and brought back the two bodies and the boatman, Ghulam Ahmed Kundoo, an old man, who had been injured in the leg by the BSF shooting. When they reached the bank, a BSF soldier took hold of Kundoo and slit his throat.

After the shooting, a number of women came out to the river bank to protest. The BSF opened fire on the protesters, killing two women, a widow named Bakti, 50, and the wife of Ghulam Mohammad Mir, 30, (name unknown).

The men in the boat were identified as Tanvir Ahmad Khuroo, 25; Mohammad Ramzan Ganai, 22; and Shaukat Ahmed Teli, 27. All were reported to be members of Hezb-ul Mujahidin.

A government press handout about the incident stated that the security forces "were fired upon by militants. The fire was returned and in the exchange of fire three militants were killed. Two women also reportedly died in the exchange of fire." The statement did not mention the murder of the boatman.

A doctor at the Sopore subdistrict hospital told PHR/Asia Watch that he was called to BSF headquarters at about 11:00 a.m. on October 18 to examine three bodies and write the police medical report. Two were the bodies of men in their 30s with bullet injuries. The third body was that of an old man whose throat had a six inch cut across it. The doctor told Asia Watch/PHR that the BSF routinely call doctors to file police medical reports, but that the security forces only permit them to note the injuries and not to perform a thorough post mortem examination in the hospital.

The Killings at Badasgam

On October 15, 1992, a BSF patrol traveling on a routine patrol on the road near Badasgam, in Anantnag district, heard the sonic boom caused by a passing aircraft and apparently mistook it for an explosion. The security forces then retaliated for what they perceived to be a militant attack by firing indiscriminately into residences and shops in Badasgam, and locking two civilians, a man named Ghulam Qadir and a woman named Sajida, into a shop which the security forces subsequently set on fire. The two civilians burned to death.

A., a student, told Asia Watch that he was going to the latrine at about 4:30 a.m. on October 15 when he saw a BSF vehicle pass by. At about the same time he heard a loud boom from a passing aircraft. Immediately after the boom, the BSF troops began firing toward the village. When A. left the latrine, he asked the BSF troops surrounding the area, who numbered about twenty, if he could move on the road. The troops would not let him leave, saying that the militants were shooting. When he told them it was just a sonic boom, the troops beat him with their rifle butts and asked him why the militants had attacked them. A. was detained by the BSF for about half an hour. Then the BSF took him to their camp, about ten kilometers away. There, they again threatened him at gunpoint to tell them about the militants. He was there about twenty minutes. At about 6:00 a.m. he returned to the village. By then fires were burning at nine shops and two houses.

Witnesses told Asia Watch and PHR that at about 6:00 a.m. a bus arrived from Anantnag. One passenger, H., a government employee, told Asia Watch and PHR that he was returning home from Anantnag when the BSF stopped the bus near the village, at a mosque. H. stated that there were about twenty to thirty BSF surrounding the bus. H. told Asia Watch/ PHR:

> The troops pointed their guns at us and made all of us, including the schoolchildren, disembark. There were 25 children, 18 women, and 20 men. They insulted us, and beat us with their gun butts. We walked about 100 meters with BSF surrounding us from all sides. When we reached the village we saw people running and three fires burning. I saw three BSF push a woman into a shop. At that time it was not burning. A short while later, the shop was on fire.

The passengers were released after they reached the village.

Z. a widow who lives across the road from the shop, said that she looked out her window after hearing a blast and saw soldiers surrounding her house. They opened fire at the house and three bullets hit the exterior walls. She saw Qadir, the shop owner, standing with folded hands in front of the soldiers and, as she watched, the security forces pushed him inside the shop. Then they pushed a woman into the shop and latched the door. She saw the security forces then sprinkle some powder.

S., a student, was standing across the road when he saw the BSF fire further up the road. He stated,

I saw Qadir come out of his shop bringing some rice to a woman who was standing there. A BSF officer and several other troops came up to Qadir and asked him, "Where are the militants?" and he told them, "I am not a militant." Then the BSF pushed Qadir and the woman into the shop, latched it from the outside, sprinkled white powder all around it and lit it. We could hear them shouting for help from inside the shop.

Later that day, an army officer came to investigate the incident. In a letter describing his findings, a copy of which was given to the residents, he stated,

The sound of the blast heard by the BSF was also heard by us, however, it was not a blast but the sound barrier being broken by the aircraft. I had personally been to scene of incident and found that there was no firing on to the BSF but the firing was done only by the BSF.

The army officer's letter also called for the release of a young man detained from the village by the BSF, Abdul Rashid Mir, son of Abdul Ahad Mir, stating:

I assure you that the u/m [under mentioned] boy is innocent and he be released. I would be grateful to you if you could kindly release him to the bearer of this letter.[88]

---

[88] The letter bore the stamp, "Gurkha Rifles FR," and was signed, Alex Thomas, Maj. OC. 'A' Coy, OC Hiller Camp. At the top right hand

Abdul Rashid Mir was released. The officer told the residents that the army had registered a complaint against the BSF. According to a press report, a court of inquiry was ordered on October 17, 1992.[89] Asia Watch and PHR have received no further information about the inquiry.

The Massacre in Batekote

On October 1, 1992, army forces conducted a search operation in the town of Bhakihaker, in northwestern Kashmir in Handwara district. The crackdown began at about 9:00 a.m. and ended a few hours later. As the troops left the town, an army vehicle came under attack by militant forces. In response, the troops entered the village of Batekote, about half a kilometer away, where they shot dead ten residents and burned down houses and grain stores.

Ghulam W., 40, a resident, told Asia Watch/PHR that he was in the courtyard of his house when he heard gunshots from the direction of Bhakihaker at about 12:30 p.m.

> I went into the house for shelter. From there I saw soldiers burning down stacks of paddy [unthreshed rice] in the fields, and setting fire to houses. They entered our village, calling out, "Come out, Kashmiri dogs." They dragged people out of their houses.

Jabbar M., a farmer, who appeared to be in his 80s or older, described the killings of his two sons and two workers:

> It happened immediately after noon. I was in my courtyard with my sons, Akbar, 40, and Mahdi, 35 and two helpers, Hamid and Ramzan, who were grading and packing apples. We could hear firing from the soldiers as they entered the village. There were about 40 or 50 soldiers. I ran to my house. The soldiers dragged

---

corner it was addressed to 512/1/A Valley, Officer Commanding, 53 BFS Kokernag. In the top left hand corner it bore the marks: 3/5 GR (FR), C/O 56 APO. It was dated October 15, 1992.

[89] "Probe into Alleged Killings by BSF," *Times of India*, October 18, 1992.

about 20 people out of their houses, both men and women, and beat them. They took my sons and the two helpers to the stack of rice in the compound next door. I followed them; they paid no attention to me. I saw them shoot my sons and the two workers several times.

A neighbor told PHR/Asia Watch that he observed the shooting from a window.

The four men -- two brothers and two workers -- were dragged from the compound of the house next door, told to stand by a stack of rice paddy and shot dead. After they had been shot, the soldiers set fire to the paddy. I went out afterwards and helped drag the bodies away so they would not burn. One of them had part of his head blown off. Another had been shot in the chest and abdomen. There were five to eight bullet wounds in each of them.

L., 60, a milk vendor stated that he and several of his neighbors watched from the compound of his house while some sixty troops poured oil and powder from cans they had brought with them and set fire to houses. Four houses in the area were burned, one after the other, along with a sawmill. Residents estimated the loss at Rs. 300,000 (U.S.$1,000).

J., 40, stated that she and about twenty men and women were huddled under the stairs and in one room of a house about fifteen yards away from the other houses. She saw the soldiers set fire to the houses and shoot indiscriminately into some of them.

We ran to this house because to get away from the fires. Then about 25 soldiers came over to the house. They dragged one man, Abdullah Dar, who was about 56, to the side of the courtyard. They said to him, "Show us the militants." When he said he did not know any, they shot him once in the chest as he was standing there. A few minutes later, they dragged another man, Ghulam Nabi Mochi, 45, into the courtyard and beat him with their rifle butts. Then they dragged him to the other side of the courtyard and shot him three times: once in the jaw, then in shoulder and chest.

J. stated that the soldiers then ordered all the other people to go to into their houses and threatened to shoot them if they shouted.

Mukhtar Dar, 70, the brother of Abdullah Dar, told Asia Watch/PHR that he heard shooting and saw smoke rising from several places in the village. When he tried to save his horse from a burning stable, he was beaten on the head with a rifle butt and then shot in the shoulder by the soldiers. He told Asia Watch/PHR:

> I wanted to escape, I wanted to get my horse and save him. But the soldiers stopped me and ordered me to come with them. One soldier had a black scarf over his face. The soldiers beat me with their rifle butts. Then one soldier fired at me. The bullet hit me in the shoulder and came out the back. I fell to the ground and he again beat me on the head. While I lay there they set fire to my house.

After the soldiers had left, Mukhtar was taken by horse-cart to a clinic about one and a half kilometers away, and the next day he was taken to Srinagar for treatment. When PHR/ Asia Watch examined him in October 1992, Mukhtar had an entrance wound in the right upper chest and an exit wound in the right shoulder. He appeared to have a fever and was suffering moderate respiratory distress. The examination suggested empyema, i.e., pus in the space between the lung and chest wall.

N., 25, a tailor and a resident of Batekote, was in the nearby town of Handwara when the incident took place. He told Asia Watch/PHR that when he returned home at about 7:00 p.m., he saw that several buildings on his property had been burned. The body of his father, Ghulam Rasool, 55, was lying on the ground with bullet wounds in the left side of the neck, the right thigh and a large wound to the abdomen, from which his entrails were protruding. He also had a deep cut nearly severing one arm below the shoulder. Two buildings, rice fields and orchards had been burned.

Three women were also killed in Batekote on October 1. H., 25, testified about the killings of her neighbors, Khonmi, 70; Shahmali, 35, daughter of Khonmi; and Saja (a blind relative), 60.

> When I saw that my house was burning, I checked the house next door and saw Saja's body lying in the courtyard. She had been shot in the neck. Shahmali's body was inside the door; she had

been shot in the chest. Khonmi was lying inside a room; she had been shot in the chest. All three were fully dressed.

An official statement about the incident claimed that

[T]he incident actually relates to a village called Bhaki Haker near Handwara in Kupwara District. When the army was engaged in cordon and search operations in the village it was fired on by militants as a result of which one army personnel was killed and two injured. During exchange of fire the militants managed to disengage and escape. While escaping they were intercepted by another column of army located outside the village. The militants discharged a heavy volume of fire including fire from rocket launchers. Due to the firing a thatched hut with paddy stocked outside caught fire. Before the fire could be contained with the help of fire tenders, which were rushed to the scene, 40 houses had been gutted. During the exchange of fire 10 civilians including three women also died. Senior District officials visited the site and an ex gratia relief of Rs.100,000 to the next of kin of the deceased villagers and one month's free ration to those whose houses had been affected was immediately announced. During the search 1 AK 47 rifle was recovered from the area.

In fact, the government version is at variance with the location of the killings. The path taken by the troops as they entered and left the village formed a U pattern. The first killing, that of Ghulam Rasool, occurred near the road where the troops first turned into the village. The killings of the two brothers and two workers occurred several hundred yards further as the troops followed a path into the village. The third killings of Ghulam Nabi Mochi and Abdullah Dar occurred at the point where the troops turned right, parallel to the main road. The last three killed were in a house just at the point where the troops turned right again to exit the village and return to the main road. Such a pattern, and the manner in which the victims were killed, makes the possibility that the victims were killed in "cross-fire" highly unlikely. In addition, there was evidence of fire at at least four separate locations along the U-shaped path.

An editorial in the *Kashmir Times* had this to say about the incident:

According to reports, the militants attacked an army convoy returning after combing operation. While one *jawan* [soldier] was killed, the militants managed to escape. This was enough provocation for the security forces to act in revengeful manner against the local citizens. The army laid seige of the village for a retaliatory action in which it resorted to killings of innocents and even in acts of arson and rape. The typical official hand-out after the incident claimed that ten persons were killed in crossfire even though official sources could not explain the cause of arson and were silent about the claims of gang-rape. However, subsequently the police admitted that those killed were innocent villagers and none of the deceased was a militant. The Kupwara SP told newspersons who visited the village that FIR [First Information Report][90] had been lodged, cases of murder and arson had been registered and the girls allegedly gangraped have ben sent for medical examination. ... The assurance about inquiry into the carnage has no meaning if those found guilty cannot be punished sternly and such excesses on innocent persons continue unabated. ... To make false statements, as the officials do by claiming that ten villagers were killed by crossfiring is not only to condone the excesses committed by the security forces but also to add fuel to the fire. These can only make the people believe that what has happened is a part of state policy.[91]

The Killings in Safakadal

On the morning of September 29, 1992, BSF troops launched a crackdown in the Tarabal neighborhood of Srinagar. Witnesses told Asia Watch/PHR that shortly after the crackdown ended at around noon, they heard gunshots from the nearby area of Nawakadal. Ghulam Nabi Mahajan, a writer at the offices of the newspaper *Hamdard*, and his son, Aijaz Hussain, 25, were in their home in the adjacent neighborhood of Safakadal, about half a kilometer away. At about 2:15 p.m., eight BSF troopers entered the house and ordered Mahajan to come out. Mahajan called Aijaz, who was upstairs doing electric work at the time, to come out because "a crackdown was beginning." As Aijaz came downstairs, one of

---

[90] A First Information Report (FIR) is the starting point of any criminal prosecution.

[91] "Batekote Carnage," *Kashmir Times*, October 6, 1992.

the BSF troopers grabbed him by the hair and pulled him about 50 meters in front of house.

Two witnesses, H. and a neighbor, N., described what happened next.

One of the BSF officers accused Aijaz of being a militant, and when Aijaz denied it, the officer ordered him to stand in the road and close his eyes. When Aijaz stood up the officer fired three shots. He hit Aijaz in the left eye, left leg and chest. When Mahajan heard the shots he came out of the house and when he saw that Aijaz had been shot, he turned back and cried out, "My son is dead." As he did so, the BSF shot him in the back.

When his wife tried to retrieve Aijaz's body, another BSF soldier from a bunker down the street fired around the body to stop her. As one BSF officer dragged Mahajan's body out of the doorway, a number of the troops entered the house and asked, "Where are the militants?" When she said that there were no militants in the house, one of the BSF officers said, "Show us the militants or we will kill you." When she asked if she could cover the bodies, the BSF told her that no one could go outside the house. After about fifteen minutes another BSF group came into the house and broke the window panes and television set. These BSF troops were joined by additional security forces who sealed off the neighborhood and conducted a search until 8:30 p.m. The bodies of Aijaz and Mahajan were taken to the police control room and the family was not permitted to retrieve them until after the crackdown was over at about 9:00 p.m. The next day, an official statement in the newspapers claimed that "two militants" had been killed in an exchange of fire with the security forces.

The Massacre at Nasarullahpora

On July 13, 1992, at about 3:15 p.m., an army patrol of four vehicles came under fire on a bridge as it approached the town of Nasarullahpora, about 12 kilometers from Srinagar. Seven soldiers were reportedly killed during a gun battle which continued for the next two hours. At about 5:15 p.m., reinforcements arrived in some thirty jeeps and other vehicles. According to local residents, the soldiers parked the vehicles near the bridge and then entered the village. A resident who lives just outside the village near the road told PHR/Asia Watch that the troops left the village at about 7:00 p.m. Shortly afterwards, the Jammu and Kashmir police arrived with about fifteen men and a number of medical personnel. The witness was asked to accompany them into the village. He told Asia Watch/PHR:

> As we entered the village, we saw the bodies of six men on the roadside. Each of them had been shot a number of times. They were still bleeding. All six were wood cutters from Shulipora, about six kilometers from here, who had come here to do a job. About forty meters further we saw two bodies of a father and son on the veranda of house; they had also been shot. The medical staff with the police took photographs of the bodies. About fifty meters further, we found two more bodies of a farmer and another man. They had also been shot. The bodies were lying in the room of a house. One had been shot in the abdomen and chest. The police told the medical staff to take bodies of the six wood cutters to their families in Shulipora. We buried the others on July 14.

The father and son killed were Sulaiman Mir, 75, and Abdul Majid, 35. Witnesses said that at about 3:00 p.m., five soldiers came to the house. Abdul Majid and Sulaiman had been doing plastering inside the house and their hands were covered with mud. Abdul Majid's wife, A., was in the house with four or five neighbor women. A. said she warned her husband not to go outside because there was some firing. She told Asia Watch/PHR:

> Some of the shots came into the house, so he went out to check. A soldier grabbed him by the neck and pulled him off the verandah. I jumped down to him but the soldiers beat me with their rifle butts on the back and shoved me aside. Then they shot him twice in the abdomen and once in the back. My father-in-law was inside the house. A soldier stabbed him in the abdomen with a bayonet, then one shot him in the back and one in the arm.

H., another witness, said that the women tried to stop the bleeding with gunny sacks. She said that the soldiers said nothing. After the army left, the police came several hours later and photographed the bodies. The bodies were buried the next day.

R., the wife of Mohammad Ramzan, told Asia Watch/PHR that many men and women had fled the soldiers and gathered in a house at the far end of the village. Twenty of them were crowded on the veranda. R. was sitting in front of a door leading to a small room on the side of the house. She told Asia Watch/PHR:

> The soldiers came and started shooting all around. They pulled two men from the veranda into the side room. One of the men, Hamid Bhatt, a tailor, put up his hands and begged the soldiers to spare his life. They accused him of being a militant. He said "I am not a *dilawar* (militant)." Then the soldiers shot Hamid in the knees. He fell to the floor and they shot him in the chest. Then other soldiers grabbed Mohammad Yusuf, a singer, and as they pushed him into the room, a soldier shot him in the back. Then the soldiers shot all around the room. When they left, they dragged the bodies into the yard.

The Killing of Tajuddin and Imtiazuddin Farooqi

On July 31, 1992, at about 7:00 p.m, Tajuddin Ahmed Farooqi, 18, a student who was home on vacation from college in Bangalore, and his brother, Imtiazuddin Ahmed Farooqi, 14, were watching the Olympic games on television at their home in Lal Bazar, Srinagar, when they heard gunfire outside the house. They turned off the television, and shortly after the gunfire stopped, there was a knock at the door. Imtiazuddin, who thought it was his father returning from Friday prayers at the mosque, opened the door and a BSF soldier shot him in the chest. Despite pleas from the boy's mother and sister, the soldier then shot Imtiazudddin in the head. When Tajuddin and his sister tried to reach Imtiazuddin, a BSF soldier dragged Tajuddin outside the gate and shot him in the abdomen two or three times. The soldiers would not let the family go to him, and beat Irfan, the boys' sister and threatened her, "Don't come outside or we will kill you." Then they bolted the gate from the outside and left. After the soldiers left, Irfan climbed over the wall to Tajuddin, who died shortly afterwards. The next day, a BSF officer came around and asked Irfan if she could identify the soldiers, but she could only tell him that they were wearing black scarves around their faces.[92] After that, a Deputy Superintendent of the Jammu and Kashmir police

---

[92] Such scarves are typically worn by commando units.

came and told the family, "This was an innocent killing. Tell us what help we can give."

Shortly before the BSF came to the Farooqi house, two BSF vehicles had been ambushed by militants, killing one soldier and injuring six.

Although official sources claimed at first that the boys were killed in "cross-fire," publicity about the case since then has led some officials to acknowledge that the killing was unlawful. In an interview with the Indian periodical, the *Illustrated Weekly*, published in October 1992, Director General of Police Bedi stated:

> Yes, that was a very bad case. A case has been registered and is under investigation. The men have been suspended. This has been done on my initiative.[93]

According to a report in the *Times of India*, four BSF soldiers were suspended and charges of murder filed against them.[94] The officer named to handle the investigation was Deputy Superintendent Masood Ahmad Nagin.

On the same evening that the Farooqi brothers were killed, a BSF search party came to the door of a house near the Farooqi's and kicked it open. There were seven family members at home. The soldiers came inside and ordered them to go outside. They pushed two young men, Sh., 22, who is a government employee, and S., 27, a businessman, outside a gate. They shot S. in the abdomen and broke Sh.'s jaw by beating him with a rifle butt. When S. and Sh.'s uncle came home and pleaded with the BSF to allow him to take the men to the hospital, the soldiers shot him in the arm and side. After about half an hour, neighbors came and took all three men to the hospital. All three survived.[95]

---

[93] Sukhmani Singh, "'I Have Already Restrained My Men', An Interview with Director General of Police B. S. Bedi," *Illustrated Weekly of India*, October 10-16, 1992, p. 9.

[94] M.K.Tikku, "Srinagar A City of Two Extremes," *Times of India*, September 30, 1992.

[95] For more on this case, see p.115.

Indiscriminate Use of Lethal Force

The Killing of Ashiq Hussain

On April 1, 1993, during a funeral procession for the assassinated JKLF leader, Dr. Abdul Ahad Guru,[96] Jammu and Kashmir policemen opened fire on the crowd, shooting Dr. Guru's brother-in-law, Ashiq Hussain, in the head and wounding several others.

According to witnesses, the funeral procession started from the Saura Institute in Srinagar at about 11:00 a.m. When it reached Dr. Guru's house at about 2:30 p.m., the crowd, estimated to number several thousand, demanded to be permitted to carry the procession to the town of Sopore, about 50 kilometers from Srinagar were blocked by security forces who refused to permit the procession to proceed to Sopore. According to witnesses, as the crowd broke into angry protests, Jammu and Kashmir policemen posted as bodyguards to Superintendent of Police Rajendra Kumar then opened fire. Asia Watch has examined photographs taken at the time of the shooting, which show many in the crowd taking cover behind parked vehicles or along the sides of the roads during the firing. The photographs also show Ashiq Hussain, Dr. Guru's brother-in-law, as he was shot in the head during the police firing.

According to one press report, the "angry crowd jostled [SSP] Rajendra Kumar, whose bodyguards opened fire." In a press release issued shortly after the incident, the government stated that,

> Mourners for Dr. Guru's funeral procession had been advised to take a particular route. However, as the procession was about to leave on April 2 [sic], a section of the mourners insisted on following a different route. Attempts were made by District Administration officials to persuade them to follow the route already decided. Nevertheless, a section of the people gathered there tried to force their way through the police cordon. At that time, some shots were heard in the vicinity. They are suspected to have been fired by unknown militants. Some persons tried to snatch the rifle from a policeman of the J&K Police. The police also fired a few rounds in the air. During the incident Mr. Ashiq

---

[96] See p.141.

Hussain, brother-in-law of Dr. Guru was hit by a bullet and died on the spot."

According to reports from journalists, the firing was so intense that even that even Inspector General of Police (IGP) Suri was forced to take cover on the ground, from which, according to witnesses, he implored the police forces to stop firing. Photographs taken at the time of the shooting show Ashiq Hussain crouching in a half-sitting position in the middle of the road, along with three other men who were lying on the ground, covering their heads. When Hussain was shot, the burst of gunfire tore a hole in the top right side of his skull.[97] It is evident that a shot fired into the air or over the heads of the crowd could not have struck Hussain while he was in that position. Although the evidence does not indicate that the police targeted Hussain, it is evident from the testimony and photographs that they fired directly into the crowd. The government has stated that an investigation was ordered into the incident. Asia Watch and PHR have received no details about the investigation.

Torture[98]

International human rights law prohibits torture and other cruel, inhuman or degrading treatment or punishment. Torture is widely practiced in Kashmir as a means of extracting information from detainees, coercing confessions, punishing persons believed sympathetic to the militants and creating a climate of political repression.[99] One

---

[97] The three photographs that show the sequence of events are included in the middle section of this report.

[98] The following material was previously published in Physicians for Human Rights and Asia Watch, *The Crackdown in Kashmir: Torture of Detainees and Assaults on the Medical Community*, (March 1993).

[99] Torture is widely used by Indian police and other security forces, not only in areas of insurgency but throughout the country. It is used not only against political detainees, but also against petty criminals and persons who have committed no crime at all. Those most vulnerable are the poor, members of "scheduled" castes and tribes, "dalits" (untouchables), landless laborers and women. *See* Amnesty International,

doctor in Srinagar who has treated torture victims estimated that he had seen four times the number of torture cases in 1992 than in previous years. He attributed the increase to intensified government operations. The PHR/Asia Watch investigations indicate that most detainees taken into custody in Kashmir are tortured.

Lawyers interviewed by Asia Watch/PHR stated that security personnel routinely ignore procedural safeguards when taking persons into custody. Although Indian law requires that everyone taken into custody must be produced before a magistrate within 24 hours, in fact, detainees are rarely produced at all.[100] Prohibitions and safeguards against torture in the Indian Penal Code (IPC) and the Code of Criminal Procedure (CCrP),[101] which prohibit the use of coerced confessions and prescribe inquiries into deaths in custody and prison terms for officers guilty of torture, are also routinely disregarded. To the knowledge of PHR and Asia Watch, the government has never made public any action it has taken to hold security personnel responsible for torture in Kashmir criminally liable for their actions. The U.N. Code of Conduct for Law Enforcement Officials (Resolution 34/169, December 17, 1979) states, in Article 5, that "no law enforcement officials may inflict, instigate, or tolerate any act of torture or other cruel, inhumane or degrading treatment or punishment nor may any law enforcement official invoke superior order in exceptional circumstances such as . . . internal political instability or any other public emergency . . . as justification for torture."

India: Torture, Rape & Deaths in Custody, (London: 1992). Article 3 of the Code of Conduct for Law Enforcement Officials states "In the performance of their duty, law enforcement officials shall respect and protect human dignity and maintain and uphold the human rights of all persons."

[100] Under Article 9 of the ICCPR, "Anyone arrested or detained on a criminal charge shall be brought promptly before a judge or other officer authorized by law. . . and shall be entitled to a trial within a reasonable time or released."

[101] Sections 330 and 331 prescribe prison terms and fines for officers guilty of torture. Section 176 of the CCrP requires a magisterial inquiry into any death in custody. The Indian Evidence Act and the CCrP also prohibit the use of coerced confessions.

Every security force has its own interrogation centers in Kashmir, which include temporary detention centers at BSF, CRPF and army camps, hotels and other buildings that have been taken over by security forces. Detainees are first interrogated by the detaining security force for periods of time which may range from several hours to several weeks. During this time the detainee is not produced before a court or given access to anyone outside the interrogation center. Those suspected of being militants are then usually handed over to Counter-Intelligence Kashmir (CIK), and interrogated at Joint Interrogation Centres (JICs) at which each security force is represented. Detention at the JIC may last for months. If a First Information Report (FIR) is to be made out, it is not done until after the detainee is handed over to the CIK.[102]

The following list of interrogation centers represents only a portion of those in operation:

1. Old Airport (BSF)
2. Hari Niwas Interrogation Center (CRPF)
3. Papa I (CRPF)
4. Papa II(BSF)
5. Red 16 (BSF)
6. Badami Bagh (Army Cantonment)
7. Gogoland -- between the old and new airports (CRPF)
8. Joint Interrogation Center (BSF and CRPF)
9. Bagi Ali Mardan (Nowshera) (BSF)
10. Lal Bazaar Police Station (BSF)
11. Hotel Mamta, Dal Gate (BSF)
12. Shiraz Cinema, Khenyar (BSF)

Lawyers in Kashmir told PHR/Asia Watch that they have filed some 15,000 petitions since 1990 calling on state authorities to reveal the whereabouts of detainees and the charges against them. However, the authorities have not responded, and the petitions remain pending in the

---

[102] Detainees are generally detained outside the state under one of two laws: the Jammu and Kashmir Public Safety Act or the Terrorist and Disruptive Activities Act (TADA). Both laws suspend safeguards against arbitrary arrest and grant the authorities sweeping powers to detain persons even for the peaceful expression of their political views. For more on these laws, see Asia Watch, *Kashmir Under Siege*, pp. 108-125.

courts. A large number of bail applications are also pending. Even when the High Court has ordered state authorities to produce detainees in court or release those against whom no charges have been brought, state and security force officials have refused to comply. Lawyers have also filed petitions charging officials with contempt for non-compliance, but these petitions have also received no response.

Under pressure from the authorities, the courts routinely grant government officials extended time to respond to petitions. After that, judges generally refer the case to the "larger bench." According to lawyers in Kashmir, that bench must be constituted by the Chief Justice. Despite the referrals, it has not been constituted. One judge, S. M. Rizvi, who managed after great resistance from the security forces to obtain records for 14 detainees -- but only after they were released -- determined that no procedural safeguards had been followed in any of the cases. Detainees who had been held for up to a year had not been granted access to legal counsel. In some cases, after a year had passed without formal charges being brought, the security forces filed another FIR to hold the detainee on the pretext of a new investigation. Shortly after Rizvi had succeeded in obtaining these records, he received orders that he was to be transferred out of the state. After the Bar Association threatened to strike in protest, the orders were withdrawn. However, since then, judges have been reluctant to challenge the actions of the security forces.

It is also clear that civil and security officials in Kashmir are aware of the widespread use of torture. Asia Watch and PHR obtained copies of numerous petitions brought on behalf of torture victims before the Jammu and Kashmir High Court, and other documentation, including a letter from the Deputy Superintendent of Police of the Crime Branch in Srinagar confirming that medical evidence supported charges of torture and the subsequent death in army custody of a resident of Baramullah, Abdul Jabir Mir, in 1992.

A great number of methods of torture are practiced in Kashmir. One method is so widely used that a prominent physician told Asia Watch:

Electric shock is nothing. That's routine here.

At the time, the physician was treating a torture victim, Masroof Sultan, 19, who had been taken into custody by the BSF on April 8, 1993, and tortured at the Papa II interrogation center at Hari Niwas. Masroof was severely beaten and given electric shocks to his chest, genitals and feet.[103] Torture and assaults on a number of health professionals is documented below.[104]

Other commmon methods include suspension by the hands or feet, stretching the legs apart, and burning the skin with clothes irons or other heated objects. Victims have also been kicked and stomped on by security forces wearing spiked boots. Another common form of torture is the crushing of the leg muscles with a heavy roller.[105] Extensive muscle damage (rhabdomyolysis), such as that caused by the roller treatment, releases toxins that may result in acute renal (kidney) failure and has in several instances required dialysis.

---

[103] Masroof Sultan's case is described in detail on p. 43.

[104] See p. 120.

[105] Some of the other methods, such as sexual molestation, placing chili powder in the eyes and elsewhere in the body, and methods of psychological abuse are documented in Asia Watch, *Kashmir Under Siege* (May 1991).

Torture Victims with Acute Renal Failure [Rhabdomyolysis]

According to doctors interviewed at the Saura Medical Institute, 37 torture victims have been diagnosed with torture-induced acute renal failure since July 1990. Three patients with acute renal failure died, two as a consequence of pulmonary edema and one from a ruptured spleen. Approximately ten patients required dialysis; the remainder of patients with rhabdomyolysis did not.[106]

• During a crackdown in the Telbal neighborhood of Srinagar on October 13, 1992, BSF forces detained fifteen young men. All of the detainees were taken to an empty house where they were interrogated and tortured. Several of the detainees were later admitted to the hospital with acute renal failure. F., 22, who works as a private driver in Srinagar, was beaten with *lathis*(canes) on his buttocks, arms and hands. His feet were tied, and he was beaten on the soles of his feet with lathis while being suspended. There were approximately twenty BSF soldiers present while he was being beaten, among them three officers who ordered the others to carry out the torture. The officers, identified as Yadav, Chander and Qadiri, each had two or three stars on their uniforms. While beating him, the soldiers accused F. of being "a commander of the militants." F. was also tortured with the roller on his thighs, and was beaten so severely he began vomiting. He was detained for about three hours.

F. stated that a doctor, whom F. identified by his medical bag and stethoscope, was present when they were tortured. The doctor ordered F. to take some medicine, but F. refused. The doctor then said to him, "If you don't take the medicine, I'll put a shoe in your mouth." F. was admitted to the hospital with signs and symptoms of acute renal failure.

• B., a sixteen-year-old student, was also taken into custody during the Telbal crackdown. He was beaten with *lathis* on his buttocks, arms and hands and was also subjected to the roller treatment. The torture lasted approximately five hours, and he was released at about 2:30 p.m. Soon after his release, he experienced diffuse body aches, shivering and vomiting. He was admitted to the hospital with the symptoms of acute renal failure and subsequently required dialysis. When PHR examined him in October, B. appeared to be improving. However, extensive bruises

---

[106] See also G.H. Malik, "Acute Renal Failure Following Physical Torture," (Nephron, forthcoming).

were visible on his shoulders and back and diffuse, moderate bruises over the buttocks where the roller had been applied.

• H., a seventeen-year-old student was at home when the Telbal crackdown began. When he came out of his house at 7:00 a.m., he told the BSF soldiers who stopped him that he was a student. They assured him, "We will not harm students who have identification cards." H. requested to be allowed to leave because he had an examination that day, but he was made to join a group of students in the area who had been separated from the men assembled outside. The students were detained until 3:00 p.m. H. noted that some soldiers were videotaping the group of students as well as the other detainees.

H. and twelve other students were taken in jeeps to a nearby house. There each of them was beaten and tortured in turn. The methods of torture included roller treatment, suspension upside down by both hands and feet, and beating. H. was tortured for approximately one hour. In addition to the methods mentioned, H. was also beaten with a strap approximately 100 times while suspended. After he was released he began vomiting. The vomiting persisted for three days before H. was admitted to the hospital. When PHR examined H. on October 19, H. had extensive and marked bruises which were confluent and extended from the mid-posterior thighs to the upper back. The injuries were consistent with the crush-type injury that results from the roller treatment.

Additional Torture Cases

• Dr. H., a surgeon at the Srinagar Medical College described the case of Muzaffar Ahmed Mirza, 35, an Arabic teacher, who died as a result of torture. Muzaffar Ahmed Mirza was arrested on October 4, 1991, in a crackdown in Tral, a village about four kilometers south of Srinagar. He was beaten and given electric shock to the genitals. After that, an iron rod was inserted into his rectum and pushed through to his chest. He was found by the side of a road and taken to the Medical College hospital the next day in severe pain, coughing up blood and showing signs of peritonitis (inflammation of abdominal cavity). The physicians performed a laparotomy (opening up the abdomen) and a portion of Mirza's rectum was repaired. Shortly afterward Mirza began to have difficulty breathing, and an X-ray of the chest showed a ruptured lung. An aspiration of the chest cavity was positive for bile, indicating that the metal rod had perforated the liver and ruptured the diaphragm. The next day, Mirza underwent chest surgery which revealed a large laceration of the diaphragm and left lung. Within two or three weeks, he died of subsequent internal infection. A PHR examination of the abdominal and chest X-rays of the patient and confirmed the finding of a ruptured lung and signs of bowel perforation.

Mirza was interviewed by several journalists before he died, and the case has been widely reported in the international press. The Indian video news program *Eyewitness* also interviewed Mirza, but the edition was censored.[107] A writ petition was filed in the Jammu and Kashmir High Court while Mirza was still alive calling for a judicial inquiry into the allegation of torture. A second petition was filed after his death calling for a judicial inquiry and for the registration of criminal cases against the security personnel responsible for Mirza's death. To Asia Watch and PHR's knowledge, the government has never publicly commented on the incident or prosecuted those responsible for Mirza's death.

• G., 56, who ran a fruit business and taught in a *madrassah* (religious school) in Reban, about four kilometers from Sopore, was arrested from his home at 6:00 a.m. on March 22, 1991, by the 6th Rajput Regiment of the Indian Army. He was taken to an army camp in Sopore where he was ordered to undress. Army officials questioned him, asking "Why do you want to leave India? We feed you and you are ungrateful." He was beaten on his shoulders, back and legs with lathis. He was then forced to stand in a tank filled with cold water up to his waist as soldiers poured buckets of water over his head. This went on for about two hours. G. was then blindfolded and taken to the army cantonment in Badami Bagh, Srinagar, which he learned after the blindfold was removed and he was able to ask other detainees at the camp where he was.

G. was then taken to a room about twelve feet square where 30 young men were detained. After a short time, he was taken to another room where he was again told to undress, and he was beaten with lathis. There were four soldiers, one of whom he recognized as one of those who beat him in Sopore. An army doctor, wearing a stethoscope and apron who was in the room told the soldiers not to beat him. Two other young men, who were also undressed, were waiting in the room. They did not appear to have been beaten. The soldiers stopped beating G. and left. The doctor examined his chest and back with the stethoscope. Then he told him to

---

[107] *See* Edward W. Desmond, "Himalayan Ulster," *New York Review of Books*, March 4, 1993, p. 26; Edward A. Gargan, "Behind its Mountain Walls, Kashmir Wages Vicious War," *New York Times*, October 28, 1991.

get dressed. After the examination G. was taken to small cell, about three feet by five feet, where he was held for three days. After that he was again blindfolded and taken to an interrogation center near the Old Airport in Srinagar where he was punched, kicked and beaten severely with a cable half an inch in diameter for about half an hour. While he was being beaten the soldiers told him to identify militants. The soldiers also applied electric shock to his chest and temples using a wire attached to a hand crank generator. He was tortured intermittently in this way for two weeks. G. was released on April 16, 1992. He was made to sign a statement which he was told said that the army had not taken any of his belongings. He was then taken by the soldiers to a police control room, where his relatives signed papers which stated that he had been handed over to them.

G. was again arrested by the 6th Rajput Regiment on November 4, 1991, during a crackdown in Lorihama, an adjacent village where he has his orchards. He was taken to an army camp at Panzgam. There he was beaten several times a day. As a result of the beatings on the soles of his feet, his feet became swollen and turned black. The soldiers then applied salt on the feet and wrapped them in bandages, after which the skin peeled off. Some soldiers inflicted further injury by stomping on his feet and grinding their boots into them. By this point, the bones of the feet were visible and the feet stank. Two weeks after G.'s arrest, an officer came to his cell and, seeing the condition of G.'s feet, asked the soldiers, "Why didn't you bring this to my attention? Take him to a hospital and save his life. I am accountable to my superiors." The soldiers told the officer that G. was "a dangerous militant", but they took him to the medical center. From there, he was transferred to the army hospital. He was admitted to the army hospital on November 20, 1991 and on November 22 both of his feet were amputated. He was released from the army hospital on September 22, 1992. G. has filed an application with the High Court seeking redress, but as of October 1992, had received no response.

Rape by Indian Government Forces in Kashmir[108]

Reports of rape by Indian security forces in Kashmir emerged soon after the government's crackdown began in January 1990.[109] Despite evidence that army and paramilitary forces were engaging in widespread rape, few of the incidents were ever investigated by the authorities. Those that were reported rarely -- if ever -- resulted in criminal prosecutions of the security forces involved. Since 1990, reports of rape by security forces and army soldiers have continued. In the vast majority of cases, no investigation tales place. In the few cases where the government has ordered inquiries and courts-martial, the findings and the punishments are not made public, leaving the victims to believe that such abuse is committed with impunity.

Rape by security personnel is a gross violation of international human rights and humanitarian law. Until recently, rape has often escaped international scrutiny and condemnation, including rape committed in the context of armed conflict. In the past, rape has often been accepted as "spoils of war" or mischaracterized as incidental to the conflict or as a privately-motivated form of sexual abuse rather than an abuse of power that implicates public responsibility. Reports of the widespread use of rape as a tactic of war in the former Yugoslavia have been instrumental in focusing attention on the function of rape in war and have provoked international condemnation. Such condemnation must be extended to the use of rape in internal conflicts as well.

Moreover, India's own criminal law makes torture a crime and explicitly prescribes punishments for members of the police or other security forces who have committed rape. Under section 376(1) of the Indian Penal Code (IPC), a minimum term of seven years' imprisonment may be imposed for rape. In addition, the Criminal Law (Amendment) Act of 1983, which for the first time provided for the offense of custodial rape, prescribes a mandatory 10 years' imprisonment for police officers

---

[108] The following material was previously published in Asia Watch and Physicians for Human Rights, *Rape in Kashmir: A Crime of War*, (May 1993).

[109] Numerous incidents of rape have been reported by Indian and Kashmiri human rights groups. See, for example, Committee for Initiative on Kashmir, *Kashmir Imprisoned* (July 1990).

who rape a woman in their custody.[110] The sentence may be extended to life, and may also include a fine. Commissioned officers of the paramilitary and military forces are included under Section 376(2)(b) of the IPC and are thus also subject to this mandatory sentence. The Criminal Law (Amendment) Act (1983) also shifts the burden of proof regarding consent to the accused.[111]

However, despite the changes in the law, there is no evidence to show that the authorities have been willing to enforce it.[112] Moreover, Section 155 (4) of the Indian Evidence Act remains in effect. It states:

> The credit of a witness may be impeached in the following ways by the adverse party, or, with the consent of the Court, by the party who calls him ... when a man is prosecuted for rape or an attempt to ravish, it may be shown that the prosecutrix was of generally immoral character.

A survey of rape case judgements in the seven years following the adoption of the Amendment Act reveals that judges continue to base their decisions largely on the "character" of the rape victim.[113]

India's military laws, notably the Army Act and equivalent legislation governing the federal paramilitary forces, also prescribe courts-martial

---

[110] Custody is customarily understood to include situations where the victim is effectively under the control of the police or security forces and is not limited to conditions of detention in a prison or lock-up.

[111] Indian Evidence Act, Section 114-A. The inclusion of this provision in the Criminal Law Amendment Act provoked considerable controversy among civil liberties groups, women's organizations, bar associations and others. See Flavia Agnes, "Fighting Rape -- Has Amending the Law Helped?" *The Lawyers*, February 1990, p. 6.

[112] See Amnesty International, "India: New Allegations of Rape by Army Personnel in Jammu and Kashmir," p. 3.; and Flavia Agnes, "Fighting Rape -- Has Amending the Law Helped?" *The Lawyers*, February 1990, pp. 4-11.

[113] Flavia Agnes, "Fighting Rape -- Has Amending the Law Helped?" *The Lawyers*, February 1990, pp. 4-11.

and punishments for members of these forces responsible for rape. In general, military courts in India have proved incompetent in dealing with cases of serious human rights abuses and have functioned instead to cover up evidence and protect the officers involved. In this report, Asia Watch and PHR recommend that all military or paramilitary suspects in rape cases be prosecuted in civilian courts.

A Pattern of Impunity

In one well-publicized case, in May 1990 a young bride, Mubina Gani, was detained and raped by BSF soldiers in Kashmir while she was traveling from the wedding to her husband's home. Her aunt was also raped. The security forces had also fired on the party, killing one man and wounding several others. The government claimed that the party had been caught in "cross-fire." After the incident was publicized in the local and international press, Indian authorities ordered an inquiry. Although the inquiry concluded that the women had been raped, the security forces were never prosecuted.[114] In response to requests from Asia Watch and PHR, the government of India provided the following information on this case:

> Contrary to the assertion that the security forces were never prosecuted in the Mubina Gani case, seven Border Security Force personnel have been suspended after a criminal case was registered and investigated. ... The inquiry was not held by the police but by a Staff Court of Inquiry.

Far from contradicting Asia Watch and PHR, the government's statement confirms what we have said. Despite the fact that the investigation concluded that the women had been raped, and that it has been three years since the incident, the BSF personnel responsible have only been "suspended" for a crime which carries a minimum ten-year sentence under Indian law.

In July 1990, police in Sopore registered a case against the BSF for the rape of Hasina, a 24-year-old woman from Jamir Qadeem, on June 26, 1990. According to doctors at the Subdistrict Hospital in Sopore, the

---

[114] Amnesty International, *India: Torture, Rape and Deaths in Custody*, (London: March, 1992), p. 21.

BSF had entered the neighborhood at about 11:00 p.m. after an exchange of cross-fire had taken place between their forces and some militant groups. The BSF had then conducted a search of the neighborhood. The doctors stated that when Hasina was brought to the hospital she had vaginal bleeding. The medical superintendent's report also recorded bite marks on her face, chest and breasts and scratches on her face, chest and legs, and injuries to her genital area. A police report filed on July 5, 1990, charged members of the BSF with rape.[115]

In its response to Asia Watch/PHR about this incident, the government of India has stated, "This case has been raised for the first time ... and was not among the two [sic] allegations ... sent to the Indian government in advance of the publication of this report." As the case was documented in the May 1991 Asia Watch report, *Kashmir Under Siege*, the authorities have had two years to investigate the charges. The cases sent in advance of this report were new cases, the documentation of which was not previously made available to the Indian government.

The reported rape on February 23, 1991, of a large number of women from the village of Kunan Poshpora by army soldiers of the Fourth Rajputana Rifles became the focus of a government campaign to acquit the army of charges of human rights violations. The incident provides a telling example of the government's failure to insure that charges of human rights violations committed by members of its armed forces are properly investigated and those responsible held to account.

The rapes allegedly occurred during a search operation in the village conducted by the army unit. The village headman and other village leaders claimed that they reported the rapes to army officials on February 27, and that the officials denied the charges and took no further action. Officials countered that no clear complaint was made. A local magistrate who visited the village requested that the commissioner order a more comprehensive investigation, only to be told that officials in Delhi had denied the charges without checking with officials in the state. A police investigation that was eventually ordered never commenced because the police officer assigned to conduct it was on leave at the time and was then transferred by his superiors.

In response to criticism of the government investigation, army officials requested the non-governmental Press Council of India to investigate the incident. A committee sent by the Council visited the

---

[115] See Asia Watch, *Kashmir Under Siege*, p. 87.

village more than three months after the incident occurred. After interviewing a number of the alleged victims, the committee concluded that contradictions in the women's testimony, and the fact that the number of alleged victims kept changing, rendered the charge of rape "baseless." The committee examined medical reports based on examinations conducted on 32 of the women two to three weeks later, on March 15 and 21, 1991, which confirmed that the hymens of three of the unmarried women had been torn. The committee concluded that the medical evidence was "worthless", that "such a delayed medical examination proves nothing" and that such abrasions are "common among the village folk in Kashmir." The torn hymens, the committee argued, could be the result of "natural factors, injury or premarital sex."

While the results of the examination by themselves do not prove the charge of rape, they do raise serious doubts about the army's version of events in Kunan Poshpora. The alacrity with which Indian military and government authorities in Kashmir discredited the allegations of rape and their failure to follow through with procedures that would provide critical evidence for any prosecution -- in particular prompt independent medical examinations of the alleged rape victims[116] -- undermined the integrity of the investigation and indicates that the Indian authorities have been primarily concerned with shielding government forces from charges of abuse. The report echoes the government's concern about international criticism by arguing that the charges against the army constituted "a massive hoax orchestrated by militant groups and their sympathisers and mentors in Kashmir and abroad ... for reinscribing Kashmir on the international agenda as a human rights issue."

In response to the Asia Watch/PHR report, *Rape in Kashmir: A Crime of War*, report, the Indian government stated that the Kunan Poshpora case

> was investigated not only by the government but by an independent and highly regarded body, the Press Council of India. The Divisional Commissioner, Wajahat Habibullah, after his inquiry into the allegation stated, "While the veracity of complaint is thus highly doubtful, it still needs to be determined why such a complaint was made at all .... I am of the opinion that

---

[116] For example, the investigation could have availed itself of internationally-accepted forensic procedures to substantiate such charges.

the allegation of mass rape cannot be sustained." Another investigation at the level of Superintendent of Police concluded that the case was not fit to be prosecuted because of contradictions and gaps in the evidence.

In this statement, the government merely repeats claims made earlier withour answering questions about the government's actions which have been raised by human rights groups.[117] It is significant that the government uses only selective comments from D.C. Habibullah's report, omitting the fact that he criticised the authorities in Delhi for dismissing the reports before any investigation had taken place, and recommending a thorough inquiry, which never took place. The Press Council does not constitute a judicial investigative body, and it had no medical component. Had the authorities conducted a competent investigation, which would have included prompt medical examinations of the victims and the taking and presevation of semen samples from the accused, it would be possible to determine the truth about what happened in Kunan Poshpora. In fact, a senior government official familiar with the incident revealed to Asia Watch that although the number of women alleged to have been rape may have been inflated, he believed that, in fact, several of the women were raped by the soldiers.

Even when investigations are ordered, they rarely result in prosecutions. A magisterial inquiry was ordered in the case of five women reportedly raped near Anantnag on December 5, 1991, but the magistrate's report has never been submitted. According to the *Kashmir Times* of January 14, 1993, the state government has ordered inquiries into 87 incidents of killings, rape and arson. None has resulted in criminal prosecutions. In seven courts-martial held between April 1990 and July 1991 involving incidents of rape, deaths in custody, illegal detention and indiscriminate firing on civilians by army soldiers, only one officer has been dismissed. The most severe punishment for the remaining officers was either a suspended promotion, or marks of "severe displeasure" in their files.[118]

---

[117] See in particular, Asia Watch, *Kashmir Under Siege*, (May 1991), pp.

[118] See South Asia Human Rights Documentation Centre, "Massacre in Sopore," January 31, 1993, p. 12.

Those who have attempted to document incidents of rape have also been abused by Indian security forces. In November 1990, Dr. K., a surgeon at the Anantnag District Hospital, was arrested after he had made arrangements for a gynecologist to examine seven women who had alleged that they were raped by security forces. The women, who were brought to the hospital while Dr. K. was on night duty, reported that the security forces raped members of a wedding party, including the bride. On November 29, Dr. K. was arrested from his home by members of the CRPF who surrounded his house. The CRPF blindfolded him along with two friends who were with him at the time and took them to a military camp. The security forces asked Dr. K., "Why did you call the gynecologist?" When he replied, "I treat people irrespective of who they are," they proceeded to beat him with *lathis* (canes) and a metal belt. His friends were also beaten in this way. The three men were detained for four days.

The impunity with which Indian security forces commit rape can also be gauged by the function the threat of rape plays when security forces attempt to intimidate local civilians into carrying out their orders. After killing several reported militants in Sopore on October 18, 1992, BSF troops then ordered five men from the area to bring in the bodies, threatening that if they did not do so, the soldiers would "rape their women." When the men complied, and towed in the boat carrying the bodies of the dead militants and a boatman injured in the shooting, the BSF took the bodies and then slit the throat of the boatman.[119]

During the October 1992 mission to Kashmir, Asia Watch and PHR documented fifteen individual cases of reported rape by forces of the Indian army and BSF. Thirteen occurred during two incidents which took place in the two weeks prior to the Asia Watch/PHR team's visit to Kashmir; the other two occurred in July 1992. To our knowledge, government authorities have ordered an investigation into only one of these incidents. As of March 1993, the results of that investigation had not been made public.

---

[119] For a full discussion of this case see p.73.

Rape in Shopian

On the night of October 10, 1992, an army unit of the 22nd Grenadiers[120] entered the village of Chak Saidapora, about four kilometers south of the town of Shopian, district Pulwama, on a search operation for suspected militants. During the operation, at least six and probably nine women, including an eleven-year-old girl and a 60-year-old woman, were gang-raped by several of the army soldiers.

Asia Watch and PHR interviewed a gynecologist and assistant surgeon at the Shopian District Hospital who examined seven of the women on October 11 and the remaining two on October 12. The doctor stated that seven of the women were brought to the hospital at 1:30 p.m. by the Station House Officer (SHO) of the local Jammu and Kashmir police station in Shopian.[121] She told PHR/Asia Watch:

> All of the women were weeping. They told me that "something bad" had happened at about midnight, that 25 army men had come into the village and into their homes. They told me that the soldiers had accused them of feeding and sheltering the militants, and asked them how many militants stay there.

The doctor conducted sperm tests and examined the seven women separately that day.[122] Because the SHO had mentioned nine cases, the next day, October 12, the doctor went to the village where the rapes reportedly occurred to locate the other two, N., 20, and her sister A., 18. She examined both of the young women, but did not conduct a slide test for sperm at that time. On October 14, the Assistant Subinspector of the Jammu and Kashmir police station in Shopian, Ghulam Nabi, brought A.

---

[120] A military unit that traditionally was armed with grenades.

[121] The local Jammu and Kashmir police are not generally not involved in counter-insurgency operations in Kashmir. Their functions are generally limited to collecting bodies of persons killed during such operations and informing the families.

[122] The presence of sperm can only be detected within 48 hours of ejaculation.

and N. to the hospital for complete examinations. The doctor described to PHR/Asia Watch the following findings for all nine women:

> Z., 11, had abrasions and bruises on her chest and face. Her vaginal area was tender, and she had a ruptured hymen with a one half centimeter vaginal tear. Blood from the tear had coagulated. The sperm test was positive.
> S., 60, had no marks of injury elsewhere on her body but was very tender around the vagina. The sperm test was positive.
> H., 30, had abrasions and bruises on her face and in the genital area. The sperm test was positive.
> N., 20, was also tender around the vagina and had a torn hymen.
> P. had marks on her chest and abdomen. The sperm test was positive.
> A., 18, was very tender around the vagina. Her hymen had been torn.

The sperm tests for G., S., and A.B. were negative, but they exhibited similar tenderness and some marks of injury.

The doctor told Asia Watch/PHR that she gave a copy of the medical report to the local police Station House Officer. On October 12, an army official came to the hospital to ask about the incident and she told him the findings of the examinations.

Asia Watch and PHR interviewed the nine women, who narrated following accounts:

S., about 25, testified that on the night of October 10 she was in the house that was owned by her father in law, who is about 70, and his wife. Both of her in-laws in the house at the time. S.'s father-in-law told Asia Watch/PHR that during the night, there was knocking at the door and three soldiers entered and asked, "Where are the womenfolk?" S. continued,

> I told them they are sleeping. They went into that room to search it and as they started searching they told me to get out. I was taken away by other soldiers.

S. told Asia Watch/PHR:

> One soldier kept guard on the door and two of them raped me. They said, "We have orders from our officers to rape you." I said,

"You can shoot me but don't rape me." They were there about half an hour. Two raped me and two raped [her sister-in-law] H. Then they left.

Their father-in-law was released about half an hour later.

A. and N. told Asia Watch/PHR that they lived nearby and were asleep around midnight when about eight or nine soldiers came to the house. Their brother went to the door and said, "The army has come to search our house." Four soldiers entered the house and ordered the father and brother to be taken out of house. The soldiers entered a room where the women were sleeping. A. and N. told PHR/Asia Watch:

They did not say anything when they came in but they were talking among themselves but we could not understand. They covered my eyes and mouth with cloths and told us to lie down.

N. and A. said they had been raped by each of the soldiers. The soldiers struck their 10-year-old sister-in-law with rifle butts and sent her out of the room.

P. told PHR and Asia Watch that there was a knock at the door of her in-laws' house at about midnight.

When my father-in-law answered, he was sent away. Three soldiers came into the room, and told me to put my daughter aside. When I refused, he picked her up and put in her in a corner. I told him not to touch me and he said, "We have orders, what can we do?" All three of them raped me.

Z. told Asia Watch and PHR that four soldiers came to the house, but only two came inside while two remained outside. She said that when her father opened the door, the soldiers kicked him and sent him away. At that point, Z. broke down and was not able to continue.

G. stated that three soldiers entered her house and took her husband outside. Only one came into her room.

He told me, "I have to search you." I told him women are not searched, but he said, "I have orders," and he tore off my clothes and raped me.

S.B. stated that three soldiers came into her room and told her to take off her clothes. When she protested that she was an old woman, one of them kicked her in the chest and she fell. Then he put one hand over her mouth pulled off her *salwar* (loose trousers), and raped her.

In response to requests by Asia Watch and PHR for information from the government about the incident, authorities have stated that the army unit, normally stationed in Chak Saidapora, "conducted search operations in the village on specific information that some militants were hiding there." They stated that the search was carried out "from 0010 hours to 0145 hours during which seven houses were searched in the presence of an elderly man." Senior government officials have also admitted that the search was carried out in violation of military regulations prohibiting soldiers from entering villages after dark.[123]

In the statement provided to PHR/Asia Watch, Indian authorities have claimed that "the residents of the 7 houses identified and confirmed that the same 3 army persons had entered and searched each house and hence it is difficult to believe that the same persons could have indulged in acts of rape in different houses within an hour and 35 minutes." The government statements adds that, "Two of the women who have been alleged to have been raped were wives of terrorists viz. Takub Hussain a Platoon Commander of Hizbul Mujahideen and Mohd. Yakub a Group Commander of the same militant group."

To Asia Watch/PHR's knowledge, the women did not identify the soldiers as being the same three in each case.[124] As we have noted above, one of the ways security forces in Kashmir use rape is as a weapon against women suspected of being sympathetic to or related to alleged militants. While Asia Watch/PHR do not know whether such suspicions motivated the soldiers responsible for the rapes of these women, it is clear that the authorities intend to use the accusation that the women associated with "terrorists" both to discredit the women's testimony and -

---

[123] See Amnesty International, "India: New Allegations of Rape by Army Personnel in Jammu and Kashmir," AI Index: ASA 20/02/93, January 1993.

[124] PHR and Asia Watch have received no further details from the government about how the soldiers were identified by the residents, i.e. by unit, rank or other marking. If any individuals were identified, a semen and blood test could provide corroborating evidence.

- implicitly at least -- shirk responsibility for the abuse. Moreover, even if the women were affiliated with any militant group, that in no way justifies the use of rape by security personnel. In response, the government has claimed that, "the statement that two of the alleged victims in the Shopian case were wives of terrorists is by no means an attempt to shirk responsibility. The Government's intention in bringing this fact to light was to caution Asia Watch about the possible motivations behind the allegations which would be to malign the security forces."

The government statement also claims that only four of the women were medically examined, and have questioned the credibility of their testimony on these grounds. PHR/Asia Watch were provided with specific medical evidence and testimony on all nine cases. Hospital authorities also stated that the evidence was also provided to army officials and was, presumably, a significant factor in the government's decision to order a police investigation into the case.

The government statement has specifically attempted to discredit the testimony of the 11-year-old Z., stating that "During the enquiry she was not found to have any visible signs or marks of injury or any physical excesses nor did she display any fear or anger and appeared to be oblivious of the alleged incident." In fact, the doctor who examined Z. the day after the incident confirmed that her hymen was torn, that blood had coagulated around the tear and that she was very tender around the vaginal area. When Z. described to PHR/Asia Watch how she was raped, she broke down and was unable to continue speaking.

According to the English language daily, *Kashmir Times* of October 14, 1992, police in Shopian registered a criminal case of gang-rape against the BSF on October 13.

After Asia Watch/PHR published this case in the report, *Rape in Kashmir: A Crime of War*, the government of India provided a statement claiming that

> The case was enquired into by a senior officer of the army as well as by an officer of the level of Senior Superintendent of Police M.M. Rafiqi who concluded that the complaints and the evidence were both unreliable and the allegations could not be sustained. Two independent enquiries thus came to the same conclusion, exposing the efforts of the militants to make false charges and terrorise or otherwise use innocent citizens to discredit the security forces.

This statement provides no explanation for the claim that the evidence -- presumably including the medical report -- was "unreliable." Neither of the two investigations were "independent," since they were conducted by the army and the police. Under Indian law, the government should have insured that the investigation was conducted by a judicial magistrate.

Rape in Haran

Another reported rape occurred on July 20, 1992, during an army search operation near the town of Haran, approximately 25 kilometers west of Srinagar. Asia Watch and PHR interviewed J., a resident of Haran, who stated that at about 6:30 a.m., five soldiers came into a courtyard and ordered her to give them some water. Two of the soldiers then dragged her into her room. One of them removed her clothes while the other stood at the door. She stated,

> The first soldier slapped me and then pushed me to the ground where I fell on a wooden stake and hurt my back. Both of the soldiers raped me. At some point I fainted, and when I regained consciousness, I discovered that my husband had placed a blanket over me.

A second woman, H., told Asia Watch/PHR that she was at home at about 9:00 a.m. when two Sikh soldiers entered the house. H. was pregnant at the time. Other soldiers remained outside in the compound. She stated,

> They told me that I had to go to a shop with them to search it. My father said he would come, but they said, "No, she has to come." I refused. Then one of them asked for some milk but when I gave it to him, he touched my breasts and pushed me into a corner. One covered my mouth with his hand while the other held a gun. They ordered me to lie down. One of them raped me. Then I fainted.

Three days later H. saw a doctor.

F., H.'s mother, stated that she was in bed when the soldiers came. She tried to run away when she saw the soldiers enter H.'s room, but other soldiers caught her and took her back to the room. She was not raped or assaulted. Asia Watch/PHR requested information from the government of India about this incident, but as of April 1993 we had received no response.

In response, the government of India has only stated, "At the time of the search operations, conducted by the army, no complaint of rape was made." The statement implies that the women should have complained about the rape to the very soldiers who raped them. The government has also stated that a complaint has now been filed with the Deputy Commissioner of the district.

Rape in Gurihakhar

The security forces have committed rape as a form of retaliation against civilians, most of whom are believed to be sympathetic to the militants. Such reprisals have occurred frequently after militant attacks on security patrols. In one such case, on October 1, 1992, a BSF patrol returning from a crackdown in the village of Bakhikar, in Handwara district, came under attack by militant forces. One member of the BSF patrol was killed. Following the ambush, BSF forces rampaged through the nearby village of Batekote, killing ten people and burning houses and grain stores. After leaving Batekote, the BSF forces entered the village of Gurihakhar.

B., 35, a resident of Gurihakhar, testified that on October 1 at about noon, she was in her home with her sister-in-law and mother-in-law, when security forces came to the house. One stayed outside while the other came inside the room where she was with her child. She told PHR/Asia Watch,

> He put his gun to the baby and told me to put him aside. I refused, and he beat me with the gun butt on my back and covered my mouth with his hand. Then he forced me to the floor and took off my clothes and raped me. Then we heard a gunshot outside and he left.

R., 25, stated that two security men came into her room where she was feeding her child. She told us,

> One of them forced me to the floor and covered my mouth with a cloth, and blindfolded me with a scarf. He threatened me, "If you scream, we will shoot your children." Then he raped me.

On October 2, 1992, local police took the women to a female doctor in Handwara who confirmed that the women had been "severely molested," but that because they were not virgins, she could not confirm whether rape had occurred with the tools at her disposal.[125]

Asia Watch and PHR also interviewed the mother of a 13-year old girl in the same town who provided an account of the rape as if she, and not her daughter were raped, apparently to protect her daughter from public humiliation. As a rape victim, the daughter may be socially ostracized and unable ever to marry. A fourth woman in the village, S. who had given birth on August 18, was also reportedly raped during the same attack, although Asia Watch and PHR could not directly investigate her case.

About this series of reported rapes, the government of India has stated that, "There was an exchange of fire between security forces and militants in which one army personnel was killed, two injured and a number of civilians died in cross fire. There was no report of rape as alleged even when senior district officials visited the site after the incident."[126] In fact, that authorities almost certainly would have been aware of the charges. An editorial in the *Kashmir Times* which appeared five days after the incident specifically mentioned the charges and the fact that local police had not only received the complaints, but that the Kupwara superintendent had sent the women for medical examinations.[127]

Indiscriminate Attacks and Assaults on Civilians

The security forces have frequently engaged in indiscriminate attacks on civilians, shooting unarmed civilians at times when there was no fighting going on and the action appears to be entirely unprovoked. They have also assaulted civilians with the clear intent of causing injury or pain. In some cases, these incidents have occurred during crackdowns

---

[125] See footnote 116.

[126] The civilians who were killed were deliberately shot by the soldiers in reprisal for a militant attack which had occurred outside the village. See p. 76.

[127] "Batekote Carnage," *Kashmir Times,* October 6, 1992.

when security forces have conducted search operations in residents' homes.

- On October 14, 1992, S., 31, a resident of Srinagar, who was five months pregnant at the time, was at home, when BSF troops posted at a bunker some 70 to 100 meters away opened fire. She was shot in the left thigh. Neighbors took her by auto rickshaw to a hospital. Two other women and a young man were also wounded. One man, Abdul Aziz, was killed and another, S.N. Islam, was wounded. Witnesses reported no other firing in the area at the time. When PHR examined S., her left thigh was bandaged, and the X-ray showed injury to the soft tissue.
- On October 5, 1992, R., 19, a resident of Nowhatta, Srinagar, was participating in a funeral procession when two security vehicles arrived at about 12:30 p.m. and the security forces ordered the crowd to disperse. R. heard someone in the procession say, "We have to take the bodies to the martyrs' graveyard." One of the soldiers replied, "Do what you will," and then the soldiers opened fire. R. was shot in both arms. When examined at the hospital on October 15, R. had comminuted (shattered) fractures to both arms.
- In April 1991, Z., 60, a resident of Fatehgar, Baramulla, was at home along with her son during a crackdown by the security forces. She stated that troops entered her house and grabbed her son. When he pleaded that he was not involved with the militants, they shot him point blank in the leg. He suffered a fracture of the lower leg. He has repeatedly been in the hospital for a comminuted fracture of the right lower leg.
- On October 12, 1992, at 2:00 p.m., Z., a resident of Anantnag, had just left her home when she was shot from a security force bunker. She stated that there was no crackdown underway at the time. She suffered a comminuted fracture of the right upper arm.
- On October 15, 1992, Mohammad R., a resident of Sopore was beaten by BSF troops when they came to search his house. He stated that they accused him of being a militant and that they forcibly removed his clothes and beat him with rifle butts. He was dragged to a nearby river where a CBI officer named Malik put sand in his mouth. He was released and at about 6:00 a.m. on October 16 and treated at the hospital for abrasions and contusions on his face and extremities.
- M., 30, a resident of the Tara Bal Idgah area of Srinagar, was shot during a crackdown in the area on September 29, 1992. The area was cordoned off by the army at 6:00 a.m. M. was made to line up for the identification parade, and afterwards released and allowed to go home.

At about 2:30 p.m., five to seven soldiers came to his house and broke the door open without warning and opened fire. M. suffered a penetrating abdominal wound. Both his brother and father were also injured. When PHR examined him in October 1992, he was in the intensive care unit.

• On February 2, 1990, T., 17, a resident of Narwarah Idgah, Srinagar, left her house to visit her teacher's house at about 10:00 a.m. As she crossed the street an Indian Army soldier approached her and shot her in the head from about 20 feet. The soldiers then left the area. T. suffered brain damage resulting in speech impairment and paralysis of the right side of her body.

• On March 11, 1990, F., 9, had entered a sweet shop when security forces entered the area, and without warning shot the proprietor dead. F. sustained three gunshot wounds; one to the right arm and two to the neck region. He came to the hospital in cardiopulmonary arrest, but survived. His larynx was badly injured.

• On July 16, 1992, S., 27, from Magam Kupwara, who was nine months pregnant at the time, was shot without warning in her home by security forces who were conducting a crackdown in the area. Although she survived, the fetus did not.

• On October 14, 1992 at 1:00 p.m., S., a 16-year-old student from Shopian, was shot by CRPF soldiers as he was walking home from school when he was approached by five CRPF soldiers. They said nothing to him but opened fire from approximately 15 feet away. He was shot twice in the right and left lower legs.

• On June 11, 1991, B., a resident of Khana Wari Zaildagar, Srinagar, his two uncles, Sayeed Mirak Shah, 78, and Sayeed Mohammed Sayeed, 75, were driving near the Srinagar Medical College at about 5:45 p.m., when they and their driver were shot by security forces from a distance of approximately seven feet away. B. and his uncles were shot multiple times as they sat in the vehicle. Two of the men died, and B. was treated for compound fractures.

Assaults on Journalists

• On September 25, 1992, Yusuf Jameel, a reporter for the British Broadcasting Corporation (BBC), Reuters and the Indian daily, the *Telegraph,* was beaten when he, along with several other journalists, attempted to obtain the names of several women being detained during a demonstration against custodial killings. A Jammu and Kashmir policeman struck Jameel on the head, just above his right eye, with a baton and then other police began beating him with rifle butts on his legs and back. When Jameel, who by this time was bleeding profusely, approached Senior Superintendent of Police K. Rajendra Kumar, Kumar told him, "Get lost. I don't owe any explanation to you." Immediately after SSP Kumar said this, CRPF forces began beating the journalists. Jameel stated that he believed he was particularly singled out because he argued with the security forces, telling them that the reporters were just doing their jobs. Jameel was hospitalized for two days. Another reporter, Muktar Ahmed, also received injuries.

Violations of Medical Neutrality by Government Forces[128]

Since the escalation of the conflict in Kashmir in early 1990, Indian security forces have exhibited blatant disregard for international laws protecting the medical neutrality of health care workers and medical facilities in Kashmir. Their actions have made an already dangerous situation for health care workers in the state increasingly desperate and have contributed to the deaths of those needing medical care in the region.

The evidence gathered by the Asia Watch/PHR team indicates that the Indian security forces have deliberately prevented injured persons from receiving medical care. PHR and Asia Watch interviewed doctors, ambulance drivers and other health care workers who testified that security forces have shot ambulance drivers, arrested patients from hospitals over the objections of doctors, and even removed them from intravenous medications or other treatments, and opened fire within hospitals. The security forces have not only prevented health care workers from carrying out their duties, but have arrested and tortured medical professionals because they have carried out those duties. While it is not possible to say with precision how many persons have died or suffered serious injury as a result of deliberate interference with the

---

[128] The following material was previously published in Physicians for Human Rights and Asia Watch, *The Crackdown in Kashmir: Torture of Detainees and Assaults on the Medical Community*, (March 1993).

delivery of health care services by the security forces, that number is certainly in the hundreds.[129]

Preventing Medical Personnel from Transporting the Wounded

Article 7 of the Code of Medical Neutrality in Armed Conflict requires that "Medical facilities, equipment, supplies and transport shall be respected and protected, regardless of whom they serve, and shall not be destroyed." The Code also provides, under Article 6, that "Medical workers shall have access to those in need of medical care, especially in areas where civilian medical services have been disrupted. Similarly, persons in need of medical care shall have access to such services." Indian security forces in Kashmir have systematically violated these provisions by preventing medical personnel from evacuating injured persons for medical treatment. Ambulance drivers have been among the principal victims of these actions. Drivers are frequently stopped while on duty, and a number have been fired on and beaten by security personnel. In some cases, the drivers have been detained, tortured and killed. The following cases are taken from Asia Watch/PHR interviews.

• Ambulance driver A., 39, described an incident in April 1992, in which he was used as a shield by the security forces as he was driving through an area where armed militants and government troops were engaged in a gun battle. The incident occurred at about 8:00 a.m., when A. was bringing emergency room staff to the Saura Medical Institute, a 540-bed care center in Srinagar. The security forces ordered A. to remain in the hospital bus which was positioned in such a way as to shield a military bunker from sniper fire by militant forces. A. stated that the bus sustained damage from the gunfire, and security forces intentionally broke many of the windows as well.

Two months later, on July 31, 1992 at about 6:30 p.m. A. was sent to pick up Dr. A., a gynecologist consultant, from her home. He was stopped at Lal Bazar by Border Security Force (BSF) soldiers, who opened fire into the air, forcing him to back up. They ordered him to stop, then removed the keys from the vehicle, and struck him in the forehead with the butts of their rifles. He was then beaten with kicks and fists, and only

---

[129] The PHR/Asia Watch team reviewed the personal data on hundreds of persons injured or killed in custody that was compiled by health professionals and human rights activists in Kashmir.

then was he permitted to show his identification papers. He explained to the BSF that he was on emergency duty. At this time, A. observed that three injured persons were lying on the road in front of his vehicle. The BSF ordered him to leave the area, but before he did so, he asked if he could take the injured persons with him. The BSF told him that he could, but when he proceeded to back up, the BSF opened fire on the ambulance, shooting through the windshield. A. was shot in the abdomen and right wrist. He managed to drive himself back to the hospital where he was treated for his injuries. At the time he was interviewed in October, he had scars on his abdomen and wrist consistent with his testimony and stated that he was still unable to work because of ongoing disabilities related to his injuries.

A. had been an ambulance driver for the Medical Institute for ten years. Prior to the July 1992 shooting, he had frequently been stopped by security forces while transporting patients and medical personnel in clearly marked medical vehicles. The incidents occurred approximately one to six times every month and generally lasted for more than 30 minutes. He also stated that, in the past year, security forces beat him about twelve times while on duty. In each of these cases, he had been in a well-marked ambulance and had shown his identification card and curfew pass to the authorities. His vehicle is also marked with a prominent red cross.

• On July 19, 1992, at about 10:00 p.m., doctors at the Srinagar Medical College Hospital, a 700-bed care center, called the Badami Bagh Army Hospital to arrange for an ambulance to pick up anti-serum for a patient who had gas gangrene, a wound infection which spreads quickly and can cause death within a short time. Ghulam Nabi Bhat, 30, the ambulance driver, was accompanied by two of the patient's attendants in an official hospital ambulance, which was clearly marked with a red cross. When the vehicle reached the gate of the army hospital, a soldier opened fire, shooting Ghulam Nabi Bhat and one of the attendants at point blank range. The attendant survived, but Bhat died at the scene and was later buried on the grounds of the Medical College Hospital. Since this incident, the hospitals have voluntarily adopted a strict policy, out of fear, that no ambulances travel after 8:00 p.m.

• On April 19, 1992, M., an ambulance driver, drove a pregnant patient from the Bone and Joint Hospital in Srinagar for an appointment at the Maternity Hospital. At about 2:00 p.m., as he was waiting to transport her back to the Bone and Joint Hospital, some 60 Indian army soldiers surrounded the Maternity Hospital. At the time, M. was alone in an official hospital ambulance. When he showed the soldiers his identification card, one of the soldiers said to him, "You have managed to get this card from somewhere because you are a militant." When M. attempted to explain that he was an ambulance driver and was waiting to transport a patient, the soldiers ordered him to accompany them, saying, "You come with us until we find out who you really are."

M. was taken to a nearby army hostel. At about 5:00 p.m. he was forced to strip naked in the presence of eight army soldiers and two officers, one of whom was referred to as "Dedwal." They accused him of being a militant and ordered him to tell them the names of other militants. The soldiers beat him with *lathis* (canes) on his back and knees even after he fell to the floor. They forced him to swallow some alcohol.[130] The soldiers pulled his legs apart at a wide angle, causing him great pain,[131] and applied electric shocks to his wrists, ankles and toes.

M. was detained for two weeks, during which he was tortured about six times in a similar fashion. On the sixth day, he was taken to a military doctor at Badami Bagh Army Hospital in Srinagar and examined. Then he was returned to the army hostel. He was released on May 2.

M. stated that he had been detained or harassed by security forces while on duty "about one hundred times" in the past year. On two occasions, his ambulance was seized and his identification card taken.

• On July 31, 1992 at about 7:00 p.m., a BSF search party came to the door of a home in the Lal Bazar neighborhood of Srinagar and kicked it open. At that time there were seven family members at home. N., 17, a student, stated:

> The soldiers came inside, there were many of them, and ordered all of us to stand up and go outside. Then they started beating us with their rifle butts. Then they pushed my two cousins, Sh., 22, who is employed by the government, and S., 27, a businessman, off the veranda and outside a gate in the wall that surrounded our

---

[130] Islam prohibits the consumption of alcohol. The act was particularly cruel since the incident also occurred in the month of Ramadan, when devout Muslims fast during daylight hours.

[131] Stretching the legs in this fashion is a common torture technique in India.

house. All the BSF went outside with them. We heard four or five shots. At that time my father, who works as an ambulance driver, came home and saw the situation. He pleaded with BSF to allow him to take my cousins to the hospital, saying, "You have done your work, now let me do my duty." But instead they shot him.

N.'s father was shot in the arm and side. After about half an hour, neighbors came and took all three men to the hospital. S. had been shot in the abdomen, and Sh. had a broken jaw from being beaten with rifle butt. They were hospitalized for six weeks and then released. The government has given no explanation for the incident.

Refusal by Security Forces to Provide or Permit Medical Care for Wounded

• On September 29, 1992, there was a crackdown[132] in the Tara Bal area of Srinagar. Security forces entered a house where M., 22, a businessman in Srinagar, lived with his parents. Without warning, the soldiers opened fire with automatic weapons. M. received numerous bullet wounds. After the soldiers left, the family transported M. to the hospital. As they passed security forces on the way, one soldier said to them, "You mean this bastard is still living?" and began striking M. with the butt of his rifle. The soldier stopped after several women interceded and the family was able to get M. to the hospital. When PHR examined him in October 1992, M. was in intensive care.

• One day in April 1991, at approximately 11:30 a.m., while a crackdown was underway, G., 70, was sitting at home when soldiers forced the door open and, without warning or question, shot him once in the chest. His wife pleaded with soldiers to transport him to the hospital or allow the family to transport him, but the soldiers refused. After the crackdown ended about four hours later, the Jammu and Kashmir police transported G. to the Saura Medical Institute in Srinagar, where doctors treated him for a hemothorax (collection of blood in the chest) resulting from the gunshot wound. He survived.

• On August 14, 1992, M., 74, a resident of the village of Daksum, 100 kilometers from Srinagar, went into the fields at about 6:30 a.m. to

---

[132] Crackdown is the term commonly used in Kashmir for cordon and search operations.

relieve himself, not realizing that the village had been surrounded by the security forces. As he was leaving his house, he was shot in the foot. Despite his injury, he was detained with all the other men from the village. At 9:30 a.m. he was seen by an army doctor but was not permitted to get the injury treated. Despite his requests to be allowed to get medical care, he was not permitted to go to a hospital until 3:00 p.m. when the crackdown ended. At that time, he and his son, G., were made to travel in a military truck which was also used to transport the bodies of twelve villagers shot by the security forces during the crackdown. M. and G. were dropped off at Kukernag, 15 kilometers from the village, and the bodies were taken elsewhere. They traveled by bus and taxi to Srinagar where they were able to get an ambulance to take them to the hospital. When PHR's Dr. Iacopino examined him in October 1992, M. had a large, 15-centimeter, infected wound in the left foot which extended to the level of the bone. At the time of the visit, M. was awaiting amputation of the foot.

Contrary to international humanitarian law, medical vehicles have also been prevented from transporting wounded patients due to curfew restrictions. International humanitarian law exempts medical vehicles and personnel from such restrictions. Doctors described numerous cases of patients with traumatic injuries who died after being arbitrarily delayed in transit, or whose injuries or illnesses worsened because of the delays. Even when the injured received assistance from local residents, they were not able to reach hospitals in a timely manner since the roads are sealed during crackdowns.

Doctors and other health professionals are also unable to be present when and where they are needed. Doctors reported that staff are often unable to reach the hospitals until 10-11:00 a.m. and must leave by 3-4:00 p.m. to avoid being caught outside after curfew. Even so, they are often caught in crackdowns. The absolute restriction on travel after dark has interfered with the transport of consultants and medical technicians needed for emergencies. If surgery cannot be postponed, others not trained for special procedures must fill in, which has hurt the quality of patient care. For example, doctors described repeated incidents where anesthesiologists and cardiothoracic surgeons were called on to perform cesarean sections. One consultant now sleeps in one of the hospitals in Srinagar because it has become impossible for him to travel during curfew hours.

Curfew restrictions have also prevented the transport of blood products, oxygen and other emergency supplies. Travel restrictions have also hindered communication between doctors at different hospitals. Because the hospitals have not had a reliable telephone system since the conflict began, doctors must send messengers or travel themselves to consult with colleagues.

Raids on Hospitals

Since the escalation of the conflict in 1990, the security forces operating in Kashmir have repeatedly violated the neutrality of hospitals, clinics and other facilities. Doctors in Kashmir described frequent raids[133] during which security personnel have cordoned off hospitals, sometimes for days at a time, to search for injured patients whom they suspect of militant activity. During hospital raids, injured patients have been arrested from hospitals, in some cases after being disconnected from intravenous medications or other treatments. International humanitarian law does not preclude such searches, but it does prohibit the security forces from engaging in abuses while conducting them.[134] If the security forces have received information that someone who has committed a crime is receiving treatment in a hospital, they may search for and arrest the person, but only if they do so without endangering the patient's health.

Witnesses testified that in one particularly cruel incident early in 1990, Indian army doctors ordered the medical staff at the Saura Medical Institute to transfer all patients with recent injuries to them so that their cases could be reviewed. Physicians at the Institute complied with the order, but objected to the transfer of one patient in the intensive care unit who was awaiting surgery for a liver abscess. At the time, the infection had spread to the bloodstream (a condition known as sepsis) and the patient required life-sustaining cardiac pressor agents to maintain his blood pressure. Despite the patient's precarious condition, the hospital staff were forced to remove him from the intensive care unit and pressor support. The patient died three hours after he was disconnected from his medication and before he was able to be returned to the intensive care

---

[133] Raids or cordon-and-searches are commonly referred to as crackdowns.

[134] See for example Geneva Conventions Protocol I, Article 10 and 11 (1); Protocol II, Article 5/2 (e) and Article 7 (2).

A teacher from Bandipor, Kashmir, who had just been released from detention where he was tortured.

The following series of photos depict an encounter with security forces that took place on April 1, 1993 during the funeral of Dr. Abdul Ahad Guru. The people under attack were mourners attending the funeral. The incident is described on pages 85-86.

Ashiq Hussain, Dr. Guru's brother-in-law, is shot in the head.

House burned by Indian army troops during a reprisal attack against villagers in Batekote. The case is described on pages 76-80.

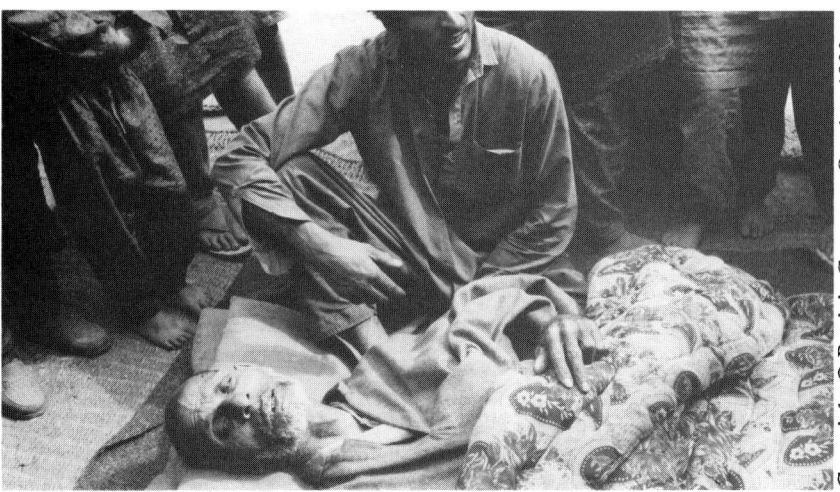

Mukhtar Dar, 70, who was shot in the shoulder by Indian army troops during a reprisal attack against villagers in Batekote. The case is described on pages 76-80.

In repeated instances, security forces have refused to provide or permit medical care for the wounded. This man was shot in the foot during a crackdown. By the time he arrived at the hospital, several hours later, the wound was seriously infected. In October 1992, the man was awaiting amputation of his foot. The case is described on pages 116-117.

Rubble from buildings burned by security forces in Lal Chowk, Srinagar on April 10, 1993. The incident is described on pages 59-63.

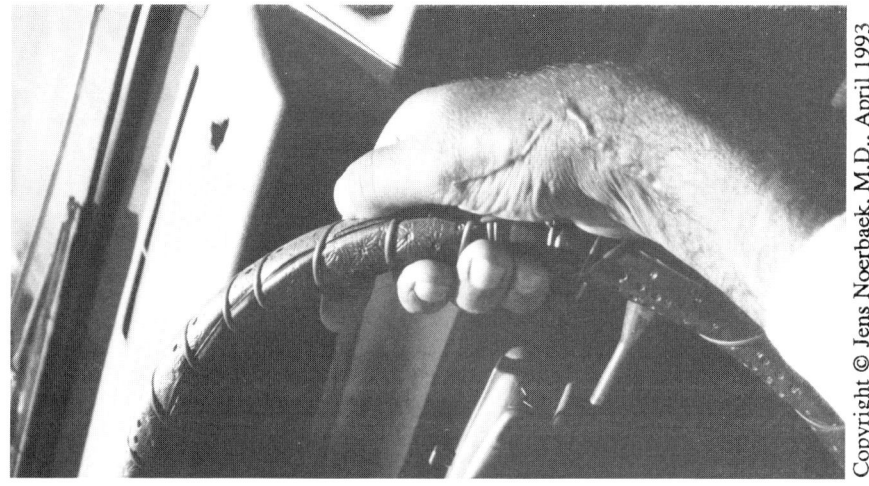

On July 31, 1992, Border Security Force troops opened fire on this ambulance as the driver attempted to pick up several injured persons who were lying on the road. The driver was shot in the abdomen and his right wrist. The case is described on pages 113-114.

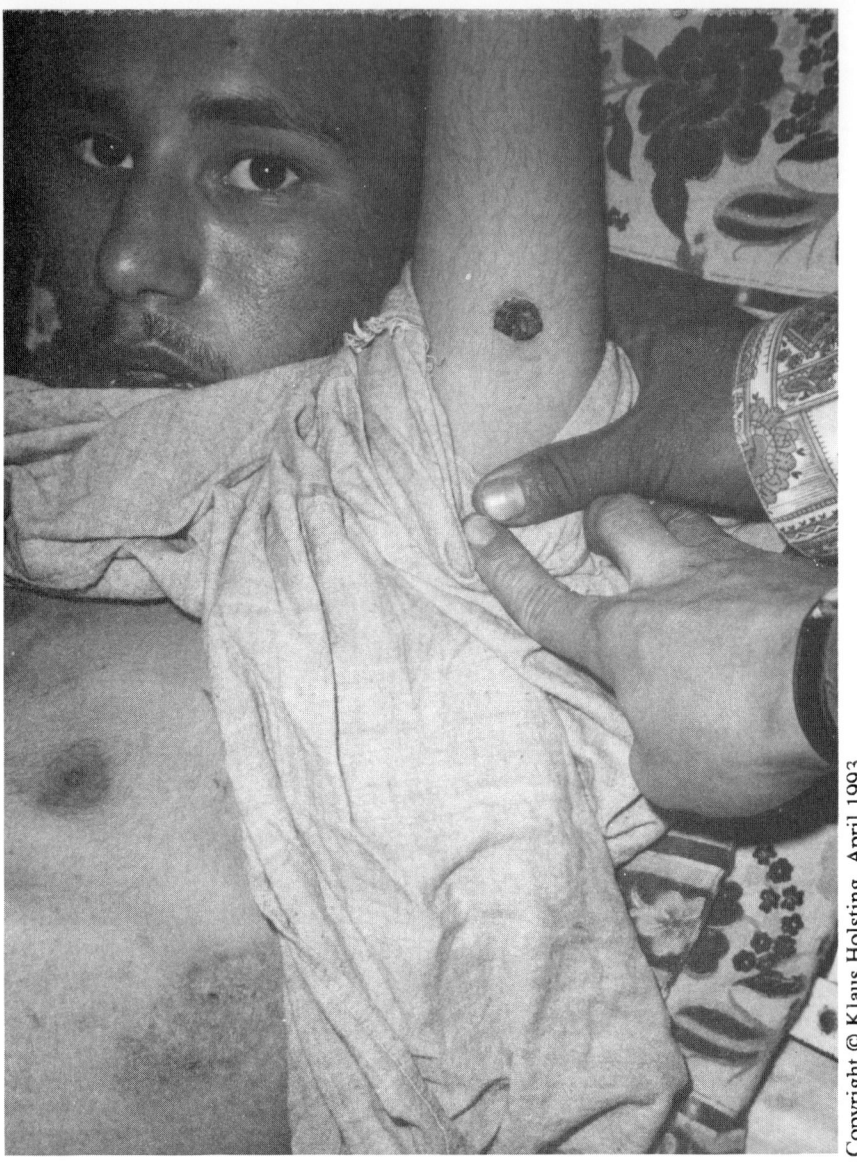

Masroof Sultan, a 19-year-old college student who was taken into custody on April 8, 1993 by Border Security Force troops, beaten and tortured with electric shock and then taken to a field where he was shot and left for dead. A burn from the electric shock is visible on his right arm. The case is described on pages 43-47.

unit. The crackdown reportedly lasted for seventeen days, during which time no one was allowed to enter or exit the hospital grounds. According to hospital staff, five dialysis patients who were not permitted to enter the hospital compound died as a result.

Medical workers are routinely verbally harassed and some have been beaten and detained. The security forces have also deliberately destroyed medical equipment and supplies, and have opened fire within hospital premises and inside hospitals, apparently to intimidate hospital staff.

These raids have continued. Doctors interviewed by the PHR/Asia Watch team in October 1992 at the sub-district hospital in Shopian described two raids on the facility in the two months prior to the PHR/Asia Watch visit. The security forces had confiscated medications, destroyed equipment, and forced doctors to identify the injured. No patients were detained during those raids, however.

A doctor who worked at the emergency center of the district hospital in Sopore told Asia Watch/PHR that the hospital had been raided ten times between August and October 1992 and that security forces had opened fire inside the hospital even as physicians were attempting to care for patients. He described one crackdown in which the staff had been trapped inside the hospital for three days.

A physician at the Saura Medical Institute stated that the facility was subjected to more than twelve raids between April 1991 and April 1992. On five occasions, hospital employees were detained during these raids. During a six-hour crackdown at the hospital hostel in April 1991, an Indian army contingent of some 800 surrounded the facility. The forces which entered demanded the medical staff to "show us the arms." They beat three attendants with the butts of their rifles. An ambulance driver was also beaten.

According to a doctor at the Srinagar Medical College, during a raid in August 1992, no personnel were allowed to enter or exit the hospital grounds for three days and night, which severely interfered with patient care. The doctor estimated that there had been twenty raids on the hospital since April 1992. During these crackdowns, the security forces first surrounded the premises, then entered the hospital while discharging their weapons both outside and inside the building, and searched for recently injured patients. An inspection of the hospital by the PHR/Asia Watch team revealed bullet marks at the building's entrance and around the windows of the hospital. There were half a dozen such marks outside the doctors' emergency on-call room. Gunshot marks were also visible inside the hallways of the Medical College hospital and inside its wards.

Doctors at the Bone and Joint Hospital, an orthopedic hospital, reported that the hospital had been raided three or four times between May and October 1992 and that on several occasions, patients were forcibly taken from the hospital, even from the operating theater. During these raids, the hospital was surrounded by as many as one hundred soldiers, and the entire complex searched, including the residents' and doctors' living quarters.

One doctor who witnessed numerous raids told PHR/Asia Watch that security officers often check the surgical registries themselves and rifle through medical records and admission documents to seek out recent cases of injuries, apparently because they believe that anyone injured may be a militant. Consequently, patients with injuries often refuse to be admitted to the hospital. Another doctor estimated that one third of those injured who required hospitalization refused admission and are examined only as outpatients because they fear they may be accused of being militants. If they are admitted, many leave at the first sign of a raid because they fear they may be arrested. He said that patients who have injuries resulting from torture or beatings request that the physician attribute the cause to a motor vehicle accident for the records and not to the security forces out of fear of reprisals.

- On June 23, 1991, Dr. R. was on duty at the Bone and Joint Hospital at about 2:30 p.m. when twelve BSF troops, accompanied by Deputy Superintendent of Police (DSP) Sharma, entered the emergency unit. DSP Sharma asked Dr. R. if "any militants were admitted" that day. Dr. R. pointed to an old woman in the emergency room. Unsatisfied, Sharma told Dr. R., "You show us the militants," while three of the BSF troops held him at gunpoint. At gunpoint, they escorted Dr. R. into the operating theater where A., an eighteen-year-old man with a gunshot wound to the leg, was under anesthesia and undergoing an operation. Six of the BSF troops removed A. from the room. BSF troops also searched the hospital for "weapons and ammunition." They found neither, but deliberately destroyed surgical instruments and supplies of medicines during the search. A. was released from custody later that night at about 10:30 p.m. and survived.

Detentions, Harassment and Assaults on Health Care Workers

Health care workers have been murdered, assaulted, illegally detained and harassed by government security forces. They are routinely subjected to such abuses because they are suspected of treating militants, and are therefore believed to be supporting the demands of the militant groups. They have also been forced to falsify reports of deaths. Doctors and other health care workers told PHR/Asia Watch that they may have to travel past fifty or more military bunkers and checkpoints on their way to and from hospitals. The fact that they carry identification cards or travel in clearly marked medical vehicles has not protected them. In fact, the cards are often confiscated and several doctors who have been stopped by security forces have been told, "The only use for this card will be to identify your dead body."

In one of the most recent cases, Dr. Farooq Ahmed Ashai, Chief Orthopedic Surgeon at the Bone and Joint Hospital in Srinagar, was returning home from his brother Nazir Ashai's home in Rambagh, Srinagar, at around 7:30 p.m. on February 18, when he was shot and killed by Indian paramilitary troops. The car in which he, his wife and daughter were traveling is marked by a three-inch cross on the front and rear windows. Government officials have stated that Dr. Ashai was killed in "cross-fire" following a militant grenade attack on the security forces. According to other reports, the grenade attack occurred a half-hour to an hour earlier.[135]

The cases described below represent a small sample of other instances of attacks on medical workers that have taken place in Kashmir.

• In late September 1992, there was a crackdown in the Kamar Wari neighborhood of Srinagar. Dr. Q., 28, was waiting near his home for the hospital bus when army troops surrounded the area at about 9:15 a.m. and began beating local residents and ordering them to go to their homes. There was no shooting at the time. At about 1:00 p.m., all the men of the neighborhood were ordered to assemble on the mosque grounds. There were about 45 to 55 men altogether. Dr. Q. identified himself as a physician and asked to leave. The soldiers told him that they had strict orders that no one could leave. The men were paraded before a masked informant, and four individuals were selected and taken away.

At 3:00 p.m. there was a second identity parade. Dr. Q.'s younger brother, a pre-medical student, was one of those selected. When Dr. Q. attempted to intervene and showed one of the officers, Captain Rana, his own identity card, the captain threw the card away and said, "You doctors in the Institute are militants because you treat militants." Dr. Q. replied, "We Kashmiris are being tortured and killed," and he rallied the other

---

The case is discussed in detail on p. 66.

men assembled there to chant slogans in protest. The troops surrounded the men, pushed them together and began to beat them. Captain Rana slapped and punched Dr. Q. several times and kicked him in the chest until he fell to the ground. The crowd of detainees was then told to turn away as the captain put a gun to Dr. Q.'s head and cocked the trigger, saying, "I'm going to shoot him." As Dr. Q. pleaded with the captain not to shoot, Colonel Dhadwani arrived and accused Dr. Q. of being an "instigator." The colonel and captain then let Dr. Q. and his brother go. Dr. Q. was later treated for a perforated left eardrum which had begun bleeding after he was beaten.

- On October 2, 1992, BSF troops surrounded the Nowhala Area of Srinagar in a crackdown at 12:30 p.m. Soldiers entered the home of Dr. F., and ordered him to go outside. He informed the soldiers that he was an anesthesiologist in the emergency service and that his shift began at 4:30 p.m. that day at the Saura Medical Institute. He also stated that the ambulance used to transport medical personnel would soon arrive for him. The soldiers refused to permit Dr. F. to leave and forced him to line up to be paraded several times in front of informants along with all the other men of the neighborhood. The crackdown did not end until October 4 at 6:30 p.m., more than two days later. Dr. F. later learned that the ambulance driver who had come for him had been turned away at the crackdown site and told not to return.

As a result of Dr. F.'s absence, certain surgical cases were delayed. The most urgent of these was that of a patient with a small bowel obstruction. When Dr. F. was unable to come to work, one of the surgical residents attempted to assume the responsibilities of the anesthesiologist because the doctors feared that if the surgery were delayed, the obstruction might progress to a state of bowel perforation. However, the resident was unable to successfully intubate[136] the patient and ultimately the surgery had to be postponed. Over the next 48 hours, the bowel obstruction did progress to perforation and although the patient underwent surgery on October 5, the operation was complicated by sepsis, a serious blood-born infection brought on by the bowel perforation. Patients who have experienced bowel perforation often have chronic problems with subsequent bowel obstruction because of scar formation in the abdomen, and sometimes require additional surgery.

---

[136] Major abdominal surgery requires the placing of a breathing tube during anesthesia.

The delay in this patient's surgery may cause the patient to suffer long-term health problems.

- In October 1992, we interviewed Dr. S. a resident at the Bone and Joint Hospital who lives on the hospital grounds in the men's dormitory. He said that since the beginning of 1992, the security forces have launched three or four early morning raids on the residents' living quarters and in the hospital. Sometimes the soldiers conduct the inspection by themselves; in other cases they have forced physicians to identify those recently admitted because of gunshot wounds.

- Dr. S. described one incident which occurred about six months prior to the PHR/Asia Watch interview. He and two other doctors were returning from the hospital in an official hospital vehicle marked with a red cross. They were stopped by several CRPF soldiers who ordered them out of the vehicle. The CRPF soldiers then proceeded to slap the men and strike them with their rifle butts. When one of the doctors objected, saying, "I'm a doctor," a soldier replied, "Any doctor can be a militant," and the doctor was again beaten. Before releasing the doctors, one of the soldiers warned them, "We will kill you if we see you again."

- Dr. R., of the Bone and Joint Hospital, reported to us in October 1992 that during his 50-kilometer round trip commute to the hospital every day, he is frequently detained and harassed by security forces at checkpoints on the way. Several times, his identification card has been confiscated and thrown away by soldiers and he cannot travel to or from work.

- On September 28 or 29, 1992, Dr. K. had just left his house on his way to Anantnag when the house was surrounded by security forces. Dr. K. was blindfolded and taken to a military camp. When the security forces accused him of "treating militants." He replied, "I am a doctor and I have to treat everyone." The security forces began kicking Dr. K. and beating him with *lathi*s, and their fists. They forced him into a sitting position and pulled his legs apart several times causing intense pain in his inner thighs. They also pressed a heavy wooden roller over his thighs and applied electric shocks to his arms, chest and back. At one point he asked them, "Why are you doing this to me? I am a surgeon." He was released after two days and hospitalized at the Saura Medical Institute where he was treated for acute renal failure. When PHR's Dr. Iacopino examined him in October 1992, he had scars on his forearms and wrists that were consistent with superficial burns from electric shock.

Dr. K. previously had been detained in November 1990 after he had made arrangements for a gynecologist to examine seven women who had alleged that they had been raped by security forces. The women, who had been brought to the Anantnag District Hospital while Dr. K. was on night duty, reported that the security forces had broken up a wedding and raped all of them, including the bride.[137]

Shortly afterward, on November 29, Dr. K. was arrested from his home by members of the CRPF who had surrounded his house. Even though Dr. K. showed them his identification card, the CRPF blindfolded him along with two friends who were with him at the time. They were taken to what they later saw was a kind of military camp. The security forces asked Dr. K., "Why did you call the gynecologist?" When he replied, "I treat people irrespective of who they are," they proceeded to beat him with *lathi*s and a metal belt. His friends were also beaten in this way. Later all three men were moved to another place where they were again interrogated and beaten. On one day, a CRPF soldier intentionally shot at Dr. K.'s foot, grazing it with a bullet. The three men were detained for four days.

- In another incident in the winter of 1991, security forces surrounded the Bone and Joint Hospital complex. About 10 soldiers came to the residents dormitory as Dr. L. happened to be passing in front of it with a medical book in his hand. The soldiers approached him and accused him of being a militant even after he showed them his medical card. He was detained there for about half an hour while some of the soldiers searched the men's and women's dormitories for "militants and weapons." Dr. L. was finally released after the matron from the nurses' quarters vouched for his identity. No one else was arrested that night.

- M., 36, a worker in the medical records department at the Saura Medical Institute was arrested along with several colleagues during a crackdown by the BSF on October 14, 1992. The BSF surrounded the area at about 7:00 a.m. During an identification parade, he and three other hospital workers were selected along with 300 men detained that day, even though they had shown the BSF their identity cards. They were taken to a BSF bunker where two soldiers beat each of them with *lathi*s, fists, and kicks. Their hands were tied behind their backs, and the soldiers demanded, "Where are the guns?" They accused the men, saying, "The hospital is a den of militants, and you are supporting them." M.'s left elbow was fractured and dislocated after he was beaten for thirty minutes.

---

[137] See also p.101.

The men were detained for approximately eight hours and were given no food or water during that time.

- Dr. W. told PHR/Asia Watch that he was first detained in March 1990 by CRPF troops who took him to an interrogation center and accused him of "treating militants." He was detained for twenty-four hours. Before he was released, his interrogators told him, "We will annihilate all Kashmiris."

After that, there was a crackdown in his neighborhood. He asked one of the soldiers if he could speak to an officer, but he was not allowed to do so. He and several other men were then ordered to sit in cow dung. They refused, and Dr. W. told the soldiers, "You are bringing shame to this uniform. I was once in your uniform, and what you are doing is wrong." He was then beaten with fists and rifle butts and kicked and sustained injuries to the chest and thighs. After he was beaten, one soldier told him, "There are ten thousand people here. We'll kill all of them, and you will be responsible."

- On June 11, 1991, during a raid on the Srinagar Medical College on June 11, 1991, Dr. Maqbool Dar, an ENT [ears, nose, throat] resident, was shot in the neck while he was standing at the entrance of the hospital. According to a report by the Government Medical College in Srinagar, he had shown the security forces his identity card. He survived. The same day, the keeper of the laboratory animal facility was shot dead while on duty on the hospital grounds.

- A doctor was called to BSF headquarters in Sopore following an incident in which three suspected militants and a civilian had been killed by BSF forces. The doctor was told to write the post mortem report based only on an external examination of the bodies, and the BSF provided no explanation for the deaths. The report was then filed with the police.

Other Medical Consequences of the Conflict

The conflict in Kashmir has devastated basic health services in the state. Many community health care programs which had been in place for years have ceased to operate or have been severely curtailed. The main reason for the breakdown in medical services is that travel has become too dangerous for health care workers trying to visit rural towns and villages, or even attempting travel between major cities. Militant ambushes and gun battles between militants and security forces occur frequently. Vehicles traveling on the roads are stopped and searched repeatedly at numerous security checkpoints. Security officials at these checkpoints frequently detain passengers, or refuse them permission to proceed further and order the vehicles to turn back. Convoys of army soldiers and other security forces which move along the roads often delay other vehicle traffic.

The programs that have suffered the most as a result of the conflict have been the rural immunization, maternal and child health care and family planning programs.[138] Before the conflict, immunizations in rural areas had been carried out under a nation-wide program called "Door to Door." Doctors in Kashmir reported that in 1989-90, before the conflict worsened, approximately sixty percent of the children in Kashmir were successfully immunized in this program and the dropout rate was very low. However, since the escalation of the armed conflict in 1990, health workers responsible for the program have not been able to visit rural areas and the program has been suspended.

Community health programs in larger cities have also been disrupted by frequent crackdowns and curfews. Although immunizations continue to take place in Srinagar, even these efforts are impeded by crackdowns and transportation difficulties. One doctor cited the example of a recent immunization drive in the suburb of Batsapura, which was disrupted when BSF forces launched a crackdown and the area was inaccessible for three days. When doctors requested to be allowed to continue the immunizations, the BSF refused. Doctors reported that the normal immunization rate in Srinagar area has been markedly reduced since 1990. Doctors in Kashmir have expressed fear that this may result in epidemics of diseases that previously had shown signs of declining. For example, physicians have had to respond to an outbreak of diphtheria and have treated sporadic cases of mumps, neither of which had been reported for several years.

In addition to immunization problems, nutrition programs and maternal and child health programs have virtually been discontinued in rural areas and have been sharply reduced in Srinagar and surrounding areas.

The violence has also resulted in the attrition of health care professionals, both Hindu and Muslim, from the state, which is estimated at 30 percent for doctors and 80 percent for nurses since 1990. The

---

[138] According to government sources, militant groups have been primarily responsible for disrupting the family planning program. For more on militant attacks on health workers, see Chapter VII.

attrition has been compounded by a 30 percent decrease in the number of medical school graduates in the state since 1990. Drastic reductions in professional and ancillary staff, together with shortages of supplies and equipment, have hurt rural areas in particular and have rendered many primary health care centers, clinics and district hospitals non-functional. Their loss, together with the increase in traumatic injuries as a result of the conflict, has seriously overburdened hospitals in Srinagar, which are also short-staffed, overcrowded and experiencing serious shortages of essential supplies.

Doctors at the obstetric hospital in Srinagar reported that because of transportation difficulties, the hospital frequently runs out of supplies. For example, between July and October 1992, the hospital was unable to obtain nitrous oxide for general anesthesia, and was forced to substitute spinal anesthesia, or in some cases, ether. On other occasions, the hospital has run out of intravenous adrenaline and steroids. It no longer has any working respirators; all are non-functional and the hospital has not been able to get them repaired or replaced.

Doctors at the Saura Medical Institute reported that their CAT scan has been out of order for two years. They have been unable to get it repaired because trained engineers are not available in Srinagar and those from outside refuse to travel to Srinagar for safety reasons. The Srinagar Medical College's CAT scan has been non-functional for the past year. The chemistry laboratory has only one instrument to measure basic electrolytes and serum chemistries, and it has been out of order for the past several months. As with the CAT scan, outside engineers have been unwilling to come to Kashmir to repair the equipment.

The Srinagar Medical College has two plain X-ray machines for the entire hospital; in 1990, there had been at least six. The fluoroscopy service -- another kind of diagnostic imaging device -- is also disabled and has not been repaired. At the same time, the need for X-rays has grown with the increase in traumatic injury cases.

Dr. H., a surgeon at the Srinagar Medical College, described one preventable death which had resulted from the hospital's lack of critical resources. A thirteen-year-old boy was brought in for an elective lobectomy (partial lung removal) due to bronchiectasis. During the procedure, the electricity went off, which has become a common occurrence since the conflict began. The hospital's generator was not working, nor was the foot pedal-operated aspiration device. Without electricity, the doctors could not maintain proper suction, and, according to Dr. H., "the boy drowned in his own secretions while on the operating table."

Doctors also reported that because telephone communications are unreliable, the only means of communication is personal contact, but because that depends on reliable transportation which is impossible during crackdowns and curfews, doctors cannot obtain the advice of or consult with their colleagues.

Nearly all of the hospitals in Srinagar are overcrowded. The Srinagar Medical College has a 700-bed hospital, but between May and October 1992, it had been running a census of over 1,000 patients. The hospital has four operating theaters. Theater No. 4, which doctors described as representative of the other three, was used for 2,276 cases of gunshot wounds and blast injuries between January and mid-October 1992. The Department of Surgery, which lost 60 percent of its staff in 1990, remains 30 percent understaffed. There are approximately ten nurses during the day and approximately five at night for all patient services for 1,000 beds. In 1990, there were fifty for each shift.

Medical education has also suffered. Medical students have expressed concern that the attrition of doctors has reduced the overall quality of the teaching at the medical school. Doctors' preoccupation with clinical problems and practical issues like transportation has also affected the quality of teaching. Curfew restrictions have severely restricted students' ability to participate in clinical rotations. The conflict, which has disrupted regular mail delivery throughout the valley, has made it impossible for the Srinagar Medical College to receive medical journals and updated texts. Finally, like all other health professionals, medical students are subjected to routine detention, harassment, and assault on their way to and from their studies and work.

The Indian Red Cross provides no medical assistance in Kashmir. The International Committee of the Red Cross (ICRC), which has its regional headquarters in New Delhi, has not been permitted to carry out any of its protection and medical services in Kashmir. Although the ICRC has been allowed to carry out general educational programs in India, even that activity has not been permitted in Kashmir. In mid-1992, the medical community in Srinagar sponsored a symposium on the treatment of trauma. ICRC speakers who were invited were not allowed to attend.

The Government's Comments and Asia Watch/PHR's Response

Before this report was published,[139] Asia Watch and PHR provided the government of India with information about all of the cases and issues and requested an official response.[140]

The government's response begins by questioning our use of the terms "armed conflict" and "medical neutrality" in the context of the conditions prevailing in Kashmir:

> because terms like "armed conflict" and "medical neutrality" are not only deceptive but could give actual respectability to terrorist organisations and their activities. ... Since 1989, what the Indian State of Jammu and Kashmir has been experiencing is an externally aided "Proxy War" of massive dimensions. The parties to this are not two opposing armies, but the forces of a motley group comprising over 100 terrorist outfits and pernicious religious extremism and propaganda, on the one hand, and the law enforcement Agencies of the State, which has [sic] desisted from reacting to this violent aggression and threat to its very sovereignty and integrity, by anything like a war but, through civilian law and order methods.

---

[139] Two parts of this report were previously published: *The Crackdown in Kashmir: Torture of Detainees and Assaults on the Medical Community* was published in March 1993; *Rape in Kashmir: A Crime of War* was published in May 1993. Asia Watch and PHR received comments from the government on both reports. Where the comments refer to individual cases, we have included them in the appropriate sections of the report.

[140] For the complete text of the Government of India's response to the PHR/Asia Watch report, please see Appendix C. The Government of India also provided a number of annexures, including press clippings, statistics on killings, arson and other acts of violence which, in consideration of space, are not included in this report.

Asia Watch and PHR believe that the Kashmir situation constitutes "an armed conflict not of an international character" to which both international human rights and international humanitarian law apply. However, even if the security forces in Kashmir are involved in what the government describes as "civilian law and order methods", that does not justify the methods that have been used in Kashmir, which have included torture, rape, and extrajudicial executions. These abuses violate rights guaranteed under the International Covenant on Civil and Political Rights (ICCPR), to which India is a party. By attempting to excuse such gross violations as legitimate means of "law enforcement", the government has signalled that these abuses are condoned as a matter of policy in Kashmir.

Moreover, international humanitarian law applies not just to declared wars but to any armed conflict of this scale, including an internal one. Indeed, the severity of the Kashmir conflict is underscored by the government's characterization of it as a "proxy war." The laws of war in question are the Geneva Conventions -- which India has ratified and is obligated to uphold -- in particular, Common Article 3, which governs the conduct of government forces and armed insurgents. The primary purpose of Common Article 3 is to insure humane treatment of those persons who do not or who no longer participate actively in hostilities, including the sick and wounded, and those taken into custody.[141] Common Article 3 explicitly states that the application of its provisions "shall not affect the legal status of the Parties to the conflict," and thus does not confer legitimacy on militant groups. Moreover, medical neutrality, as defined by international law and codes of medical ethics, provides that medical personnel can render medical care to populations on all sides of the conflict.

The government cites abuses by militant organizations, stating that "[t]he blatant misuse of religion has inspired acts of gruesome brutality on the minority population in the Kashmir Valley, leading to the exodus

---

[141] The fundamental principle that the wounded and sick should be respected and protected is part of customary international law. Protocol II to the Geneva Conventions provides further authoritative guidance for implementing the provisions of Common Article 3 by forbidding attacks against medical personnel, units and transports, unless they are used to commit hostile acts, outside their humanitarian function.

of nearly two hundred and fifty thousand innocent people ... abduction, rape, torture, extortion, looting and killing ..."

In this report, PHR and Asia Watch have documented such abuses, including indiscriminate attacks and targeted assassinations of members of minority groups. Asia Watch and PHR hold these militant groups accountable under international law for these violations. We have also discussed Pakistan's role in arming or providing shelter to militant groups in Kashmir. PHR and Asia Watch fully recognize India's right to prosecute persons responsible for the murder, rape and other crimes so long as it affords them the rights of due process. However, the Indian government cannot excuse itself from abiding by international human rights and humanitarian law on the grounds that the militants have also committed abuses.

The government condemns the "willing gullibility of the authors" and the questions the credibility of those interviewed by PHR and Asia Watch. As noted above, Asia Watch and PHR are aware that many of those interviewed had sympathies with one side or the other in the conflict. However, the findings contained in this report are based on our independent analysis of the testimony of over one hundred witnesses, medical examinations and other physical evidence of the incidents described. Asia Watch and PHR are aware that many witnesses to abuse by either security forces or militants may have a motive to fabricate or exaggerate reports of abuse. For this reason, the investigators took a variety of steps to insure the reliability and honesty of the accounts they were given. The investigators sought out eyewitnesses to events, interviewed them individually, and probed them for details they were unlikely to have planned or coordinated in advance. In most cases, that testimony was corroborated separately by other witnesses. Whenever possible, the PHR/Asia Watch team also visited the sites of the incidents and asked witnesses to re-enact the events they had described, again with the goal of probing their accounts and clarifying details. On the strength and consistency of this testimony, and the irrefutable medical and other physical evidence we gathered, PHR and Asia Watch have determined that the Indian security forces have committed widespread and systematic human rights violations in Kashmir.

The government also states that two incidents described in the report are fraudulent: the transfer of Judge Rizvi and a crackdown in 1990 which lasted 17 days. According to human rights activists and lawyers in Kashmir, the transfer order for Judge Rizvi was cancelled after the Bar Association threatened to strike in protest. In the early months of 1990, curfews lasted alomst continually from January 21 through May, which according to doctors interviewed by Asia Watch and PHR, had devastating consequences for health care.

The government states that "terrorists may have forced themselves into hospitals to use them as sanctuaries ... This has been made possible both by connivance on the part of the doctors and medical staff and the sheer fear of the gun ..." The government also lists medical personnel killed by militants. In the report, Asia Watch and PHR have documented killings by militants of medical workers, including health professionals suspected of giving information on injured militants to officials. As we have stated, these abuses represent serious violations of international law. We have also stated that if any militants who have not required medical treatment have used hospitals as sanctuaries, thereby violating the neutrality of the hospital and endangering the lives and security of civilians in the hospitals, they have committed serious violations of international humanitarian law.

The government states that

> terrorists who have sustained injuries in counter-insurgency operations have surreptitiously got themselves admitted into some hospitals, and the staff, mostly out of fear and sometimes due to connivance, have not reported such cases to the police, which must be done under the law in all medico-legal cases ... Against this background occasional searches, based on specific information, have had to be made in the premises of certain medical institutions. It is also necessary in some cases, where terrorists are suspected to feign injuries, to have bandages etc. removed for verification.However, at no stage have any patients, reported to be critically ill, been subjected to such examination, and also in no case, at any stage, have life-support systems been disconnected as alleged in this report.

According to the information obtained by PHR and Asia Watch, when security forces conduct search operations in hospitals in Kashmir, they do not always do so on the basis of specific information. Rather, they routinely conduct searches to look for any recently admitted injured patients whom, because of their wounds, they suspect of being militants. The government has admitted that security forces may "remove bandages" when "terrorists are suspected to feign injuries." The government has provided no evidence that militants in any hospital in

Kashmir have done this. Given the fact that hospitals are subjected to frequent searches, they are unlikely places for many militants to seek refuge unless they are genuinely wounded. In fact, doctors in Kashmir have stated that militants not uncommonly force doctors at gunpoint to treat injured colleagues outside hospitals. Threatening medical workers in this way constitutes a serious abuse on the part of the militants.

Removing bandages or otherwise interfering with medical treatments is in clear violation of international human rights and humanitarian law, both of which prohibit any cruel and inhumane treatment, including abuses against the sick and wounded. In fact, because searches of hospitals have become so abusive, many injured persons are too afraid to seek medical care. International humanitarian law does not preclude searches of hospitals, but it does prohibit the security forces from engaging in abuses while conducting them. If the security forces have reason to believe that someone who has committed a crime is receiving treatment in a hospital, they may search for and arrest the person, but only if they do so without endangering the patient's health. The authorities may also require that a guard be posted for the duration of the patient's treatment.

While such measures are not precluded under international humanitarian law, international codes of medical ethics are equally clear about the role of physicians and other health professionals when confronted with acts that may potentially harm their patients. Article 1 of the Declaration of Tokyo, adopted by the World Medical Association in 1975, states: "The doctor shall not countenance, condone or participate in the practice of torture or other forms of cruel, inhuman or degrading procedures, whatever the offence of which the victim of such procedures is suspected, accused or guilty, and whatever the victims beliefs or motives, and in all situations, including armed conflict and civil strife." Article 4 provides: "A doctor must have complete clinical independence in deciding upon the care of a person for whom he or she is medically responsible. The doctor's fundamental role to alleviate the distress of his or her fellow men, and no motive whether personal, collective or political shall prevail against this higher purpose."

Therefore, those physicians who choose not to divulge information about their patients to authorities (1) solely out of concern for their patient's safety and or (2) for no other reason, in the current context of widespread human rights abuses in Kashmir, are, in the opinion of PHR and Asia Watch, upholding their professional duties and responsibilities as physicians.

While the Indian authorities may prosecute health professionals for failing to provide information about persons in their care whom they believe may have committed crimes, they cannot physically abuse them for failing to do so. In this report, PHR and Asia Watch have documented numerous cases of doctors and other medical workers who have been arrested, beaten and tortured to reveal information about suspected militants. PHR and Asia Watch also documented a number of cases where patients were removed from life-support systems or while in critical condition. Such abuse constitutes cruel and inhuman and degrading treatment, and as such violates fundamental human rights guaranteed under the ICCPR.

In one such case described in the report, A., an eighteen-year-old man with a gunshot wound to the leg, was removed from the operating room while under anesthesia for an operation. The government, after acknowledging that the security forces did remove the patient from the hospital, has attempted to justify this abuse by stating that the patient, "Riaz Ahmed Wani, a Pakistan-trained militant of the 'Al-Umar' outfit, was being treated clandestinely by the medical staff in the hospital. He was however, handed over to the Police Control Room, Srinagar, who in turn got him re-admitted to the hospital." This abuse of a patient undergoing medical treatment represents a serious violation of human rights and international humanitarian law.

Our report describes a number of incidents in which security forces opened fire inside hospitals, apparently to intimidate the medical staff to identify suspected militants. Such actions, which needlessly endanger civilians, violate international law. The government has not provided any explanation for these incidents. The government lists one incident in which they claim that "an exchange of fire" took place when "terrorists" fired on security forces "from the premises of the SKIMS, Soura, Srinagar." Without further information, PHR and Asia Watch are unable to comment on this incident. In many cases, however, the security forces routinely resort to lethal force even when circumstances do not warrant such action. Two security laws currently in force in Kashmir, the Armed Forces (Jammu and Kashmir) Special Powers Act and the Jammu and Kashmir Disturbed Areas Act, explicitly permit the use of lethal force against people who are not combatants and who do not pose a threat to lives of the security forces. These laws also provide the security forces with immunity from prosecution for their actions, thus effectively granting them a license to kill even such non-combatants.

Torture, which is widely practiced by Indian security forces in Kashmir, is a grave violation of internationally recognized human rights. The Indian government has provided no response to the incidents of torture documented in the report, except to say that in one case described, they were unable to identify the area or the officers and so were unable to provide any details. That incident involved the torture of three young men, all of whom required medical treatment for acute renal failure which resulted from beatings and the "roller" treatment. There have been many such cases of torture-induced acute renal failure documented in Kashmir, as well as numerous cases of electric shock, beatings and other forms of torture. The Indian authorities have never indicated that they have taken action to put a stop to torture in Kashmir. Indeed, by permitting the security forces to hold detainees in undisclosed interrogation centers where they have no access to lawyers and family members, the authorities have signalled that the practice of torture is condoned. The authorities have never made public any action taken against security personnel responsible for torture. To Asia Watch and PHR's knowledge, not a single security officer has been held criminally liable for any incident of torture in Kashmir.

On the general state of health care delivery, immunization programs and other community health services, the government states that, "it is not as if the entire health net-work in the State of the Valley, has collapsed. ... hospitals in the city of Srinagar, as well as in the rural areas continue to provide effective health services to the needy." On the basis of our on-site inspections of six hospitals and clinics, and interviews with 45 health professionals, PHR and Asia Watch believe there is no question that medical services in Kashmir have been seriously impaired by the conflict. As we have stated in the report, responsibility for the crisis rests with both the government and the militants.

Although the government states that additional doctors and other medical staff have been appointed to positions in hospitals in Kashmir, the fact remains that hospitals remain seriously understaffed for the number of patients. The government acknowledges that the immunization program has suffered because of the violence, although it has not been shut down. In our report, we have stated that the program has been drastically reduced in Srinagar, and suspended in some rural areas of the valley. The government cites efforts by militants to disrupt the family planning program. PHR and Asia Watch condemn any attacks by militant groups on health workers or participants involved in the program. As with other militant abuses against health care workers documented in the report, PHR and Asia Watch consider such actions to be violations of international law.

Asia Watch and PHR have not questioned the legality of the curfew per se, but we have condemned actions by security personnel which have targeted clearly identified medical personnel and transports and have deliberately prevented the evacuation of the wounded. The government has also stated that while they believe the situation of medical supplies to be "reasonably satisfactory" and that, "if necessary, additional funds will also be provided to augment the supplies." It also states that "efforts will be made" to insure that needed medical equipment is repaired. Asia Watch and PHR would welcome these measures. The government also states that the army has launched a "civil action programme" which has included medical camps in which patients have been treated for eye ailments and dental work. Such programs are certainly welcome, and appear to signal the government's tacit acknowledgement of that ordinary civilian health services have been devastated by the conflict.

Finally, the government has stated that "Wherever there is transgression, action has been taken. By now, over the last two years, action has been taken against over 100 personnel of the security forces, and this has involved punishments including imprisonment ranging from less than a month to seven years and various forms of departmental action including suspension pending enquiry in a number of cases." As noted above, such punishments would be a sign of progress, the Indian government has never responded to requests from Asia Watch and PHR as to the specifics regarding the nature of the abuses, the identity and rank of those responsible for abuses, and what punishments have been ordered in any cases. The government's failure to properly investigate numerous incidents of abuse and hold those responsible criminally liable is the single most important reason why security forces may believe they can operate with impunity. Making public the findings of all such investigations and the punishments awarded is critical to deter future abuse.[142]

---

[142] Such publicity need not include the names of the perpatrators, particularly since there is a genuine risk of retaliation for them and their family members.

V. THE MURDER OF H.N. WANCHOO

On December 5, 1992, Hirdai Nath Wanchoo, 67, Kashmir's most prominent and respected human rights monitor, was assassinated in Srinagar. As of June 1993, no one had been brought to justice for the murder.

On the morning of December 5, Wanchoo left his house accompanied by two Kashmiri men who had met with him at his home that morning and asked for his assistance. They told him that a boy had been picked up by the security forces and asked Wanchoo to see the boy's mother, who was very sick, and reassure her that he would be able to go to court and get the boy released. According to family members, Wanchoo had never seen the two men before, but he often received visits from unknown people who came to him for help. The same men had come to Wanchoo's house on December 4, when he was not at home. They stayed for about 15 or 20 minutes. At that time the men spoke with Wanchoo's brother and told him that they wanted to talk to Wanchoo because somebody had been picked up by the security forces. They did not give their names. The two men had also come on December 3, accompanied by a third man who never returned. On the morning of December 5, the two men came back and waited for Wanchoo to return from Karanagar, a near-by neighborhood. Wanchoo came home about 9:50 a.m. An auto-rickshaw was waiting across the street. The two men got in with him and they left.

Wanchoo's body was found on a street in Karanagar at about 10:15 a.m. He had been shot three times, once in the back of the head, once in the upper back and once in the abdomen. Residents in Karanagar stated that they heard shots in the area where the body was found, and that before the killing, they saw an auto-rickshaw with three men and driver, and another man dressed in black on a scooter.

A free-lance photographer, who said that he received a call at about 10:00 a.m saying that a dead body had been found in Karanagar, went to the place and saw the body lying face down on Balgarden Street, clutching a sheaf of papers in one hand. When the photographer turned the body over, he saw that it was Wanchoo. There was blood on the face and chest, and a bullet hole in the neck. The papers in Wanchoo's hands were documents about human rights cases on which he had been working. About a half hour later the local police took the body to the police control room. The body was then returned to the family for one night and cremated on December 6 at 4:00 p.m. The funeral was attended by thousands.

On December 16, the government issued a press release stating that the Central Bureau of Investigation (CBI) had been given responsibility for the investigation. As of April 1993, the CBI had interviewed Wanchoo's family members and colleagues. Asia Watch has been unable to obtain any further information from the government of India about the status of the CBI investigation.

According to family members, since 1990, Wanchoo had received phone calls from unknown callers who told him in Kashmiri to leave Kashmir. One caller told him, "If you don't leave, we won't spare you." Three or four months before his death he had received a handwritten note bearing the insignia of a militant group which warned him not to form a Hindu organization or indulge in politics but only remain in human rights. Family members told Asia Watch that Wanchoo "was not working for any particular organization. He was just working for human rights -- asking that innocent people not be killed."

In March 1993, Madhukar Gupta, Joint Secretary in the Home Ministry, told Asia Watch that the Indian government had arrested the persons responsible for Wanchoo's murder and that they were members of "a fundamentalist organization" which opposed to Wanchoo because he was a politically prominent Hindu. When Asia Watch asked Secretary Gupta about the government's intentions to prosecute the accused persons and make it known publicly that the murder suspects had been apprehended, Joint Secretary Gupta stated that, "It was a very difficult time," and he "could not say any more."

More than three months after that meeting, and more than six months after H.N. Wanchoo's murder, government authorities have still not officially made public the names or identities of the suspects supposedly arrested. In its comments on the Asia Watch/PHR reports, the government has stated that "[I]nvestigation of Mr. Wanchoo's death has clearly established the involvement of the Jamait-ul Mujahidin, a pro-Pakistani militant group. Mr. Wanchoo was an active member of the Kashmiri Hindu Forum and was perceived as a threat by this group which felt he was being used to give a secular colour to the anti-Government movement."

The government has not stated how the involvement of this group was "clearly established." Associates of Wanchoo's told Asia Watch that Wanchoo worked exclusively for human rights, and that he was perceived only as a human rights activist by the people in the valley. Before this report went to print, Asia Watch reiterated its request for information about the investigation and prosecution, but received no response from the government.

Although the government has not made public any evidence supporting its claim that a militant group killed Wanchoo, government sources have issued statements to selected reporters alleging the involvement of named individuals in the murder. Sources in the state government told a correspondent of the Chandigarh-based *Tribune* that Wanchoo's killer had been identified as a former constable of the Jammu and Kashmir police named Ghulam Qadir, and that he had killed Wanchoo on the orders of Nisarul Islam, the head of the Jamait-ul Mujahidin. According to the government source for the story, Qadir remains at large in Kashmir.[143] In January 1993, Nisarul Islam was reportedly killed while trying to escape from the custody of the BSF. The account provided by the government in the *Tribune* report contradicts the account provided to Asia Watch by Joint Secretary Gupta, who had asserted that Wanchoo's killers were in custody in March 1993.

To date, Indian authorities have provided no credible motive for any militant group to have killed Wanchoo. In fact, a senior Indian government official told Asia Watch that Wanchoo was killed on the orders of Governor Girish Saxena, and that those orders were carried out under the direction of the Inspector General of the BSF, Ashok Patel.[144]

Wanchoo had strongly opposed the Indian government's repressive policies in Kashmir and his efforts were dedicated to documenting abuses against the predominantly Muslim population of Kashmir by Indian security personnel. For this reason, he was widely respected throughout the valley. Wanchoo had filed *habeas corpus* petitions on behalf of detainees held under security laws in Kashmir, and had petitioned the courts to investigate several hundred cases of summary executions of detainees held by the security forces. The state authorities in Kashmir

---

[143] "Wanchoo's Killers Identified," *Tribune* (Chandigarh), May 19, 1993.

[144] In March 1993, Governor Saxena was recalled by central government authorities and replaced by Governor Krishna Rao, as part of an effort to restart negotiations toward a political settlement. In May, Ashok Patel was transferred out of Kashmir for the same reason.

repeatedly refused to comply with High Court directives ordering state security authorities to respond to the petitions by producing detainees missing since they were arrested, identifying hundreds of detainees in custody, and conducting investigations into custodial deaths. Moreover, Wanchoo had passed on information about hundreds of these killings, disappearances and illegal detentions to the international press and international human rights groups. Twenty days before he was killed, Wanchoo had met with representatives of Amnesty International. In October, Wanchoo had assisted Asia Watch and PHR in their investigations in Kashmir. According to colleagues, he planned to submit information to the United Nations Human Rights Commission in early 1993. One prominent Kashmiri lawyer told Asia Watch and PHR-Denmark that the government was particularly embarrassed by Wanchoo's activities because he was a non-Muslim.

Although the identity of the person carried out the murder of H.N. Wanchoo may never be known, Asia Watch and PHR are concerned that the government has attempted to avoid an independent investigation of the murder by sponsoring press reports implicating a militant group.

Asia Watch and PHR have urged the Indian government to order a independent judicial inquiry into the murder, headed by a high court justice or the equivalent and empowered to *subpoena* members of the security forces and police records. The government's failure to do so raises serious questions about the possibility of government complicity in the murder.

VI. THE KILLING OF DR. ABDUL AHAD GURU

Dr. Abdul Ahad Guru, a renowned Kashmiri cardiothoracic surgeon, was assassinated by unidentified gunmen in Srinagar on March 31, 1993. Dr. Guru was a member of the governing council of the Jammu and Kashmir Liberation Front (JKLF), and his political position made him a target for rival militant groups as well as elements within his own organization. He was also an outspoken critic of human rights abuses by Indian security forces in Kashmir, and met frequently with the international press and international human rights groups. While it is not possible to say for certain who was responsible for Dr. Guru's murder, there is substantial circumstantial evidence implicating militant groups. At the same time, serious questions remain about the government's actions before and after the murder.

Dr. Guru left the grounds of the Saura Institute at about 2:00 p.m., accompanied by two other doctors from the hospital. About one hundred meters from the hospital, a man wearing a *pheran* appeared in front of them and raised his hand to stop the car. He asked for a lift. Dr. Guru refused, saying he was in a hurry, but the man insisted and Dr. Guru eventually agreed. The man appeared to be about 25, was dark-skinned, and about 5' 10" in height. He wore tinted glasses, and spoke with a pronounced stammer. He got into the front seat of the car, and a second man who abruptly joined him got into the back.

After going for about one and a quarter kilometers, Dr. Guru told the driver to stop in the Nawshera neighborhood. The first man argued with Dr. Guru, insisting that they drive on a little further. When Dr. Guru declined, both men got out of the car. The first man then came around to the back of the car where Dr. Guru was sitting, opened the back door, bent down and pulled a gun out of his *pheran* and showed it to Dr. Guru. Then Dr. Guru told him he would drop the men at the next lane. The two men got back in the car, and after they had gone a little further, the first man said to Dr. Guru, "You must come with us and see some of our patients." Told that he must make an appointment, the man said, "If you don't come we will hurt you." The man again showed Dr. Guru the gun, which had a foot-long silencer attached. The gun was not a revolver. The man said, "This weapon will make no sound if it is fired, so you be careful. You must come now." Doctors in Kashmir have told Asia Watch that is not uncommon for militants to demand -- at gunpoint -- a doctor's services to care for a wounded combatant, then to return him to the place where he was taken.

At the moment that the man issued the threat, an auto-rickshaw pulled up behind Dr. Guru's car. Several men got out of the auto-rickshaw and surrounded the car. One of them, a light-skinned man in his late 20s, about 5'7", asked in Kashmiri, "Is he not coming?" The first man said no. When one of the other doctors offered to go instead, one of the men said, "No we want him [indicating Dr. Guru]. We must take him for 10 minutes."

Dr. Guru got out of the car. One of the men said, "We'll be back in 15 or 20 minutes." The men went into the lane and the auto-rickshaw pulled in behind them. Then Dr. Guru and the men got into the auto-rickshaw and drove away. The doctors waited for Dr. Guru for several hours but he did not return.

Residents of Bachpora, Srinagar, told Asia Watch that at around 9:00 p.m. on March 31, they heard a vehicle moving very fast coming from the north along Industrial Lane. The vehicle stopped suddenly. In the next two minutes, the residents heard three shots. After a few more minutes they heard the vehicle leave, again heading to the north along Industrial Lane. One resident stated that at about 7:00 a.m. on April 1, a neighbor told him that a dead body was lying in the vicinity. He told Asia Watch, "This has become a daily affair. Four years back I would have been shocked. Now it is nothing." He went with the neighbor and saw the body of Dr. Guru lying alongside the six-foot high wall of a residence on Industrial Lane. It had been lying face down but children from the neighborhood had turned it over. The body was covered with blood, and there was a pool of blood beside it. There was an entry bullet wound in the right side of the neck, and an exit wound on the left side. There was also a bullet wound in the left chest. One of the bricks in the wall had been chipped about four feet from the ground, and there was blood and flesh on the wall. Three shells were lying on the ground around the body. Rigor mortis had fully set in. The resident informed the police at around 7:30 a.m. and they moved the body to the Saura Institute, a nearby medical facility.

When Asia Watch and PHR-Denmark examined the site, there was one bullet hole visible three to four feet above the ground in a red brick wall which runs along Industrial Lane, and possibly another bullet hole five and a half feet up the wall. Dr. Guru was 5'7". There were several blood stains one centimeter across scattered on the wall. The pattern in which tissue matter had been splattered along the wall for several feet indicated that Dr. Guru had been shot in the middle of the road, not up against the wall.

Interviews with local residents and an examination of the site indicated that there are no security checkpoints along Industrial Lane, the road that the car apparently took. There are checkpoints to the south along Saura Road, which runs parallel to Industrial Lane. Although a security post bunker is only 100-150 yards from the place in the road where Guru was taken from his car, his body was found about one kilometer from the nearest security post. If one follows Industrial Lane in the direction from which neighbors say they heard the car come, one passes through an area which is flanked by houses to the east and open fields to the west along Anchar Lake. It is possible to reach the murder site directly by this road from the countryside north of Srinagar. Residents claim that this road is commonly used by militants to enter Srinagar.

The government has ordered an investigation into the killing, but Asia Watch and PHR have been unable to obtain any details about it. In its comments to Asia Watch/PHR, the government has stated that,

> Dr. Guru's killing, it is widely believed, was the work of the Hizb Ul Mujahideen, a pro-Pakistani fundamentalist group which has a running battle with the JKLF to which Dr. Guru was aligned. Only 15 days before this incident, there were cases of kidnappings and killings of important personalities as a result of this rivalry.

However, a source familiar with both organizations told Asia Watch that Dr. Guru actually had good relations with the Hezb-ul Mujahidin, but that there were significant political disagreements and rivalries within the JKLF which involved Dr. Guru.

Government sources have claimed that Dr. Guru was targeted because he was involved in negotiations with Minister of State for Internal Security Rajesh Pilot and others about a political settlement to the conflict. However, in a letter dated April 7, 1993, to Dr. Guru's son expressing condolences on the death of his father, Minister Pilot stated that he never met Dr. Guru.[145] At the same time, Dr. Guru may have been seen as being close to others involved in the Pilot negotiations.

Days before Dr. Guru was murdered, on March 25, 1993, a report by correspondent Chandra Mitra in the *Hindustan Times* publicly disclosed that Dr. Guru had met with Minister of State for Internal Security Rajesh Pilot and other government contacts as part of an effort negotiate a political settlement to the conflict. Unnamed government sources were cited in the press report. The report, which cites "informed source in Delhi," states that the"'soft-line' officers being propped up by Mr. Rajesh Pilot and Dr. Farooq Abdullah are in touch with only two go-betweens. They are Dr. Guru and Mr. Abdul Majid Wani. Home Ministry sources say that Dr. Guru's antecedents are extrmely suspect. He is believed to be in league with Pakistan's Inter-Services Intelligence (ISI) and has been trying to bring the pro-Pakistan Hizbul Mujahidin and the pro-independence JKLF together to establish at least a working relationship."[146] Some sources told Asia Watch that information about the negotiations may have been deliberately planted to discredit the named individuals.

While there may be evidence supporting charges that militant groups carried out the killing, that does not absolve the government from its responsibility to conduct a thorough, independent investigation into the murder. The fact that Dr. Guru and his family had also been harassed and assaulted by the security forces makes such an inquiry all the more important. When Asia Watch and PHR met with Dr. Guru in October 1992, he described repeated incidents of harassment, detention and assault by the security forces. On October 9, 1992, troops had shot at his clinic; on August 7, they had shot into his house, injuring his nephew. Shortly afterwards, in September 1992, the nephew was detained by CRPF forces, blindfolded, beaten and given electric shocks. The security

---

[145] A journalist told Asia Watch that Dr. Guru had met Pilot in 1991, when Dr. Guru was involved in negotiating the release of K. Doraiswamy, executive director of the India Oil Corporation, who had ben kidnapped by the Ikhwanul-Muslemin group on June 28, 1991. Doraiswamy was released on August 21, 1991.

[146] Chandra Mitra, "Pilot's Kashmir Policy Runs Aground," *Hindustan Times*, March 22, 1993.

forces interrogated him about his uncle and told him to identify militants. He was released after 24 hours.

Dr. Guru was arrested at the Delhi airport on August 12, 1990, as he was returning from a meeting in Riyadh, Saudi Arabia. He was detained for four months and charged with "participating in the release of five militants," "passing money to earthquake victims in Iran," distributing Rs. 150,000 (approximately $5,360) to "militants" and "donating Rs. 100,000 (approximately $3,570) to the JKLF on July 1, 1990." The first charge had to do with his participation as an intermediary in the government's efforts in December 1989 to negotiate the release of Rubia, the daughter of the Home Minister who had been kidnapped by the JKLF. Because Rubia's older sister, Dr. Mahmooda, had been trained by Dr. Guru, he was asked to assist in the negotiations. Rubia was released after five detained JKLF leaders were released from custody. The second charge was based on an appeal which Dr. Guru placed in a newspaper for earthquake victims in Iran. Dr. Guru reported that the Rs. 50,000 (approximately $1,785) that was donated was sent by bank draft to the Iranian Consulate in Delhi. The third charge was based on a similar appeal Dr. Guru organized in March, 1990, for survivors of two villages (Magam and Tangmarg) which were burned by security forces. The money collected, Rs. 150,000, was distributed to victims. On the date specified in the last charge, Dr. Guru stated that he was in Saudi Arabia a medical conference.

Dr. Guru was released from jail on December 23, 1990. The case was never brought to court. However, in November 1990, while he was in jail, his passport was impounded. After his release, officials from the Central Bureau of Investigation (CBI) questioned Dr. Guru on many occasions about his professional and personal activities. When PHR/Asia Watch interviewed him in October 1992, he stated that he believed he had been under surveillance for a number of months. Dr. Guru was also questioned by the CBI after meeting with PHR.

During the funeral procession for Dr. Guru, when the mourners attempted to march from Dr. Guru's home to the town of Sopore, the security forces blocked them, saying that the procession would not be permitted to take that route. During the protest that followed, one of the bodyguards of the Senior Superintendent of Police K. Rajendra Kumar opened fire with an automatic weapon, shooting Dr. Guru's brother in law in the head and killing him instantly.[147]

---

[147] For more on this, see p. 85, 141.

VII. VIOLATIONS BY MILITANT ORGANIZATIONS

Militant organizations operating in Kashmir have committed grave violations of international human rights and humanitarian law. Many of the violent attacks committed by these groups have deliberately targeted civilians. Among the worst abuses have been the assassinations of hundreds of civilians, including members of the Hindu community, civil servants and political figures, particularly Muslim political leaders associated with the National Conference party and other political groups opposed by the militants.

Militant groups have also abducted and executed civilians, both Hindu and Muslim, whom they have accused of being government informers or of otherwise supporting the government of India.[148] In many cases, those accused of being informers have first been detained for interrogation and torture by the militant group. Execution generally follows a summary "hearing", during which the detainee is given virtually no opportunity to defend him or herself. Militants have also tortured and summarily executed captured security personnel in their custody. These

---

[148] Militants have also killed and wounded members of the security forces -- the CRPF, BSF and others -- operating in Kashmir. These are not violations of the laws of war if these killings occur in combat or ambush and are not the result of perfidy. Insofar as members of the security forces have combat duties and are actively engaged in hostilities, they are military targets, subject to direct attack. Although policemen, customs agents and other government personnel authorized to bear arms are excluded from the definition of "armed forces" and are not proper military targets, policemen with combat duties are military targets. *See* Report of Working Group B, Committee I, 18 March 1975 (CDDH/I/238/Rev.1; X, 93), in Levie, Howard S., ed., *The Law of Non-International Armed Conflict*, (Dordrecht, Netherlands: Martinus Nijhoff Publishers, 1987), p. 67. BSF, CRPF and other national security forces operating in Kashmir routinely engage in combat with militants. In many situations, they are, in effect, acting in lieu of army soldiers to perform purely military functions. Under international humanitarian law applicable in internal armed conflicts, the government may try members of guerrilla forces for sedition, treason and murder in violation of state laws, but must afford them due process.

executions have reportedly increased in 1992 as a deliberate form of retaliation for the increase in custodial deaths by Indian security forces. Militant spokespersons have acknowledged that executions of captured security force personnel are carried out as a matter of policy. Such summary executions constitute grave violations of international humanitarian law.

Members of militant groups have also raped women in Kashmir. While there it is not clear that militant leaders have explicitly sanctioned such abuses, there is little indication that the militants have done anything to stop their forces from committing rape. Some incidents of rape by militants appear to have been motivated by the fact that the victims or their families are accused of being informers or of being opposed to the militants or supporters of rival militant groups. Some members of militant forces have also launched other violent attacks on women who do not adhere to prescribed dress codes and other social restrictions. These attacks, and the fact that they are carried out with impunity, have contributed to a climate of fear for women in Kashmir.

Militants have engaged in indiscriminate attacks which have injured and killed civilians. Members of militant groups have thrown grenades at buses and used rocket-propelled launchers to fire grenades into government buildings of the civil administration, injuring and killing employees. Armed militant groups have also launched targeted bomb attacks against civilians in Jammu.

Kidnappings of civilians has been a hallmark of the militants' efforts since the conflict began in earnest in 1989. Militants have kidnapped civilians and held them as hostages for detained colleagues, or to pressure rival militant organizations. Militants have also kidnapped civilians in order to extort funds from their families.

When the conflict escalated 1989, militant groups issued widespread threats to members of the minority Hindu community in Kashmir. Attacks on Hindus since 1988, and particularly in early 1990, have driven more than 100,000 Hindus to flee Kashmir to Jammu and Delhi, where most remain in increasingly desperate conditions in refugee camps. Tens of thousands of Muslims have also fled. Those militant groups which espouse an extremist Islamic ideology have also issued threats to persons associated with businesses they consider "un-Islamic," including liquor dealers and cinema hall owners. Militant groups have also issued threats to journalists whom they have accused of "biased" reporting.

All of these abuses constitute grave violations of international human rights and humanitarian law. Although some militant leaders have issued statements calling on their forces not to engage in criminal activities, to Asia Watch and PHR's knowledge, the militant groups responsible for these gross abuses have taken few if any steps to end them.

Militant Operations

At least eleven major militant organizations, and perhaps dozens of smaller ones, operate in Kashmir. They are roughly divided between those who support independence and those who support accession to Pakistan. The oldest and most widely known militant organization, the Jammu and Kashmir Liberation Front (JKLF), has spearheaded the movement for an independent Kashmir. Its student wing is the Jammu and Kashmir Students Liberation front (JKSLF). A large number of other militant organizations have emerged since 1989, some of which also support independence, others of which support Kashmir's accession to Pakistan. Although all groups reportedly receive arms and training from Pakistan, the pro-Pakistani groups are reputed to be favored by Pakistan's military intelligence, the Directorate of Inter-Services Intelligence (ISI). The most powerful of these is the Hezb-ul-Mujahidin. Other major groups include Al-Jehad, Al-Barq, Hizbollah, Ikhwan-ul-Muslimin, Jamait-ul Mujahidin, Tekriq-ul Mujahidin, Allah Tigers, Al-Umar Mujahidin and Al-Umar Commandos. According to press reports, several hundred fighters from Afghanistan and Sudan have also joined some of the militant groups.[149]

Intense rivalries among the militant groups, and particularly between the dominant groups, has sparked frequent clashes and has often prevented the miltants from coordinating military operations.[150] As of mid-1993, a Coordination Committee comprised of representatives of the leaders from the JKLF, Hezb-ul Mujahidin, Iqwan Muslim, Harkat-ul-Mujaheedin; Jamait-ul-Mujaheedin; Tahreek-ul-Mujaheedin, Hizbollah; and Muslim Mujahidin had assumed some judicial oversight for the various groups, under the authority of recognized legal and religious advisors. The committee reportedly has no written laws or regulations.

---

[149] See Harinder Baweja, "Losing Control," *India Today*, p.27.

[150] See Sumit Ganguly, "Avoiding War in Kashmir," *Foreign Affairs*, Winter 1990/91 (1990) p. 65, and Steve Coll, "Kashmiris Describe India Resorting to Arson in Rebel War," *Washington Post*, November 16, 1990.

It is not known whether the committee plays any role in coordinating military strategy.

The militant forces do not control territory in Kashmir, but certain parts of the valley have gained a reputation as strongholds of particular militant groups, particularly towns near the Line of Control which separates the Indian state of Jammu and Kashmir from the territory controlled by Pakistan. Many of these towns, notably Kupwara, are along the supply lines for weaponry from Pakistan. The Hezb-ul Mujahidin, for example, is reported to have a dominant presence in the town of Sopore where, according to recent press reports, the group has claimed to have established pockets of control from which they have launched attacks on Indian government troops trying to conduct search operations in the vicinity.[151]

The militants' military operations are generally characterized by ambushes of security force patrols and convoys and hit-and-run attacks on security force bunkers and pickets, for which they generally use grenades, rocket-propelled grenade launchers and anti-personnel and anti-tank mines. Some militant groups have organized commando units responsible for attacking specific targets, such as security force bunkers. The militants also engage army troops and other security forces in gun battles. For these operations they rely on weapons such as AK-47 and AK-56 assault rifles, light machine guns, revolvers and other light weapons. The militants are also reported to have sophisticated night vision and wireless communication equipment. State authorities claim that nearly 8,000 AK series assault rifles, 455 rocket launchers and 8,030 grenades have been recovered since 1988.

The Pakistan Conduit

Much of this weaponry reaches Kashmir from Pakistan, and militant leaders freely acknowledge that they receive support from Pakistan's ISI.[152] Pakistani leaders, while officially denying that they provide

---

[151] See Harinder Baweja, "Losing Control," *India Today*, p.27.

[152] Under Pakistan's late president Zia ul-Haq, the ISI gained increased powers over domestic and foreign intelligence operations. The ISI has also been the conduit for outside covert assistance to the Afghan resistance and has reportedly provided some of that weaponry to a

arms, cite instead their "moral and political support" of the Kashmiri militants.[153] Weaponry from Afghanistan has also reportedly reached Kashmir through Pakistan military conduits. According to one report,

> There is evidence too that at least some of the rebel factions have established ties with the mujahedin of Afghanistan, who now have time on their hands and a huge arsenal of American- and Pakistani-supplied weapons.[154]

Another report provides more detailed information about the arms source and the variety of weapons which have reached Kashmir.

> Virtually the entire insurgent arsenal points to sources close to the Afghan war. Some of the more exotic pieces seen in militant hands, such as captured Soviet AKS-74 rifles and AKR submachineguns, have evidently passed through the arms bazaars of Pakistan's tribal areas. But a high volume of weaponry, most of it Chinese -- notably Type 56-1 folding stock assault rifles, pistols, stick grenades and Type-69 rocket-propelled grenades -- suggests the diversion of bulk consignments intended for the Afghan conflict. ... Separatist sources also claim to have begun training courses inside the Vale of Kashmir area. Instructors are said to be guerrillas with both training and combat experience in Afghanistan, where several *mujahideen* factions have opened doors to the Kashmiris. Whatever the truth behind New Delhi's repeated assertions -- routinely denied by Islamabad -- that training of Kashmiris continues in camps in Pakistan, the Afghan

---

number of militant groups in Kashmir. *See* Selig S. Harrison, "Showdown in Kashmir," *Peace and Security*, Vol. 5, Number 3, Autumn 1990, pp. 8-9. *See also*, Steve Coll, "India, Pakistan Wage Covert 'Proxy Wars'," *Washington Post*, December 8, 1990.

[153] "Pakistan to Back J-K Ultras: Sharif," *Times of India*, December 25, 1990.

[154] Anthony Spaeth, "No Peace in the Valley," *Harpers*, April 1993, p. 82.

connection today would appear to provide the militants with the instruction they need at no diplomatic cost to Pakistan.[155]

According to a report in *India Today*, Indian army officials have identified 72 routes used by militant forces crossing the Line of Control from Pakistan.[156]

Another observer notes that although "incontrovertible evidence of *direct* Pakistani involvement in the training and arming of insurgents is hard to establish," other actors in Pakistan have an incentive for playing a role in Kashmir, particularly the ISI.[157]

In early 1993, after the U.S. reportedly threatened to include Pakistan on its list of countries sponsoring terrorism, Pakistani officials launched a public relations campaign to counter the charges.[158] Pakistani leaders claim that they have stemmed the flow of arms into Kashmir in

---

[155] R.A. Davis, "Kashmir in the Balance," *International Defence Review*, April 1991, p. 301.

[156] W. P. S. Sidhu, "The Challenge in the Mountains," *India Today*, June 30, 1991, p. 27.

[157] Sumit Ganguly, "The Prospects of War and Peace in Kashmir," in Raju G. C. Thomas, ed. *Perspectives on Kashmir: The Roots of Conflict in South Asia*, (Boulder: Westview Press, 1992), p. 359.

[158] As part of that effort, Nisar Ali Khan, chief political adviser to Pakistan's Prime Minister Nawaz Sharif, met with U.S. officials in Washington on April 6, 1993. See Farhan Bokhari, "Pakistan Seeks to Allay US Fears over Terrorist Links," *Financial Times*, April 7, 1993. According to an *Associated Press* report, on the eve of talks between U.S. and Pakistani officials in April 1993, the U.S.ambassador to Islamabad, John Monjo, indicated that Pakistan has not moved forcefully enough to curb assistance to the Kashmiri insurgents. George Gedda, "Christopher Raises Terrorism Issue with Pakistani Official," *Associated Press*, April 7, 1993. In meetings with Asia Watch in 1992, Pakistani officials disavowed responsibility for events in Pakistan-controlled Azad Kashmir -- where many of the training camps are reportedly based. The claim cannot be considered credible, since the Pakistani military, including the ISI, have a considerable presence in the province.

response to pressure from the U.S.[159] However, other observers report that that the government's efforts have not resulted in any discernible reduction in arms supplies to Kashmiri groups who have traditionally received such support. A report in the *Washington Post* cited a former ISI official as stating that as a result of increased pressure from the U.S., the ISI was "increasingly funneling assistance to India through third parties" and that the political party Jamaat-i Islami had "hired former employees of ISI and the Special Services Group, the army's elite commando force, to run its Kashmir operations."[160]

A number of militant organizations have claimed responsibility for some of the assassinations, kidnappings and other attacks carried out by their forces in Kashmir. There are many other cases in which no group has taken responsibility, and it is impossible to say which of the many groups operating in the state have committed these abuses. In each of the cases listed below, militants killed, assaulted or threatened civilians with death; these actions directly international humanitarian law, which protects civilians and other non-combatants from abuse. The cases listed below are illustrative; there have been many such incidents of abuse since 1989 by various militant groups.

Executions of Civilians and Other Non-Combatants

Militant organizations operating in Kashmir have repeatedly violated the strict prohibitions under international human rights and humanitarian law, particularly Common Article 3, against violence to life and person of those taking no part in the hostilities. These groups have assassinated Hindu civilians, civil servants and prominent Muslims associated with the National Conference party and other groups. The attacks appear to have been motivated as part of a campaign early in the conflict to drive out the Hindu minority and to eliminate any political leaders who could pose a challenge to the militants' aims. Many of the political figures targetted by the militants have been those associated with the former discredited administration of Farooq Abdullah. In other cases,

---

[159] Douglas Jehl, "Pakistan is Facing Terrorist Listing," *New York Times*, April 25, 1993.

[160] Molly Moore and John Ward Anderson, "After Cold War, U.S.-Pakistan Ties Are Turning Sour," *Washington Post*, April 21, 1993.

those who have been murdered have been selected apparently only because they have been employed in the civil service.

There are no precise figures for the number of killings of this kind that have taken place since the conflict began. Government sources report that as many as 2,000 civilians have been killed by militant groups. The cases described below are illustrative of the kind of murders of civilians which militant groups have committed and continue to commit.

• On March 2, 1993, Ghulam Nabi Baba, a retired assistant commisssioner, was shot dead after being abducted by militants on February 28. Ghulam Nabi Baba was a relative of the state Congress-I party leader, Ghulam Rasul Kar. On March 1, Ghulam Rasul Kar's brother-in-law, Habibullah Mirshah, was also killed by militants.[161]

• On January 19, 1993, the bodies of Abdul Razak Lone, a resident of Samthan, Bijbehara, and Abdul Rehman Bhat, a resident of Narkara, Badgam, were recovered from Bijbehara and Ichkote, respectively. Both men had been abducted by members of a militant group several days before they were killed. Lone had died from gunshot wounds and Bhat had been strangled.[162]

• On December 13, 1992, the body of Ghulam Ahmed Lone, an employee of the Military Engineering Service (MES) was found in the Trikilabal region of Kupwara. Lone had been abuducted by members of a militant group several days earlier.[163]

Many similar killings have occurred since 1990. Asia Watch documented many other cases of execution by militant forces early in the conflict, [164]including the exection of the abduction and murder of the Vice-Chancellor of Kashmir University, Mushir-ul Haq, and his personal secretary, Abdul Ghani Zargar, in April 1990. We have listed a number of other cases from this period below. There were many more killings

---

[161] "Kashmir Militants Kill Abducted Ex-Official," All-India Radio, March 2, 1993. As cited in FBIS, (NES-93-040), March 3, 1993, p. 32.

[162] *Aftab*, January 19, 1993.

[163] "4 Ultras Among 7 Killed in Valley," *Times of India*, December 14, 1992.

[164] These and other cases are documented in Asia Watch, *Kashmir Under Siege*, (May 1991).

during this period and in the years that followed than it was possible to document here.

• Lassa Koul, the 47-year-old director of the state-run Doordarshan television center for Jammu and Kashmir, was shot dead by JKLF gunmen on February 13, 1990, apparently as part of an effort to compel program changes more favorable to the militants. Koul had received more than a dozen written threats, some on the letterheads of the JKLF and others including the Hezb-ul Mujahidin, as well as telephone calls, mostly at his office at Doordarshan. The JKLF subsequently took responsibility for the killing.

• On December 13, 1990, militants of the Hezb-e Ullah killed Maulana Mohammad Sayeed Masoodi, 87, the former general secretary of the National Conference party and a leading moderate politician in Kashmir since India's independence. Masoodi was gunned down in his home in Ganderbal, a suburb northwest of Srinagar. According to press reports, the assassins fired at Masoodi from point blank range and then fled.[165]

Summary Executions and Other Abuses Against Accused Informers

The killings of suspected police informers or others accused of undermining the militants political or military objectives have been ordered by senior commanders of the militant organizations. While some individual militants may murder political rivals or carry out vendetta killings on their own, the assassinations of political figures and suspected government agents are carried out as a matter of policy under the authority of the legal advisor to the militants' coordination committee. One report noted that the assassinations of real and suspected government informers "almost certainly outnumber fatalities inflicted on the security forces."[166]

Militant leaders have stated that they conduct judicial proceedings against anyone captured by their forces who is accused of informing on

---

[165] "32 Die in Clashes After Secessionist Arrested," Agence France Presse, December 13, 1990, as cited in FBIS-NES-90-241, December 14, 1990, p. 38.

[166] R. A. Davis, "Kashmir in the Balance," *International Defense Review*, Vol. 24, No. 4, April 1991, p. 301.

the militants to the security forces or otherwise harming the political and military objectives of the militants. During interrogation of suspected informers, the militants have resorted to brutal methods to coerce confessions or other information. Although the militants claim to hold trials of those in custody, these procedures are so rudimentary and biased that they constitute a clear violation of internationally-recognized standards of due process, and executions carried out on the basis of such procedures represent gross abuses of international humanitarian law.

According to a militant spokesperson, information about the alleged violation is first brought to the attention of the Coordination Committee by local neighborhood or village committees which comprise four or five persons and who oversee the actions of members of militant groups in those localities. If a militant or resident in that area is suspected of being an informer or of cooperating with the Indian forces, the local committee informs the district committee. The local militant commander has the responsibility of deciding whether to arrange for the person to be taken into custody for interrogation.

The purpose of the interrogation is to coerce the suspect to confess to anti-militant activities. To accomplish this, the suspect is subjected to various forms of mistreatment and torture. Although militant leaders have claimed that the interrogation begins without the use of threats or force, they have also acknowledged that in order to coerce the suspect to confess, he or she is progressively subjected to more severe forms of mistreatment. First, he or she may be denied food or water for 24 hours, or forced to consume salty water, and then kept for prolonged periods in a dark room. Following that, the detainee is apparently subjected to other forms of torture.[167]

The presence of a legal or religious advisor and one to three witnesses is required before the hearing can be held. The witness is supposed to be confronted face to face with witnesses against him, and he or she is told what the charges are, but is not permitted to call witnesses in his or her own defense. The legal advisor or the religious advisor from the Coordination Committee acts as the judge. It is evident that in a hearing of this kind, the guilt of the accused has already been determined by the committee. As one militant leader stated, "There has not yet been

---

[167] One militant leader has claimed that the practice of physical torture was stopped in late 1992, but the claim cannot be considered credible.

a case where a person has been found not guilty." Such a procedure does not meet recognized standards of due process.

When the detainee is pronounced guilty, the Coordination Committee determines the punishments. Anyone determined to have been involved in abuses by the security forces, particularly as an informer on anyone subsequently killed in custody, is executed. For lesser offenses, the committee may order the person to be shot in the foot, or to have his or her head shaved. In other cases, the detainee may be released, but is kept under constant surveillance by the district committee. If he or she is reported to be engaging in anti-militant activities a second time, the punishment is death. A militant leader stated that out of 75 persons detained by the militants in March and April 1993, 67 were released on condition that they would be kept under surveillance, 59 of whom were ordered not to leave their neighborhoods. The remaining eight left Kashmir. Five others were executed, and three remained in custody.

Five executions of suspected informers carried out between March and April, 1993, included Parvez Ahmed Sheikh, alias Pareen, Deputy Chief of Iqwan Muslamin, 24; Aftab Khan of Kupwara; Riaz Ahmed Mitha, 24; Ghulam Nabi Shah, 42; Abdul Aziz, 49; and a woman named Waheeda, 27.

A number of militant organizations have claimed responsibility for executions of suspected informers, political figures and civil servants. For example, Al-Jihad took responsibility for killing Pareen, on April 9, 1993. There are many other cases in which no group has taken responsibility, and it is impossible to say which, if any, of the many groups operating in the state may have committed the crime. Such executions have been reported frequently since 1990.

• In October 1992, Asia Watch was informed about the killing of a suspected informer, Bilal, believed responsible for providing information to the security forces that led to the summary execution of Mohammad Yaqub Mir.[168] The Al-Barq militant group was believed responsible for Bilal's murder.

• Mir Ghulam Mustafa, 51, former member of the dissolved Kashmir state legislative assembly, was hanged on March 25, 1990, 34 hours after he had been kidnapped. The Hezb-ul Mujahidin claimed responsibility for Mustafa's execution, stating that under interrogation he had admitted

---

[168] For more on this case, see p.57.

"indulging in anti-Islamic activities and spying for Indian government intelligence," and for hat reason he had been hanged.[169]

- On March 12, 1990, militants of the Hezb-ul Mujahidin executed Maulana Abdul Aziz and Maulana Ayub Ali al-Qasmi, near Shopian, claiming that the two leaders (*imams*) were "tried" and "executed" under Islamic law for "spying on behalf of an intelligence agency." Police reported that the bullet-ridden bodies were found near a road at Veil village.[170]

- On July 30, 1990, unidentified armed youths killed Umkarnat Muttu, a shopkeeper, at Panpour on the Srinagar-Jammu highway. Muttu had been a supervisor in the Indian army and after retirement had opened a shop in the Badami Bagh cantonment. Militants accused Mattu of having been a government spy. The JKLF student wing took responsibility for the killing.[171]

- According to press accounts, at about 4:00 p.m. on November 16, 1989, three unidentified persons entered the tailor shop of Abdul Rashid Mattoo, 35, in Batmaloo locality, Srinagar, and asked Rashid to accompany them. As Rashid came out of the shop, one of the men fired at him and killed him. A week earlier, a handwritten notice had been placed at the main entrance of Rashid's house asking him to dissociate publicly from a "volunteer force" raised by the police. The JKLF, which accused Rashid of being a police informer, claimed responsibility for the killing.[172]

- On March 24, 1990, the body of Anwar Khan was found hanging from a tree in the village of Chandiloora, 34 kilometers west of Srinagar.

---

[169] Mustafa had acted as a go-between in December 1989 to help arrange the release of the kidnapped daughter of Home Minister Mufti Mohammed Sayeed in exchange for five detained militants.Pushpa Saraf, "The War Within," *Indian Express*, April 8, 1990; "Kidnapped Kashmir Politician Found Dead," Reuters, March 25, 1990.

[170] Yusuf Jameel, "2 WB Priests Killed in J&K," *Telegraph*, March 13, 1990.

[171] *Srinagar Times*, July 31, 1990.

[172] "Militants Gun Down One in Srinagar," *Kashmir Times*, November 17, 1989.

A handwritten note left with the body said Khan had been executed by the Hezb-ul Mujahidin for being a "CRP informer." The same day shortly after noon, a deputy superintendent of police, Gulam Hassan Tabasum, was shot dead outside his residence in Balgarden locality, and a government engineer, Ashok Misri, was shot and fatally wounded in Peerbagh. The JKSLF claimed responsibility for both killings, stating that Misri was an Intelligence Bureau informer.[173]

Summary Executions of Captured Security Force Personnel

Militant leaders have admitted that they execute members of the security forces who have been captured by their forces. Such executions represent grave violations of international humanitarian law. One militant leader admitted, "Up to eight months ago, the militants would capture members of the security forces and hold them to exchange for captured militants. But since Operation Tiger started eight months ago, Indian government will not exchange -- it just kills those it captures so we do the same. Our policy now is to execute any security forces we capture." Asia Watch and PHR have noted incidents of such killings which occurred in 1992 and 1993.

• The body of Dharmpal Singh, an army serviceman, who had been kidnapped by unidentified militant forces on June 2, 1993, was found in Srinagar on June 3.[174]

• On September 17, the JKLF announced that it had executed two army soldiers, R.K.Ghai and K.R. Kannan, who had been taken hostage by the group on August 3, 1992. In its announcement to the local press, the JKLF stated that one of its commanders killed the two men as they were trying to escape.[175]

---

[173] "Militants Execute J&K 'Informers,'" *Telegraph*, March 25, 1990.

[174] "Abducted Armyman Killed in Srinagar," *Times of India*, June 4, 1993.

[175] "JKLF Executes 2 Armymen Taken Hostage," *Times of India*, September 18, 1992.

Rape by Militant Groups

While militant threats to women were reported as early as 1990, most frequently by groups reportedly seeking to enforce their interpretation of "Islamic" culture in Kashmir, reports of rape by militant groups were rare in the conflict's early years. A July 1990 report cited frequent threats to women by one group, "warning the women that severe action will be taken if they do not maintain *purdah* (or *burqa* -- clothing which entirely conceals the body)."[176] Such threats have continued, and women who have challenged the militants have been attacked. On May 13, 1993, members of the women's militant organization, Dukhtaran-e-Millat (Daughters of the Nation) issued warnings to women in Srinagar not to come outside without wearing *burqas*. The militants sprayed paint on women who defied the order. Four students were hospitalized with eye injuries from the paint.[177]

Reports of rape by militant groups in Kashmir have increased since 1991. The reasons for this are not clear, but the increase coincides with a rise in other violent crimes against civilians, including kidnapping, extortion and murder. In some cases, women have been raped and then killed after being abducted by rival militant groups and held as hostages for their male relatives. In other cases, members of armed militant groups have abducted women after threatening to shoot the rest of the family unless she is handed over to a militant leader. The fact that local people sometimes refer to these abductions and rapes as "forced marriages" gives some indication of the social ostracism suffered by rape victims and code of silence, and fear, that prevents people from openly condemning such abuses by militant groups.

Some incidents of rape by militants appear to have been motivated by the fact that the victims or their families are accused of being informers or of being opposed to the militants or supporters of rival militant groups. One of the earliest such cases involved a staff nurse at the Saura Medical Institute, Sarla Bhat, 27, who was kidnapped from the

---

[176] Committee for Initiative on Kashmir, *Kashmir Imprisoned*, July 1990, pp.46-47.

[177] From South Asia Human Rights Documentation Centre, April 7, 1993.

institute on April 14, 1990. Her body was found four days later. A note found near the body stated that the JKLF took responsibility for the killing and accused Bhat of informing the security forces about the presence of a number of wounded militants in the hospital.[178] The post-mortem report concluded that she had been raped before she was shot dead.

Rape by militant groups is a violation of international humanitarian law under Common Article 3 of the Geneva Conventions, which prohibits murder, torture and ill-treatment of non-combatants by both government and militant forces. As noted above, in both conflict and non-conflict situations, the purpose of rape is power. Both security forces and armed militants have used rape as a weapon: to punish, intimidate, coerce, humiliate and degrade. The fear of rape has reportedly been a factor in the flight of Muslim families from Kashmir.[179] However, cases of rape by militant groups are difficult to investigate because most Kashmiris are reluctant to discuss abuses by the militants out of fear of reprisal. According to one report, the increasing number of rapes has led to an increase in abortions in Kashmir, resulting in one case in the murder of a doctor who complained about having to perform them. Militants from the Hezb-ul Mujahidin and Al Jehad reportedly accused the doctor of being an informer.[180]

A 1992 case of rape and murder by militants attracted publicity in part because the incident provoked street protests condemning the militants for the crimes. The incident involved the family of a retired truck driver named Sohanlal, 60, who lived in Nai Sadak, Kralkhud. At about 8:30 p.m. on March 30, 1992, armed militants entered Sohanlal's home. According to his son, the men demanded food and shelter. The family complied. After about two hours, Sohanlal and his wife, Bimla, heard their daughter, Archana, crying for help from a room on the ground floor of the house. When they reached the room, the militants shot Sohanlal, killing him instantly. The bodies of the two women were

---

[178] Yusuf Jameel, "Ex-Minister Shot Dead by J&K Militants," *Telegraph*, April 20, 1990.

[179] Ibid, p. 43.

[180] See Harinder Baweja, "People Turning Against Militants," *India Today*, May 31, 1992, p. 42.

later discovered in the street outside the house. According to the autopsy report, both women had been raped before being shot. According to one report, 5,000 women staged a protest march to condemn the rapes and murders.[181] To Asia Watch/PHR's knowledge, no group has claimed responsibility for the incident.[182]

---

[181] Harinder Baweja, "People Turning Against Militants," *India Today*, May 31, 1992, p. 42.

[182] Provided by South Asia Human Rights Documentation Centre, April 7, 1993.

Kidnapping

Common Article 3 prohibits the "taking of hostages." The International Committee of the Red Cross commentary on Protocols I and II of the Geneva Conventions explains that hostages are persons

> detained for the purpose of obtaining certain advantages. This means that hostages are persons who find themselves, willingly or unwillingly, in the power of the enemy and who answer with their freedom or their life for compliance with the orders of the latter and for upholding the security of its armed forces.[183]

Since the conflict began, militants have engaged in frequent kidnappings of civilians, some of whom have been held as hostages for detained colleagues, or as a means of exerting pressure on family members of the victim who support a rival militant organization. Particularly in 1991, militant groups also kidnapped foreigners, apparently as a means to attract international attention. Militants have also kidnapped civilians in order to extort funds from their families. Asia Watch has documented numerous cases of kidnappings that occurred between 1989 and 1991.[184] We have noted a number of cases below which occurred in 1992 and 1993.

• On June 8, 1993, militants adbucted Sharifuddin Shariq, a prominent National Conference leader and former member of the Jammu and Kashmir state assembly, from Lal Mandi, Srinagar. According to a press report, Shariq was considered a close associate of former Chief Minister, Farooq Abdullah. To Asia Watch and PHR's knowledge, no group claimed responsibility for the kidnapping.[185]

---

[183] International Committee of the Red Cross, *Commentary on the Additional Protocols* (1987) p. 874. Although the Additional Protocols do not bind the parties to the Kashmir conflict, as elaborations upon the principles outlined in common Article 3, they provide rules of authoritative guidance which may be used in evaluating the parties' conduct.

[184] See Asia Watch, *Kashmir Under Siege*, (May 1991).

[185] "Militants Abduct Farooq Aide," *Times of India*, June 9, 1993.

- On January 22, 1993, militants abducted two employees of the Public Works Department, Shamsuddin Malik, an executive engineer, and Mushtaq Ahmed, an assistent engineer, from Haproo in Batapora. Asia Watch and PHR have not been able to obtain information as to the fate of the two men.[186]
- On October 14, 1992, four employees of the Bharat Heavy Electrical Limited company, including M.A. Sheikh, deputy general manager, S. P. Adana, assistant foreman, S. C. Jha, branch manager, and Ramesh Singh, commercial officer, and their driver, Vijay Singh, were abducted by militants in Pampore. Two of the officers were released later that day, and the remaining men several days later.[187]

Indiscriminate Attacks

Militant groups have engaged in grenade attacks, and have detonated car bombs and other explosive devices in residential and commercial areas where these attacks have injured and killed civilians. One such attack occurred in Srinagar during the Asia Watch/PHR mission in October 1992. Common Article 3 prohibits not only murder but other forms of "violence to life and person," including violence which results in injury and not death. Militant bombings and grenade attacks on civilian government buildings and civilian transport vehicles are violations of the laws of war.

- On May 11, 1993, militants attacked the government secretariat which houses the offices of the civilian administration in Srinagar using rocket-propelled grenade launchers. According to press reports, the attack killed one employee and injred three others. The Hezb-ul Mujahidin reportedly claimed responsibility for the attack in a telephoned statement to the Press Trust of India office in Srinagar.[188]

---

[186] *Afaq*, January 22, 1993.

[187] "J & K Ultras Abduct Two Engineers," *Times of India*, October 15, 1992. Also interview with journalist in Srinagar, October 1992; "JK Ultras Free BHEL Dy GM," *Indian Express*, October 15, 1992.

[188] "Attack Sparks 4-Day 'Boycott'," Agence France Press, May 11, 1993.

- On November 7, 1992, militants hurled a grenade into Shaheedi Chowk, Srinagar, killing a Rajesh Jain, a shopkeeper, and causing minor injuries to Hamidullah Khan, an advisor to the state governor, Girish Saxena. Khan was believed to have been the target of the attack.[189]
- At about 12:00 noon on October 17, 1992, a car bomb planted by militants of the Hezb-ul Mujahidin exploded outside the State Bank of India on Residency Road in Srinagar, a popular shopping and business district of Srinagar. Asia Watch and PHR interviewed witnesses who reported that at least two civilians were killed, and several policeman of the Indo-Tibetan Police Force (ITPF) and other civilians injured. The ITPF security force personnel were posted on guard outside the bank. Witnesses reported that one of the militants warned civilians to clear the street, but that those who were killed had not been warned.

Since 1991, bomb blasts have increasingly been reported from Jammu, where militant groups have attempted to expand the conflict through attacks on government buildings and civilian targets. According to an editorial in *Indian Express*, the JKLF, Hezb-ul Mujahidin and Al-Jehad groups all have a presence in Jammu.[190] The escalation of violence has involved not only Kashmiri Muslim militant groups, but Hindu militant organizations, including the Shiv Sena and the Rashtriya Swayamsevak Sangh (RSS), as well as Sikh militant groups from Punjab.

In the incidents described below, no group has claimed responsibility.
- On the night of May 15, 1993, a grenade exploded inside a passenger bus in Jammu, killing three people and injuring seven others. It was reportedly the third such attack in May in Jammu.[191]
- On May 3, 1993, at least one person was killed and 40 injured in Jammu following the explosion of a bomb inside a cinema and another

---

[189] "Grenade Attack on Saxena's Aide," *Times of India*, November 8, 1992.

[190] "Thwart Them in Jammu," *Indian Express*, October 8, 1992.

[191] "Grenade Attack on Bus Kills Three in India," United Press International, May 16, 1993.

on a passenger bus carrying devotees returning from a Hindu shrine at Vaishno Devi, Rajasthan.[192]

- On October 7, 1992, at least 12 persons were killed and 65 injured when a bomb exploded on a bus near the town of Digina, near Jammu.[193]
- On October 14, 1992, thirteen people were injured when a bomb exploded on an empty passenger bus in Jammu. All of the injured were standing near the bus at the time of the explosion.[194]

Threats

Common Article 3 to the Geneva Conventions, which is applicable to both government forces and armed insurgents in an internal armed conflict such as that in Kashmir, expressly prohibits "cruel treatment and torture" and "outrages upon personal dignity, in particular humiliating and degrading treatment." Explicit threats to kill are barred by these provisions.[195]

Various militant groups have employed threats to force shopkeepers, businesses and the media to desist from activities considered "un-Islamic" or detrimental to the militants' objectives. Targets of such threats have included liquor dealers and cinema hall owners, among others.

Threats and Assaults on Journalists

Militant groups have also issued threats to journalists, and have assaulted or kidnapped journalists whom they accuse of "biased"

---

[192] "Bomb Blasts in Kashmir Kill 1, Injure 40," Agence France Press, May 3, 1993.

[193] "12 Die in Bus Blast Near Jammu," *Tribune*, October 8, 1992.

[194] "13 Injured in Bomb Explosion in Jammu," *Indian Express*, October 16, 1992.

[195] Article 13 of Protocol II provides, "Acts or threats of violence the primary purpose of which is to spread terror among the civilian population are prohibited."

reporting. They have also issued bans on newspapers, and have enforced these bans through kidnappings of distributors and other assaults.[196]

- In March and April 1993, militant groups in Kashmir issued death threats against employees of the state-run television corporation, Doordarshan, because of a serial on the Bible which portrayed figures revered by Muslims. The serial was withdrawn on March 14 because of the threats. It resumed on April 11 after state officials provided extra security for producers and engineers at the television station in Srinagar. According to press reports, the militants did not carry out the threats.[197]

- On February 18 and March 31, 1992, grenades were thrown into the office of Yusuf Jameel, the Srinagar correspondent for BBC, Reuters, and the Indian daily *Telegraph*. No group claimed responsibility.

- On March 31, 1992, the Srinagar correspondent of the *Indian Express*, George Joseph, was ordered by a militant group to leave the valley within 48 hours. The ultimatum, which was provided to the United News of India news service, accused Joseph of "biased and distorted reporting."

- On May 25, 1992, Ayaz Ahmed Mir, as assistant engineer at All India Radio in Srinagar, was kidnapped by members of a militant group. He was released on May 30.

- On June 18, 1992, Yusuf Jameel, and two Srinagar-based dailies, *Al-Safa* and *Aftab*, received threats from the militant organization, Jamait-ul Mujahidin. Jameel was threatened because of his alleged "misreporting" of the news, and the two newspapers were threatened because they did not publish the group's statements about Jameel.

- On June 25, 1992, the distributor of the Hind Samachar newspapers in Srinagar, Farooq Raja, was kidnapped by members of the Jamait-ul Mujahidin, who accused him of distributing a "banned" newspaper. He was released on June 28. Following the incident, the Hind Samocahr group suspended distribution of its newspapers in Srinagar.

- On June 25, 1992, the JKLF issued a five-day ban on the *Kashmir Times*, because of a disputed reference to the militant group.

---

[196] The following incidents are cited in Committee to Protect Journalists, *Attacks on the Press 1992*, New York 1992), pp. 145-150.

[197] Krishnan Guruswamy, "TV Resumes Bible Show Despite Death Threats," Associated Press, April 11, 1993.

- In September Yusuf Jameel again received threats from militant groups displeased with the BBC's coverage of events in Kashmir.

Threats Against the Hindu Minority

The militants have also used threats to compel Hindu families and suspected political opponents to leave the Kashmir valley. Beginning in 1988, many Hindus were made the targets of threats and acts of violence by militant organizations and this wave of killing and harassment motivated many to leave the valley.[198] With government assistance, a large part of the Hindu community in Kashmir, numbering more than 100,000, left the valley in 1989-90.[199] These threats have continued. According to one report in 1992, when one militant group, the Ikhwan-ul-Muslimin, appealed for the Kashmiri Hindus to come back to the valley, two others, Al-Umar and Al-Jehad, immediately issued press releases warning them not to return.[200] Such threats and violence constitute violations of the laws of war, and Asia Watch was able to document many specific cases that occurred early in the conflict. The cases listed below are illustrative.

---

[198] The government role in encouraging the exodus, particularly the part played by former Governor Jagmohan, is a matter of considerable controversy in Kashmir and among the Hindu refugees in Jammu and New Delhi. Some reports suggest that while many Hindus left the valley out of fear of militant violence, some may have been encouraged to leave by authorities who hoped to undermine support for the militant movement.

[199] The precise number of Kashmiri Hindus who fled the valley during this time is not known. Estimates vary widely. According to one press report, as of November 1990, some 50,000 Hindu families had fled. *See* James P. Sterba, "Valley of Death," *Wall Street Journal*, November 9, 1990. *India Today* previously had reported almost 90,000 Hindus having left the valley for Jammu or Delhi. *India Today*, April 30, 1990, p. 10. Many began leaving in 1988, and the migrations contined through 1990.

[200] Harinder Baweja, "Living on the Edge," *India Today*, July 15, 1992, p. 48.

- On September 20, 1989, O.N. Sharma, a 47-year-old travel agent from Srinagar found a letter written in Urdu in his mailbox, signed by the JKLF. Sharma told Asia Watch that the letter was addressed to him by name and it referred to him as an "Indian dog." The letter told Sharma to leave the valley by September 27, or he and his family would be killed. Days after he received the letter, Sharma was threatened verbally by unknown young men who told him to leave the area. Sharma left the Kashmir valley on October 2, 1989, returning briefly on December 14 for four days. The rest of his family left for good in February 1990.
- H.N. Jattu, a businessman who has served as president of the All India Kashmiri Pandit Conference for the past nine years, lived in Srinagar until March 13, 1990, when he and his family relocated to New Delhi. Jattu told Asia Watch that beginning in November 1989, he received calls daily at his home which called him a "bastard," correctly identified him as a leader of the Kashmiri pandits and told him that if he did not "take up the gun against India," he would be killed. The callers variously identified themselves as calling from the JKLF, the Allah Tigers, the Hezb-e Islami and the Hezb-ul Mujahidin. Sometimes the callers did not identify themselves. According to Jattu, in November 1989 the *Kashmir Times* published death threats against him that had allegedly been made by the Jamaat-e-Islami. From November 6, 1989, until he left Kashmir on March 13, 1990, Jattu was under police protection and did not leave his home.
- In December 1989, Joginder Nath, a teacher at the Master Radha Krishna Public School in Srinagar, found a notice hanging on the wall outside the school which named four teachers, including himself, and ordered them to leave the Kashmir valley immediately. All were accused of working for the intelligence division of the government of India. The notice was printed on paper that bore the seal of the Allah Tigers. Nath left Srinagar that day for his family home in Fathepora, in district Anantnag. A few weeks later while he was residing in Fathepora, Nath was accused of being an Indian government intelligence agent. Nath left the valley for Delhi in June 1990.
- In late 1989, C.N. Makoo, a 50-year-old businessman in army contracting from Bane Mullah, Srinagar, received three written threats on paper which bore the seal of the JKLF. Makoo told Asia Watch that in September, he found a notice stuck to the front door of his house written in Urdu with a JKLF seal, which accused Makoo of being a police informer and saying he was number 66 on a hit list. Shortly thereafter,

the *Srinagar Times* published a statement by Makoo in which he denied that he was an informer or had any links with any government agency or political party. In October a second notice appeared on Makoo's front door, again on paper with a JKLF seal. The notice disputed the veracity of Makoo's statement denying that he was not an informer and said that his "number" on the list had now been reduced to 33. Following receipt of the second notice, Makoo sought protection from the army. On November 21, a third notice on paper with the JKLF seal was placed on Makoo's front door, saying he was now number 12 on the list. Makoo, together with his wife and mother, left the valley at 2:00 a.m. on November 23, 1989.

• Jai Krishan Dar, a 35-year-old handicrafts salesman originally from the Safakadal area of Srinagar, reported to Asia Watch that he received two death threats which led him and his family to leave the Kashmir valley on April 27, 1990. In mid-January 1990, Dar discovered a handwritten note on Hezb-ul Mujahidin letterhead on the outside of his front door. The note, addressed to Dar by name, said that he would be killed because he was giving information to the police about what it referred to as the "liberation movement." The note told Dar to provide to a local newspaper written proof that he was not a government informer. A few days later on January 20, Dar left with his wife and two daughters for Jammu. On February 28, Dar returned to Srinagar with his family to conclude some financial arrangements. One day in March at about 10:30 a.m., Dar received a telephone call at his Srinagar office telling him to leave Srinagar or he would be killed. On April 27, Dar and his family again left for Jammu and from there to Delhi.

• According to family members, T.P. Dhar, 50, an employee of the Jammu and Kashmir state government, received a written death threat signed by the Hezb-ul Mujahidin in July 1990. He left the valley shortly thereafter with his brother, Soom Nath Dhar, who had been shot and injured by unknown assailants after Dhar had received the threat.

• In a statement issued in Srinagar on March 19, 1990, the Hezb-ul Mujahidin declared that if all non-Kashmiris working as civil servants for the Indian Administrative Service (IAS) and as officers of the Indian Police Service (IPS) did not leave the state by March 31, "They will become our new targets and we shall definitely punish them." The statement threatened to "roast alive" anyone found helping the central or state government and stated:

We can no more tolerate any Indian stooges or police informers here. We warn you not to take our warnings lightly. We shall carry them out and you must quit Kashmir before we do that."[201]

• In March 1990, the JKSLF issued a statement warning all non-Kashmiri traders and officials living in the valley "after acquiring citizenship rights through false declaration" to leave by the end of the month. The statement said that "after the deadline is over, we will make them our new target and the responsibility will be theirs."[202]

Violations of Medical Neutrality by Militant Groups

Militant forces have contributed to the crisis in medical care services in Kashmir. Since 1990, militants have assassinated Hindus and Muslim civilians in the Kashmir valley. They have accused some of being informers, others of supporting government policies or being otherwise opposed to the objectives of various militant groups. In early 1990, members of the Hindu minority took the brunt of these attacks. The murders and attacks drove many Hindu and Muslim professionals, including health professionals to flee Kashmir.[203]

Doctors in Kashmir have stated that militants have abducted doctors at gunpoint for the purpose of getting them to provide medical services for injured militants. Militants have also abducted patients and medical workers from hospitals. These killings, attacks and threats constitute grave violations of international law. The cases described below are illustrative; there have been many similar abuses by militant groups.

• On March 15, 1993, JKLF militants abducted the Hezb-ul Mujahidin leader Sued Ali Shah Gilani, together with his son and son-in-

---

[201] "Quit Notice to IAS Men in Kashmir," *Telegraph*, March 21, 1990.

[202] Such a certificate is required because under the Jammu and Kashmir constitution, non-Kashmiris may not own property. Yusuf Jameel, "Top CRPF Official Shifted from J & K," *Telegraph*, March 23, 1990.

[203] Government authorities, in particular then Governor Jagmohan, reportedly encouraged the exodus.

law, from the Saura Medical Institute where Gilani was undergoing treatment for a heart ailment. Gilani and his relatives were released unharmed shortly afterwards. The incident appeared to have been provoked by internecine rivalries between the two organizations. According to a Reuters report, Javed Mir, acting president of the JKLF, apologized the next day, saying he had not ordered the kidnapping.[204]

• Sarla Bhat, 27, a staff nurse at the Saura Medical Institute in Srinagar, was kidnapped from the hospital on April 18, 1990. She was shot dead four days later. Her body was found in Lal Bazar in Srinagar. Police sources claimed that a note found near the body stated that the JKLF took responsibility for the killing and that the organization accused Bhat of telling the security forces that a number of militants were in the hospital. According to one source, Bhat had revealed this information after overhearing a conversation between a doctor and a wounded militant. Four days before she was killed, Bhat was kidnapped from the nurses' hostel by unidentified men.[205]

• G.K. Muju, a lecturer at the Srinagar Medical College and a member of the working committee of the All State Kashmiri Pandit Conference, received threats in 1990 from militant groups who included his name on hit lists of prominent Hindus which had been posted in mosques around Srinagar. After rocks were thrown at his home on a number of occasions, Muju and his immediate family left Srinagar for Jammu on March 6, 1990. On July 6, Muju's parents, who had remained behind, were attacked in their home by an unknown assailant. His 75-year-old mother was stabbed in the neck; his 80-year-old father was knifed in the chest, and died at about 5:00 a.m.

Militants have also planted land mines on public roads which pose a serious risk to civilian traffic, including medical vehicles.

Members of militant groups with easy access to arms have also used their weapons to settle personal scores and engage in extortion. One doctor interviewed in October 1992 conveyed the sense of fear that he and other doctors felt inside the hospital: "The hierarchy of the hospital

---

[204] "Senior Kashmir Leader Abducted, 4 Punjab Militants Killed," All-India Radio, March 15, 1993; and Raju Gopalakrishnan, "Kashmir Rebel Groups Seem Locked in Power Struggle," Reuters, April 26, 1993.

[205] Yusuf Jameel, "Ex-Minister Shot Dead by J&K Militants," *Telegraph*, April 20, 1990.

system no longer exists. I can't even ask the floor sweeper to do his job, because you never know who's carrying a gun or who someone may be." Finally, any militants who have not required medical treatment but have used hospitals as sanctuaries, thereby endangering the lives and security of civilians in the hospitals, have committed a grave violation of international law.

VIII. CONCLUSIONS AND RECOMMENDATIONS

As this report went to press, the conflict in Kashmir had entered its fourth year, and despite some political changes in the state administration, there were few signs that the abuses were abating. Indeed, in the period covered by this report, abuses by Indian security forces escalated as government forces undertook brutal offensives in the valley aimed at killing suspected militants and crushing support for them among the civilian population. The success of any new efforts to restart a political process will hinge on the government's ability to end the abuses which have alienated and embittered a great proportion of the civilian population, regardless of their support or opposition to the militants' goals. More than any other factor, the increase in human rights violations in the past year is testament to the failure of the Indian government's policy of attempting to end the political crisis through repressive means. In the words of one long time observer, India's fight for Kashmir has become a war on the people.

Foremost among the reasons behind the human rights crisis in Kashmir has been the government's unwillingness to take effective steps to curb abuses by its security personnel. Government officials have admitted that "excesses" have been committed and that action has been taken against those responsible. But such action, when it has occurred, has happened rarely and has seldom included criminal prosecutions. Moreover, such measures have not been publicized in a way that would communicate to the civilian population of Kashmir that these abuses are not tolerated, and that would act to deter other security forces from commiting similar abuses. In the vast majority of cases, members of the security forces have not been held criminally liable for abuses that include torture, rape and murder. When confronted with the evidence of abuse, time and again the authorities have attempted to impugn the integrity of the witnesses, discredit the testimony of physicians, lawyers and other advocates or simply deny the charges -- everything except order a full, independent inquiry and prosecute and punish those responsible. When punishments have been given, they have been limited to administrative disciplinary measures.

For their part, the militant groups have continued to use their military and political power to engage in abuses against the civilian population. These groups have systematically violated international human rights and humanitarian law by engaging in summary executions, rape, kidnappings, threats and assaults on civilians. Asia Watch and PHR are also unaware of any efforts by the militant groups to prevent their forces from committing abuses. Nor, to our knowledge, have any groups publicly condemned these abuses. In fact, as noted above, some groups have continued to encourage violent attacks on women and others who do not conform to prescribed social behavior, thus creating a climate of fear for many in Kashmir, and those who have been forced to leave.

The recommendations below are crucial steps the government of India, the government of Pakistan, the militant groups and the international community should take to address the human rights crisis in Kashmir.

- The government of India should permit, at a minimum, the International Committee of the Red Cross to provide all of its protection services in Kashmir, including visits to detainees, and to provide medical assistance. The ICRC should also be permitted to carry out all of its other humanitarian activities.

- The government of India should support swift investigations of extrajudicial executions, deaths in custody, torture and rape by security forces and paramilitary forces in Kashmir. Security personnel, including police, army and paramilitary, responsible for these abuses should be prosecuted in civilian courts. Only with such trials and appropriate punishments will these forces receive the clear, unequivocal message that human rights violations are not condoned by their superiors. Those found guilty of abuse should be punished regardless of rank. The punishments should be at least as severe as those specified under civilian law. The results of these investigations and the punishments should be made public as a means of giving the people of Kashmir a reason to believe in the government's commitment to justice and the rule of law.

- The government of India should strengthen and enforce the safeguards existing in Indian law that protect detainees from torture, including requirements that all detainees be brought before a magistrate or other judicial authority empowered to review the legality of the arrest within 24 hours of arrest, and that all detainees have immediate and regular access to lawyers, family members and medical care. Security personnel responsible for torture should be held criminally liable and the victims should be compensated.

- Physicians in Kashmir should be permitted to carry out post mortems in all cases of unnatural deaths. If necessary, training should be provided to physicians to insure the consistency and thoroughness of the post mortem. It may also be necessary to provide community education to answer religious and cultural concerns about the process. Those conducting post mortems must be able to function impartially and independently of any potentially implicated persons or organizations.

• Detainees should have access to prompt medical examinations by civil medical staff. The results of those examinations and all post mortem reports should be automatically available to the courts and to the detainee's family and legal counsel.

• A centralized register of detainees accessible to lawyers and family members should be established in the state. In addition, the security agencies should require that arresting officers provide signed receipts for all detainees to family members, village elders or persons of similar status. The receipt would be retrieved when the person is released.

• To insure adequate protection against rape, the government of India should provide police training, perhaps after consultation with international experts, on adequate evidence gathering for rape prosecutions. Explicit prohibitions against rape should be included in training for all enlisted men and officers in the police, paramilitary and military as a way of sending a clear signal that rape is not tolerated by the state.

• State authorities and the headquarters of the army and paramilitary operations in Kashmir should issue public statements affirming the security of medical personnel and institutions. The statement should include explicit guarantees for the security of ambulances traveling at night and during curfews, and for neutrality of hospital premises. Removal of patients from hospital premises should be prohibited until the patient's treatment is completed. Security personnel should be trained in the principles of medical neutrality and those violating those principles should be prosecuted.

• Medical workers who have examined and treated rape victims should be protected from abuse. Medical facilities, including private licensed physicians, should be encouraged to give testimony and introduce physical evidence in court with regard to rape and other forms of sexual and physical abuse.

• Militant forces who have committed murder, rape and assault and who have issued threats to civilians have committed grave violations of international human rights and humanitarian law. These groups should abide by the provisions of Common Article 3 of the Geneva Conventions which prohibits cruel, inhumane and degrading treatment and executions. The international community should condemn these acts by militant groups and bring pressure on these groups to end all such abuses.

- The government of Pakistan should end all support for abusive militant organizations in Kashmir. The international community should condemn Pakistan's efforts to support any of these groups.
- Militant organizations should immediately desist from actions that interfere with or impede the delivery of health services, including attacks on or threats against health professionals.
- Neither the government nor militant groups should interfere with the actions of international and domestic humanitarian and other non-governmental organizations to provide relief and disseminate information about health services and human rights norms.
- A center should be established in Kashmir or in an area accessible to Kashmiris to treat victims of physical and psychological trauma resulting from the conflict, including torture. International organizations specializing in such treatment should be permitted access to the center.
- Physicians complicit in human rights violations should be appropriately charged and also disciplined by their professional associations. Medical schools should carry out programs of education on the human rights responsibilities of health professionals.

APPENDIX A: Disappearances in Kashmir[206]

1. Mohammad Rafiq Bhat, son of Abdul Rehman, resident of Nowhatta, Qutub-ud-Din, Srinagar, was arrested from the house of his uncle in Maskeenbagh, Nowpora, by the 69th and 110th Battalion of the BSF on August 19, 1992. As of June 1993, his whereabouts were not known.

2. Mohammad Shafi Dar, son of Ghulam Mohammad Dar, resident of Lachmanpora, Batmaloo, Srinagar, was arrested by the 141st BSF Battalion, headed by Deputy Superintendent Chawhan on May 23, 1990. Writ petition No. 451/90 is pending before the High Court. An inquiry conducted under the orders of the High Court established that Dar was in the custody of the security forces.

3. Syed Basharat Ahmad Shah, son of Syed Mohammad Amin was arrested at Warpora, Sopore, on October 12, 1990, by the CRPF, along with four other persons who were later released. Writ petition No. 896/91 is pending before the High Court. Justice Rizvi appointed the District Commissioner to inquire into the incident, and a report on the inquiry was submitted on May 6, 1992, but Syed Basharat Ahmad Shah has not been produced.

4. Arshad Ahmad (Babu), son of Ali Mohammad Bhat, resident of Buchwara, Dalgate, Srinagar, was arrested by the BSF during a crackdown on December 15, 1991. Writ petition No. 509/92 is pending before the Jammu and Kashmir High Court.

5. Feroz Ahmad Shah, son of Ghulam Ahmad Shah, resident of Sarafkadal, Srinagar, was arrested by the 110th Battalion of the BSF, Company E, on November 1, 1992, while traveling by bus to Nowpora. As of June 1993, his whereabouts were not known.

6. Farooq Ahmad Mir, son of Mohammad Sultan, resident of Watlab, Mallapora, Sopore, was arrested by the BSF from his residence on November 1, 1992. As of June 1993, his whereabouts were not known.

---

[206] In the cases listed below, the authorities have not acknowledged that the detainee was in custody or revealed where he is being held. Such cases constitute disappearances, an extremely grave violation of international human rights law. In many of the cases listed, witnesses identified the detaining forces, and in some cases, the commanding officer responsible. This list was compiled by human rights activists and lawyers in Kashmir.

7. Ghulam Ahmad Sofi, son of Abdul Gaffar Sofi, resident of Mlikyar Fatehkadal, Srinagar, was arrested by the BSF on June 26, 1992, in Fatehkadal. As of June 1993, his whereabouts were not known.

8. Mohammad Shafi Najar, son of Ghulam Mohammad, resident of Botengo, Watlab, Sopore, was arrested on November 1, 1992. As of June 1993, his whereabouts were not known.

9. Nazir Ahmad Bhat, son of Sonaullah, resident of Sheikhmohalla, Handwara, was arrested by the 6th Mrhatta Regiment and the 10th Garwar Regiment of the Indian Army, during a crackdown in Sopore on October 18-20, 1992. As of June 1993, his whereabouts were not known.

10. Ghulam Nabi Bhat, son of Ghulam Ahmad, resident of Kanidewar, Islamia College, Hawal, Srinagar, was arrested by the 107th Battalion of the BSF while they were on patrol near the college. Writ petition No. 88/92 is pending before the High Court.

11. Sajad Ahmad Bazaz, 22, son of Ghulam Mohammad Bazaz, resident of Hazratbal, Srinagar, a retail shopkeeper, was arrested by the 30th Battalion of the BSF under Commandant Rathore on February 12, 1992. Writ petition No. 15/92 is pending before the High Court.

12. Bilal Ahmad Bhat, son of Ali Mohammad, resident of Kursu Padshahibagh, Naikpora Srinagar, was arrested by the 95th, 137th, and 124th Battalion of the BSF during a crackdown in Padshahibagh on December 3, 1992, under the authority of Commanding Officer Sabarwal of the 137th and Commandant Sharma. A police report on this case has been filed at the Sadar police station, Srinagar.

13. Mohammad Maqbool Bhat, son of Habibullah, resident of Gangbug, Batmaloo, Srinagar, was arrested on July 21, 1990, at Machawa, Badgam. Writ petition No. 451/90 was filed in the Jammu and Kashmir High Court, in response to which the court ordered an inquiry by Srinagar Sessions Judge Bashir-ud-din. Judge Bashir-ud-din's report, dated December 4, 1992, established that Mohammad Maqbool Bhat had been arrested by the security forces. Deputy Inspector General A. K. Suri and Deputy Inspector General CRPF Nagie have filed affidavits denying that Bhat was in custody. On June 25, 1992, Justice Rizvi directed the police to register a case, U/S 364 and 365 RPC against the security forces.

14. Waheed Ahmad Ahangar, son of Mohammad Maqbool, resident of Lalbazar, Srinagar, was arrested by the 79th batalion of the BSF from his residence on May 26, 1990. His relatives visited him at the Papa II interrogation center on June 3, 1990 and again in November 1990 at the Pantha Chowk interrogation center. After that visit, Ahangar's relatives

were unable to learn his whereabouts. Writ petition 676/90 is pending before the High Court.

15. Abdul Latief Khan, son of Mohammad Akbar Khan, resident of Uri, Baramulla, Zadipora, was arrested from his residence along with his brother Bashir Ahmed on July 17, 1990. Bashir Ahmed's body was found on July 18, 1990. A writ petition is pending before the High Court.

16. Javid Ahmad Ahangar, son of Ghulam Nabi, resident of Dhobi Mohalla, Batmaloo, was arrested on August 17-18, 1990, by National Security Guards. In response to writ petitions Nos. 755/90 and 64/91, the court ordered an inquiry by Additional Sessions Judge Abdul Rehman, whose report established that Ahangar had been arrested by National Security Guards.

17. Manzoor Ahmad Zargar, son of Mohammad Sidiq, resident of Akahoon Shaib, Gojwara, Srinagar, was arrested by the BSF on July 15, 1990. A writ petition is pending before the High Court.

18. Mohammad Ashraf Khan, son of Ghulam Nabi Khan, resident of Dhobi Mohalla, Batmaloo, was arrested in April 1990. Writ petition No. 756/90 is pending before the High Court. On December 23, 1991, Justice Parray appointed an inquiry officer, but no report has been submitted.

19. Khursheed Adil, son of Wali Mohammad Adil, resident of Sopore, Baramulla, was arrested by the 50th Battalion of the BSF on August 25, 1990, from Iqbal Market Sopore. A writ petition is pending before the High Court.

20. Peer Mohammad Shafi, son of Peer Ghulam Mohammad, resident of Khoor Sheer-a-bad, Pattan, Baramulla, was arrested by the 49th Battalion of the CRPF, under the command of Deputy Commandant Pandey on August 8, 1990. A case registered at the Pattan police station, no. 193/90 U/S 364 RPC, is pending before the High Court. On the basis of writ petition No. 559/91, the court has ordered an inquiry.

21. Nazir Ahmad Khan, son of Ghulam Mohammad Khan, resident of Bachipora, Mazhane, Rawalpora, Badgam, was arrested on September 20, 1990. Writ petition No. 379/91 is pending before the High Court. On July 6, 1992, Justice Parray ordered the Chief Judicial Magistrate in Badgam to hold an inquiry. As of June 1993, Nazir Ahmed Khan had not been produced.

22. Ghulam Mohammad Dar, son of Noor Mohammad Dar, resident of Khusapora, Berwah, Badgam, was arrested on December 7, 1990. A writ petition is pending before the High Court.

23. Abdul Ahad Bhat, 70, son of Adbul Gaffar Bhat, resident of Malgonipora, Rafiabad, Sopore, was taken into custody by the 195th

Battalion of the BSF on December 14, 1990, along with eight other men at Seel Sopore. The other seven were released. Abdul Ahad Bhat's whereabouts are not known.

24. Rouf Ahmad Shah, son of Ghulam Qadir Shah, resident of Chargi, Drugmulla, Kupwara, was arrested in May 1990. An inquiry by the Divisional Magistrate ordered by the Jammu and Kashmir High Court found that Rouf Ahmad Shah had been arrested. On the basis of a writ petition filed on August 14, 1991, the High Court ordered that a police case be registered against the securty forces. The case is pending.

25. Farooq Ahmad Bhat, son of Abdul Ahad Bhat, resident of Wazabagh, Hyderpora, Srinagar, was arrested by the 102nd Battalion of the BSF under the command of Commandant Chawhan, on June 22, 1991. Writ petition No. 69/91 is pending before the High Court.

26. Riyaz Ahmad Hajam, son of Ghulam Mohammad, resident of Dalhasanyar, Habbakadal, Srinagar, was arrested by the security forces. On the basis of writ petiton No. 753/91, the High Court ordered an inquiry under the Chief Judicial Magistrate in Srinagar. As of June 1993, the inquiry had nor been completed.

27. Riyaz Ahmad Bhat, son of Ghulam Mohammad Bhat, resident of Razwan, Berwah, was arrested by 102nd Battalion on December 31, 1990 during a crackdown at Razwan. Writ petition No. 438/91 is pending before the High Court. The court ordered an inquiry under the Chief Judicial Magistrate in Srinagar. As of June 1993, the inquiry report had not been submitted.

28. Mohammad Ramzan Dar, son of Ghulam Mohiuddin, resident of Dangarpora, Baramulla, was arrested by the BSF on August 24, 1991, at Wagoora Sopore. His whereabouts are not known.

29. Bashir Ahmed Sheikh, 45, son of Ghulam Mohammad Sheikh, resident of Rakhi Zakoora, was arrested on June 16, 1992, during a crackdown in Lal Chowk, Srinagar. His whereabouts are not known.

30. Nazir Ahmad Teli, 35, son of Abdul Rashid Teli, resident of Babapora, Habbakadal, Srinagar, was arrested on September 1, 1990. A writ petition is pending before the High Court.

31. Ghulam Nabi Bhat, son of Ali Mohammad Bhat, resident of Tral, Carve, Pulwama, was arrested by the 92nd Battalion of the BSF at Natipora on August 22, 1991, along with Ghulam Nabi Baya of Dalgate, Srinagar. Baya's dead body was discovered on August 23, 1991. Writ petition 1733/91 is pending before the High Court.

32. Shabir Ahmed Bhat, 17, son of Mistari Amir-ud-Din, resident of Lal Chowk, Anantnag, was arrested during a crackdown in the neighborhood on August 28, 1991. His whereabouts are not known.
33. Tariq Ahmad Wani, son of Abdul Gani Wani, resident of Lal Chowk, Anantnag, was arrested during a crackdown in the neighborhood on August 28, 1991. As of June 1993, his whereabouts were not known.
34. Mohammad Shafi Kotwal, son of Mohammad Ishaq Kotwal, resident of Lal Chowk, Anantnag was arrested during a crackdown in the neighborhood on August 28, 1991. As of June 1993, his whereabouts were not known.
35. Mohammad Shafi Shah, 35, son of Neimatullah Shah, resident of Janbazpora, Baramulla, was arrested by the 115th Punjab Regiment of the Indian Army on September 13, 1992. The regiment was under the command of Commandant Ahuja. Shah was arrested with Manzoor Ahmed Mir, whose dead body was discovered on September 14. A writ petition is pending before the High Court.
36. Mohammad Ramzan Mir, son of Ghulam Rasool Mir, resident of Kadipora, Syed Shahib, Anantnag, was arrested by the 194th Battalion of the BSF on December 14, 1990. As of June 1993, his whereabouts were not known.
37. Mohammad Anwar Mir, 25, son of Mohammad Sultan resident of Nagbal, Yousmarg, was arrested by BSF troops under the command of Senior Superintendent S. K. Samyal, Superintendent Sharma, Deputy Commandant Chanchal Singh, during a crackdown in 1992. Writ petition No. 200/92 is pending before the High Court.
38. Manzoor Ahmad "Jana" Kachkar, 18, son of Bashir Ahmed, resident of Urdu Bazar, Fatehkadal, Srinagar, was arrested by forces of the BSF 75th Battalion, during a crackdown in Karanagar on November 14, 1991. Other detainees, including Ashaq Ahmad, son of Abdul Gaffar, and Farooq Ahmad Beg, son of Ghulam Mohammad, resident of Kazgari Masjid, were arrested with Manzoor Ahmad Kachkar, but released after four days. Writ petition No. 138/92 is pending before the High Court.
39. Javid Ahmad "Sanoo" Dar, son of Ghulam Hassan, resident of Ladura, Sopore, was arrested by the CRPF on October 3, 1990, after he pelted a stone at a security force jeep at Rajbagh. Senior Superintendent Thakur Jaswant Singh of the of Central Intelligence Kashmir (CIK) told the family that Sanoo was at the Old Airport interrogation center, but Sanoo was not found there. After that, the parents were informed that Sanoo was detained at the Joint Interrogation Center (JIC) at Jammu, but the

Superintendent at the JIC told the family that Sanoo was never in custody there. As of June 1993, his whereabouts were not known.

40. Farooq Ahmad Bhat, son of Abdul Jabbar Bhat, resident of Nawgam, Srinagar, was arrested from his residence on May 24, 1990. When the family approached the Deputy Inspector General of Central Intelligence for the JIC, Thakur Jaswant Singh, they were told that Farooq was detained at the JIC and the family was permitted to see Farooq on December 21, 1990, but when they went to the JIC the family was told that Farooq was not there. Writ petition 828/90 is pending before the High Court.

41. Nazir Ahmad Dar, son of Ghulam Mohammad, resident of Rawalpora, Badgam, was arrested on September 20, 1990. Justice Parray of the Jammu and Kashmir High Court ordered a magisterial inquiry. Further action is pending before the High Court.

42. Tariq Ahmad Lone, son of Ghulam Nabi, resident of Ranigham, Pattan, Baramulla, was arrested by CRPF forces under the command of Deputy Commandant Kirpal Singh, on September 9. 1990. On June 4, 1992, the High Court ordered state authorities to produce Tariq Ahmad Lone, but he was not produced. The petition is still pending.

43. Abdul Ahad Dar, son of Ghulam Mohammad resident of Ramielgadh, Pattan, Baramulla was arrested during a search operation on June 22, 1991. In response to a petition, numbered No. 711/91, the government advocate stated on July 2, 1992, that the detainee had not been arrested. The case is still pending.

44. Abdul Hamid Teli, resident of Panzgham, Kangan, was arrested by the BSF on September 7, 1991, and subsequently disappeared. A petition No. 998/91 is still pending, and the government has not replied.

45. On March 22-23, 1992, Javid Ahmad Shalla and Mohammad Sadiq Sofi of Khankahi Moulla, Srinagar, was arrested from a house in Bemina, Srinagar, along with ten other persons and taken to the Tatoo Ground Interrogation Center in Batmaloo. Javid Ahmad Shalla subsequently disappeared. Four of the other detainees, who were released on March 25 at 5:00 p.m., have stated that Shalla was with them up until the time of their release. In response to a petition No. 888/92, the government has stated that Javid Ahmed Shalla attempted to escape on March 24.

46. Abdul Gani Hagoo, resident of Malahnag, Islamabad, was arrested in March 1991, and subsequently disappeared. A writ petition, no. 309/91, is pending before the High Court. On August 26, 1992, Justice Parray of the High Court, appointed a magisterial inquiry.

47. Shakeel Ahmad, son of Qazi Noor-ud-Din, resident of Khankahi Moulla, Srinagar, was arrested on August 13, 1990, by the 67th Battalion of the bSFfrom his residence at about 10:00 a.m. The government has denied the arrest but on September 23, 1992, Justice Parray ordered a magisterial inquiry.

48. Mohammad Ashraf Wani, son of Ghulam Nabi, resident of Munawar, Islamabad, was ordered by the Jammu and Kashmir High Court to be released immediately on December 12, 1991. On September 23, 1992, Justice Parray appointed a district magistrate to conduct an inquiry.

49. Maqsood Ahmad Bhat, son of M. Abdullah Yorakshaipora, Islamabad, was arrested from Islamabad on May 20, 1991, and taken to an unknown place. On September 23, 1992, Justice Parray ordered a magisterial inquiry.

50. Mohammad Altaf Akhoon, son of Mohi-ud-din, resident of Nanil, Islamabad, was arrested by security forces during a crackdown in Wasoo, Kukernag, on August 13, 1992. His relatives were permitted to visit him on September 6, 1992, in the Badamibagh Army Cantonment area, but after that visit his whereabouts are not known.

51. Siraj Ahmad Misgar, resident of Safakadal, Srinagar, was arrested at about 10:30 p.m. on January 22, 1992, from Nowhatta, Srinagar. Other detainees arrested with Misgar have stated that they were held for two days at the Ikhwan Hotel interrogation center, and after that they did not know where Misgar was taken. A petition is pending before the High Court.

52. Peer Mohammad Shafi, son of Peer Ghulam Nabi, resident of Pattan, Baramulla, was arrested during a crackdown in Pattan by the 46th Battalion of the CRPF on August 8, 1991, under the command of Deputy Superintendent Ajay Panday. An First Information Report (FIR) has been registered at the Pattan police station, and the investigating officer has determined that Shafi had been arrested. A habeas corpus petition is pending before the High Court. Deputy Superintendent Pandey has been transferred to Punjab where he serves in the Governor's special guards.

53. Ghulam Rasol Bangroo, son of Ghulam Mohammad, resident of Danamazar, Safakadal, Srinagar, was arrested on July 11, 1990. A habeas corpus petition is pending before the High Court.

54. Waheed Ahmad Shora, resident of Bandiora and was arrested in July 1990 from Lal Bazar, Srinagar. A petition is pending before the High Court.

55. Reyaz Ahmed, son of Ghulam Rasool Dar, resident of Sopore was arrested from Zero Bridge, Srinagar, in August 1990. A petition is pending before the High Court.

56. Nizar Ahmed, son of Ghulam Mohammad, resident of Jogiyar, Baramulla, was arrested on May 29, 1990, from his residence by the 16th Dogra Regiment of the Indian army. The Superintendent of the Central Intelligence Kashmir (CIK) told his relatives that Nizar Ahmed had been handed over to the CRPF on August 4, 1991. As of June 1993, Nizar Ahmed's whereabouts were not known.

57. Mohammad Afzal Sheikh, 45, son of Sonaullah, resident of Muran, Pulwama, was arrested on December 28, 1990, by the 142d Battalion of the BSF under the command of Caommandant S. K. Seth. On the basis of a petition, the High Court ordered an inquiry. A report was submitted on December 15, 1992, but Mohammad Afzal Sheikh has not yet been produced in court.

58. Khursheed Adil, resident of Sopore was arrested on September 25, 1990, and reporteldy taken to the Cheek Jageer interrogation center. His whereabouts since then are not known.

59. On the basis of a petition, the Jammu and Kashmir High Court ordered the release of Showkat Ahmad, son of Habibullah, resident of Aqil-mir, Khanyar, Srinagar, in September 1991, but the detainee has never been produced.

60. Showkat Ahmad Baba, son of Ghulam Rasool, resident of Rehbab Sahib, Srinagar, was arrested by the 124 Battalion of the BSF forces from Kralpora on September 23, 1990. As of June 1993, his whereabouts were not known.

61. Latief Ahmad Khan, son of Akbar Khan, resident of Uri Balla, was arrested from his home along with his brother, Bashir Ahmad Khan, on July 7, 1990. The dead body of Bashir was discovered a few days after the arrest. The whereabouts of Latief are not known.

62. Mohammad Ashraf Yatoo, resident of Bandipora, Badgam, was arrested in May 1990. As of June 1993, his whereabouts were not known.

63. Adil Rasool, resident of Baramulla was arrested in June 1990. As of June 1993, his whereabouts were not known.

64. Farooq Ahmad Wani, resident of Solina, of Badgam, was arrested in January 1990. As of June 1993, his whereabouts were not known.

65. Atta Mohammad Kataria, resident of Kamalkot, Uri, Baramulla, was arrested in June 1990. As of June 1993, his whereabouts were not known.

66. Ali Mohammad Mir, resident of Dardpora, Kupwara, was arrested in January 1990. As of June 1993, his whereabouts were not known.

67. Ghulam Hassan Kakroo, resident of Uri, Baramulla, was arrested in September 1990. As of June 1993, his whereabouts were not known.

68. Manzoor Ahmad Bhat, 22, son of Fateh Bhat, resident of Bhagate Kanipora, Badgam, was arrested on September 28, 1990. As of June 1993, his whereabouts were not known.

69. Ghulam Rasool Bangroo, 21, resident of Danamazar, Safakadal, Srinagar, was arrested at Safakadal in July 1990. As of June 1993, his whereabouts were not known.

70. Fayaz Ahmad Gujroo, resident of Khawja Bazar, Baramulla, was arrested in May 1991. As of June 1993, his whereabouts were not known.

71. Mohammad Ramzan, resident of Muran, Pulwama, was arrested in December 1990. As of June 1993, his whereabouts were not known.

72. Abdul Salam, resident of Suiteng, Srinagar, was arrested in a crackdown in September 1992. As of June 1993, his whereabouts were not known.

73. Ghulam Ahmad Shagoo, resident of Suiteng, Srinagar, was arrested in a crackdown in September 1992. As of June 1993, his whereabouts were not known.

74. Mohammad Yousuf Mir, resident of Bangh Bagh, Kangam, Srinagar, was arrested by the 162d field regiment of the Indian army on July 31, 1992. As of June 1993, his whereabouts were not known.

75. Mohammad Shau Bhat, son of Abdul Razaq Bhat, resident of Abiguzar, Tral, Pulwama, was arrested in September 1990. As of June 1993, his whereabouts were not known.

76. Altaf Ahmad Sheikh, son of Ghulam Nabi, resident of Amdakadal, Srinagar, was arrested by the BSF at a carpet shop owned by Ali Mohammad Beg in Botakadal, Srinagar. A writ petition is pending before the High Court. As of June 1993, Altaf Ahmad Sheikh's were not known.

77. Fayaz Ahmad Mir, son of Mohammad Sultan, resident of Batmaloo, Srinagar, was arrested in June 1990 at By-Pass Road in Srinagar. As of June 1993, his whereabouts were not known.

78. Farooq Ahmad Kashoo, son of Ghulam Mustafa, resident of Syeed Hamdanipora, Nawabazar, Srinagar, was arrested in July 1990. As of June 1993, his whereabouts were not known.

79. Gulzar Ahmad Tabardar, son of Ghulam Mohammad, resident of Bemina Colony, Srinagar, was arrested on October 21, 1990. As of June 1993, his whereabouts were not known.

80. Manzoor Ali Wani, son of Mohammad Amin Wani, resident of Banipora, was arrested in July 1990. As of June 1993, his whereabouts were not known.

81. Javid Ahmad Zargar, son of Mohammad Amin Zargar, resident of Safakadal, Srinagar, was arrested in November 1990. As of June 1993, his whereabouts were not known.
82. Abdul Qayoom Sheikh, son of Ghulam Nabi, resident of Mandrowa, was arrested in April 1990. As of June 1993, his whereabouts were not known.
83. Mohammad Asraf Malik, son of Abdul Samad Malik, resident of Mandrowa, was arrested in April 1990. As of June 1993, his whereabouts were not known.
84. Ghulam Mohi-ud-din Lone, son of Mohammad Shaban Lone, resident of Poswari, Kupwara, was arrested on October 15, 1990. As of June 1993, his whereabouts were not known.
85. Mohammad Ayub Khan, son of Mehda Khan, resident of Karipora, Kupwara, was arrested on October 15, 1990. As of June 1993, his whereabouts were not known.
86. Ghulam Hassan Wani, son of Ghulam Rasool Wani, resident of Karipora, Kupwara, was arrested on October 15, 1990. As of June 1993, his whereabouts were not known.
87. Mushtaq Ahmad Zargar, son of Ghulam Ahmad Zargar, resident of Sazgaripora, Srinagar, was arrested in June 1990. As of June 1993, his whereabouts were not known.
88. Abdul Majid Sajad, son of Ghulam Hassan Wani, resident of Charishrief, Badgam, was arrested at Poonch in September 1990. As of June 1993, his whereabouts were not known.
89. Abdul Khaliq Shah, son of Syed Shah, resident of Garura, Bandipora, Baramulla, was arrested in July 1990. As of June 1993, his whereabouts were not known.
90. Feroz Ahmad Qureshi, son of Abdul Rehman Quereshi, resident of Batmaloo, Srinagar, was arrested in December 1990. As of June 1993, his whereabouts were not known.
91. Nazir Ahmad Mir, son of Ghulam Mohammad Mir, resident of Zoogiyar, Baramulla, was arrested in May 1990. As of June 1993, his whereabouts were not known.
92. Abdul Khaliq Pir, son of Sayed Pir, resident of Wandgam, Bandipora, Baramulla, was arrested on September 2, 1990. As of June 1993, his whereabouts were not known.
93. Abdul Rashid Lone, son of Mohammad Sultan Lone, resident of Keeri, Pattan, Baramulla, was arrested on August 24, 1990. As of June 1993, his whereabouts were not known.

94. Sonaullah Wani, son of Abdul Gani Wani, resident of Aloosa, Canalpora, Kupwara, was arrested on July 27, 1990. As of June 1993, his whereabouts were not known.

95. Habibullah Lone Chopan, son of Ghulam Mohammad Lone, resident of Malangam, Bandipora, Baramulla, was arrested on December 14, 1990. As of June 1993, his whereabouts were not known.

96. Shabir Ahmad Reshi, son of Abdul Gaffar Reshi, resident of Khamadbal, Kupwara, was arrested on September 9, 1990. As of June 1993, his whereabouts were not known.

97. Mohammad Ashraf Yatu, son of Khalil Mohammad Yatu, resident of Chadura, Badgam, was arrested on December 13, 1990. As of June 1993, his whereabouts were not known.

98. Abdul Qayoom, 8, a resident of Rustum Colony, Rajahbagh, Srinagar, was arrested on February 12, 1990. As of June 1993, his whereabouts were not known.

99. Mushtaq Ahmad, resident of Safakadal, Srinagar, was arrested in November 1991. As of June 1993, his whereabouts were not known.

APPENDIX B: The Code of Medical Neutrality

(These standards are based on rules and principles concerning medical neutrality set forth in the four Geneva Conventions of 1949 and their two additional protocols of 1977, and apply to all situations of international and internal armed conflict.[207])

1. Sick and wounded combatants and civilians shall be protected, treated humanely, and provided with medical care without delay.
2. Medical workers shall be respected, protected, and assisted in the performance of their medical duties.
3. The sick and wounded shall be treated regardless of their affiliations and with no distinction on any grounds other than medical ones.
4. Medical workers shall not be punished for providing ethical medical care, regardless of the persons benefiting from it, or for refusing to perform unethical medical treatment.
5. Attacks on defenseless sick or wounded combatants or civilians are prohibited. Upon detention, they shall receive thorough and responsible medical exams and medical care.
6. Medical workers shall have access to those in need of medical care, especially in areas where civilian medical services have been disrupted. Similarly, people in need of medical care shall have access to such services.
7. Medical facilities, equipment, supplies and transports shall be respected and protected, regardless of whom they serve, and shall not be destroyed.
8. A recognized medical emblem, such as the red cross or the red crescent, shall be displayed by all medical units, personnel, and transports provided it is used for medical purposes only.
9. Parties to an armed conflict shall cooperate to make and support practical agreements for the care of the sick and wounded.
10. No party to a conflict can legitimately claim to serve the interests of its nation's citizens if it violates this code, which is based on moral, ethical and legal principles.

---

[207] The code was formulated by the International Commision on Medical Neutrality, 1747 Connecticut Avenue NW, Washington D.C. 20009.

APPENDIX C: The Comments of the Government of India

EMBASSY OF INDIA
2107 Massachusetts Avenue N.W.
Washington, D.C. 20008

PRESS RELEASE

**INDIAN GOVERNMENT'S COMMENTS ON ASIA WATCH-PHYSICIANS
FOR HUMAN RIGHTS REPORT "THE CRACKDOWN IN KASHMIR"**

FEBRUARY 1993

...

The Indian Government had given detailed comments to Asia Watch-PHR on the findings in their Report on "The Crackdown In Kashmir - Torture of detainees and assaults on the medical community". Some of these comments have been incorporated, along with rebuttals by AW-PHR, in the main body of the Report which is being released on February 28. A few of them have been distorted by AW-PHR to draw erroneous conclusions about Indian Government policy while some have been less than fairly interpreted.

In view of this it is felt necessary to respond to AW-PHR's observations on the Indian Government's initial response so as to put the facts in their correct perspective.

It is unfortunate that the Press Release starts with an attack against the Indian forces for having stepped up their "campaign of terror" against civilians. The use of the word "terror" to describe the difficult combat of the security forces against the large-scale violence in the Valley is all the more surprising because AW-PHR have carefully avoided using this word to describe the murderous activities of Pakistan-backed Muslim fundamentalist groups in Kashmir. To suggest that the only terrorism in Kashmir is the one at the hands of the security forces is to make a travesty of the real situation there. Apart from countless reports in the international media on terrorism in Kashmir by Muslim groups and recognition of this fact by several Governments, even the latest Report on Human Rights issued by the State Department has noted that the militants have maintained a reign of terror in the Kashmir Valley. The true picture is that the violence unleashed by the terrorists in Jammu and Kashmir has grown and in 1992, as compared to 1991, the total number of incidents of terrorist violence increased from 3122 to 4971 (Annexure-I). The question to ask is who is sustaining this growing terrorist activity? Where are the terrorists obtaining their arms and equipment, training and strategic direction from? What is the responsibility of the terrorists and their increasing activity in disrupting civilian life in the Valley, including health and medical services?

The manner in which AW-PHR's report seeks to pass instant judgement in the case of Dr. Farooq Ahmad Ashai by insinuating that his death might have been caused deliberately by the security forces is a matter for concern. Should AW-PHR seek first to elicit information from responsible sources on such incidents, or should they virtually within hours of their taking place thousands of miles away in circumstances they can have no authentic information on immediately, widely publicise their a priori conclusions? Details in the case borne out also by local press reports, clearly show that this was a case of Dr. Farooq, unfortunately, getting caught up in cross-firing. The Indian Government is unable to understand the basis and the intention for deliberately projecting this as a case of his having been shot by security forces at a checkpoint, in the face of evidence to the contrary, and the nexus sought to be drawn with a claim that he was a human rights activist. A terrorist group has even claimed responsibility for the grenade attack that was mentioned in the context of this incident. Even so, the investigation of the case has been entrusted to the Crime Branch and will be conducted by a Superintendent of Police. The Divisional Commissioner has also been asked by the Governor to conduct an enquiry and ascertain the full facts of the case.

A claim has again been made that patients in hospitals have been disconnected from life sustaining treatments which had earlier been categorically denied. A similar claim has been made regarding shooting doctors on duty and torturing some others, which is also categorically denied. It is unfortunate that AW-PHR continue to make these groundless charges based on hearsay.

While dwelling at some length on the issue of medical neutrality and the Geneva Conventions, the Release accuses the Government of violations and denies that any legitimacy is being provided to terrorist groups, as indicated in our preliminary response. It goes on to say that as per the norms of medical neutrality medical personnel should be able to render medical care to all populations, on all sides of the conflict. While not entering into any argument on issues of principle, it may be mentioned that nowhere does the Report care to acknowledge the fact that treatment has been provided to the apprehended terrorists even in army hospitals, quite apart from the question that nothing in their Report or in our response suggests that the Government or the security forces as a matter of policy prevented treatment of injured terrorists in the hospitals.

To the best of our knowledge, the visit of the Team was extremely brief and the effort to show the extent and nature of painstaking investigations that were made must be qualified and seen in this perspective. As for two specific statements which had been called false in our earlier comments, to indicate that there may be false claims made before the Team (as distinct from exaggerated claims), it may be reiterated that Justice Risvi has not been transferred out of the State till this date. As for duration of a crackdown which allegedly lasted for 17 days, the comment in the Release appears more like a leading question.

A perturbing aspect of AW-PHR's Report is its tendency to reject evidence which may not fit in with the case it wants to project, or make categorical statements on matters that clearly they are not qualified to do as they cannot have full information with them. While the Release acknowledges killings of medical workers by the terrorists, it goes on to say that "there is no evidence that militants have done this" in the context of our observation that militants have used hospitals as sanctuaries and have even feigned injuries in this process. In fact, it claims that "hospitals are unlikely places for militants to seek refuge unless they are genuinely wounded". AW-PHR make this claim in the face of evidence of the recoveries made from the hospitals in the searches that were conducted in some of them. They assert that when security forces conduct such operations in hospitals in Kashmir, they don't do so on the basis of specific information. If such a format of reporting were to be acceptable, just about anything can be said and any claim could be made without there being any need for evidence for and to the contrary.

The Report says that while the authorities may prosecute health professionals for failing to provide information about persons in their care whom they believe may have committed crimes, they cannot physically abuse them for failing to do so. In fact, in our comments we had not referred to prosecution of health professionals but to conditions in which most of them out of fear and some due to connivance, may not report medico legal cases as required under the law, which may lead to situations where it may become necessary to look for such criminals inside hospitals.

In the specific case of Riaz Ahmed Wani, our earlier comments did not provide any acknowledgement that the patient was removed when he was under anesthesia and, instead, the facts of the case were mentioned.

The Release says that the Report describes a number of incidents in which security forces opened fire inside hospitals, apparently to intimidate the medical staff to identify suspected militants. The Report mentions such incidents at two places and the number of times that a hospital may have been searched, but no specific incident has been narrated. The question of providing any explanation for such incidents, therefore, does not arise. However, in our comments, the incidents in which searches did take place in the hospitals were mentioned, including those cases where such searches may not have ended up in any recoveries. Once specific incident taken out of our response and included in the Report, about firing from the premises of SKIMS, is only one of the numerous illustrative incidents that had been mentioned in our comments to show the type of activities that the terrorists have been indulging in from the premises of hospitals in Srinagar.

The Release also mentions two security laws currently in force in Kashmir, viz., The Armed Forces (Jammu & Kashmir) Special Powers Act and the Jammu & Kashmir Disturbed Areas Act, and has stated that these acts explicitly promote the use of lethal force against people who are not combatants and who do not pose a threat to the lives of the security forces. It has also been claimed that these laws permit immunity from prosecution to the security forces. Elsewhere it refers to our claim that we are trying to fight the terrorist menace by civilian law and order methods and concludes that the Government, by saying so, attempts to justify and excuse acts of gross violations as legitimate means of "law enforcement". Such a conclusion is astounding, to say the least. The fact of the matter is that the security forces in Kashmir or elsewhere are not a law unto themselves and none of these Acts provide any immunity to them. What they require is prior sanction for prosecution as ls also provided under India's Criminal Procedure Code (Section 197). In actual fact, as mentioned in our previous comments, action has been taken against over 100 personnel of the Army and Para-Military forces which includes officers. This shows that neither does the Government excuse violations nor is there any immunity for errant officers or personnel who may be acting even within the powers conferred under these Acts. The suggestion that Government policy condones excesses is totally baseless.

The warning of the medical catastrophe, unless the Government grants immediate access to the ICRC, is deliberately alarmist. All the details in the AW-PHR's Report together do not point to any impending medical catastrophe. Despite all the difficulties created by terrorist activities, the authorities will continue to do their best to meet their responsibilities for providing health, medical and other facilities to the population of the affected areas.

A statement showing the number of cases registered and the number of persons arrested, released and still under arrest under TADA and the Public Safety Act is enclosed at Annexure-II. This would show not only that there are judicial safeguards available, but they are also being used liberally, and in a number of cases the authorities themselves have released persons on parole even where bail may not have been granted. It may be mentioned here that Screening Committees have been set up both at the District and State levels to ensure that persons who may be deserving sympathetic treatment can be expeditiously released from custody.

Brief comments have been given above only with respect to some of the specific points mentioned in the Release. There are many others which are general and speaking about wide-spread torture, maltreatment by the security forces etc., on which no specific comments are being made again. We would, however, like to strongly state that we do not make any excuses for violations of Human Rights just because the terrorists may be indulging in abuses. At the same time, the extremely difficult environment created by the indiscriminate and massive level of violence perpetrated by the terrorists has to be understood to appreciate that it may not be possible to deal with the situation, under the normal laws. Over 500 security force personnel have been killed by the terrorists, apart from a large number of politicians, press persons, Government officials and innocent citizens in the State (figures have been given earlier). Even so, the Special Laws referred to in the Release are not passed by any ad hoc draconian fiat, but after full deliberation in the Parliament, and are only temporary measures. In the prevailing environment, there can be possibilities where harassment may be caused to the civilian population on account of security operations and there may also be occasional cases of excesses. At the same time, we reiterate that we do not hesitate to take action against security force personnel where deliberate acts of excesses and cases of gross negligence and over-reaction etc., come to notice. The swift and firm response in the recent unfortunate incident at Sopore would bring this out clearly.

Finally, we note that in the chapter "Conclusions and Recommendations" of the Report, AW-PHR have made several critical comments against the Government of India of an all-embracing political nature on the problem in Kashmir, but have no advice to offer to militant groups to put an end to terrorist activities in the context of Human Rights, other than merely urging them to desist from attacks against health services and health professionals. Can it be concluded that AW-PHR encourage or condone all other forms of violent activities by Muslim fundamentalist terrorist groups?

Washington,
February 27, 1993

Comments on the Asia Watch - PHR Report "Medical Consequences of the conflict in Kashmir and cases of torture and violations of medical neutrality."

While describing the conditions of medical services and facilities in Jammu and Kashmir the Asia Watch - PHR Report has accused the security forces of gross abuses of "medical neutrality" in "armed conflict."

2. Before responding to some specific, and the much larger number of general allegations, it would be in order that the nature of the "armed conflict" mentioned in the report is briefly described because terms like "armed conflict" and "medical neutrality" are not only deceptive but could give actual respectability to terrorist organisations and their activities.

3. Since 1989, what the Indian State of Jammu and Kashmir has been experiencing is an externally aided "Proxy War" of massive dimensions. The parties to this are not two opposing armies, but the forces of a motley group comprising over 100 terrorist outfits and pernicious religious extremism and propaganda, on the one hand, and the law enforcement Agencies of the State, which has desisted from reacting to this violent aggression and threat to its very sovereignty and integrity, by anything like a war but, through civilian law and order methods.

4. A set of charts depicting the profile and dimension of terrorism in Jammu & Kashmir are   . Among other things this would show that over 11,000 sophisticated weapons have been recovered from the terrorists including nearly 8,000 AK-series rifles. All this would show the sheer scale and dimension of the "Proxy War" that has been unleashed by the terrorists and their mentors in the State of Jammu & Kashmir.

5. The blatant misuse of religion has inspired acts of gruesome brutality on the minority population in the Kashmir Valley, leading to the exodus of nearly two hundred and fifty thousand innocent people who are today living in other parts of the State and the Country virtually as refugees for nearly three years. This is "ethnic cleansing" at its worst, and through it an attempt has been made to change the very demographic profile of a particular region of the State, as a part of the desperate efforts of a hostile neighbour and its terrorist proteges to annexe territory on the basis of religious fanaticism.

6. Acts of enforcement of codes of conduct, abduction, rape, torture, extortion, looting and killing have been perpetrated by the terrorists on a massive scale. The victims have been innocent citizens dubbed as "informers" or those who may have surrendered after being disillusioned with their masters; politicians and political workers and their relatives,

lest they dare to try and get the normal political and democratic processes to work at the cost of the so-called "militants"; the press and the media, so as to gag those who are not willing to go along, and force others to act as their mouthpiece and to echo their disinformation; members of the judiciary to prevent the law from taking its course; Government servants, to prevent them, by the fear of the gun, from discharging their duties and to extort government and development funds; prominent citizens with the aim of striking terror generally in the population; and members of the police and the security forces, over 500 of whom have been killed and a much larger number injured in the past two years.

7. Hundreds of schools and colleges, other than those run by banned extremist outfits, have been burnt down; banks have been looted; tourist centres, bridges and other government buildings have been destroyed; telecommunication links have been sabotaged; and thousands of private houses/property, particularly those belonging to the minority community, have been torched. Every now and then the terrorists have, through the fear of the gun, forcibly imposed "hartals" in the Valley thereby bringing normal life to a standstill. Posters routinely appear warning people against going to or talking with Government authorities.

8. At the same time the terrorist gangs have frequently fought amongst themselves to gain superiority and dominance in this macabre dance of death and destruction. Predominant among them have been some of the rabid groups like the Hizb-ul-Mujahideen, openly supported from across the border and, in turn, propagating their cause through the gun, in this sensitive border state of India. Anyone coming in the way is eliminated without compunction.

9. It is unfortunate that while detailing and lamenting the disruption of medical services and stating unmitigated condemnation of the security forces, it has not been considered necessary to give any hint of the real situation, which has been referred to only obliquely "Convoys of army soldiers and other security forces also move frequently along the roads, delaying other vehicle traffic. Because these convoys are frequent targets of militant ambushes, other vehicles risk running into gun battles or reprisal attacks. Militant forces have also planted land mines along some of the roads, although Physicians for Human Rights (PHR) and Asia Watch learned of no incidents in which medical vehicles had struck a mine."

10. Statements like "The crackdown lasted for seventeen days, during which time no one was allowed to enter or exit the hospital grounds," and "One Judge, S.M. Rizvi, who managed after great resistance from the

security forces to obtain security records for detainees... <u>was transferred out of the State</u>", both of which are patently false, show the willing gullibility of the authors - while no satisfactory explanation exists why these, and indeed all the other allegations made in the report, could not be cross-checked or verified during the course of the "investigation" itself. Instead alleged statements of unnamed doctors, ambulance drivers and some others have been taken as the gospel truth and all that there is to see and tell.

11. That the terrorists may have forced themselves into hospitals to use them as sanctuaries has been overlooked. This has been made possible both by connivance, on the part of some doctors and medical staff, and the sheer fear of the gun and the threat of elimination imposed on the majority of them - there are documented cases of elimination and killing of medical staff on allegations of informing the security forces of terrorists taking sanctuary in hospitals. Some illustrative incidents showing the activities of the terrorists in, and out of, the premises of various hospitals are as under:

(a) A Staff Nurse at Sher-e-Kashmir Institute of Medical Sciences, Srinagar (SKIMS), Sarla Bhatt, was abducted from the Institute on 17th March, 1990. She was gang-raped and tortured and her body, with broken limbs, was found abandoned on the road. She is suspected to have been killed for having given a clue regarding connivance by some doctors in an attempted escape of a leader of one of the major terrorist outfits.

(b) One Mohd. Yusuf, Head Cashier, SKIMS, was kidnapped from the Institute on 25 February, 1991. He was tortured and the keys of the cash chest were taken away. He later died as a result of injuries inflicted on him by the terrorists.

(c) An ambulance belonging to SKIMS, Soura, Srinagar was found to have been used in the kidnapping of Mrs. Khemlata Wakhloo, ex-Minister and her husband, Dr. O.N. Wakhloo on 4, September, 1991.

(d) One Mohan Lal, a Librarian was killed by the terrorists in the Medical College, Srinagar in 1991.

(e) A MBBS student, Sajjad s/o Mohd. Shafi, an ex-Minister was abducted from Jhelum Valley Medical College, Srinagar on 23 October, 1991.

(f) Mr. Hafizullah Dar, an Additional DIG of Police was abducted from the SKIMS premises when he had gone there to meet an ailing relative on 24th January, 1992.

(g) Dr. S.N. Dhar, Superintendent, Chest Diseases Hospital, Srinagar was abducted by terrorists on 31 March, 1992.
(h) Mr. A.R. Khan, a Deputy Superintendent of Police was killed by terrorists when he had gone to meet his daughter in the Girls Hostel of the Medical College.
(i) It May, 1992, a security force party, led by senior officers, which was proceeding from the UNDP Complex to the Police Station, Soura was subjected to heavy firing by the terrorists from the premises of SKIMS, Soura, Srinagar, leading to an exchange of fire.

12. Besides using the hospital premises for actual criminal activities, the terrorists have been using certain medical institutions in the Valley as safe havens to hide themselves and to store weapons and ammunition. It is also a fact that in many cases terrorists who have sustained injuries in counter-insurgency operations have surrepti-tiously got themselves admitted into some hospitals, and the staff, mostly out of fear and sometimes due to connivance, have not reported such cases to the police, which must be done under the law in all medico-legal cases.

13. Against this background occasional searches, based on specific information, have had to be made in the premises of certain medical institutions. It is also necessary in some cases, where terrorists are suspected to feign injuries, to have bandages, etc., removed for verification. However, at no stage have any patients, reported to be critically ill, been subjected to such examination, and also in no case, at any stage, have life support systems been disconnected as alleged in the report. It has also been categorically denied by the State Government and the Army authorities that any medical institution was at any stage asked to transfer their patients to the Military hospitals, as alleged in the report. Transfer of cases is accepted only in cases where the life of any patient is in danger from the terrorists, or in any other emergency, on the specific request of the State Administration.

14. During 1992 the following searches were conducted, on the basis of specific information, in various hospitals in Srinagar, the details of which are given below:
(a) On 22 January, 1 AK series rifle with a magazine and 26 rounds were recovered from the residential quarters of SMHS Hospital.
(b) On 5 March, the security forces recovered 10 AK series rifles, 6 Grenades, 16 Magazines, nearly 1100 rounds of ammunition and apprehended five terrorists from the SMHS Hospital, Srinagar.

- (c) On March, 23rd, 1992, 3 AK series rifles, 5 magazines and 138 rounds of ammunition were recovered from the Lalded Hospital, Srinagar; and 3 AK series rifles and incriminating documents were recovered from SMHS Hospital, Srinagar;
- (d) During April, 1992, 3 AK series rifles were recovered from Lalded Hospital, Srinagar;
- (e) During April, 1992, 3 AK series rifles and incriminating documents/literature were recovered from SMHS Hospital, Srinagar;
- (f) During September, 1992, 17 AK series rifles were recovered from the Canteen of Sher-e-Kashmir Institute of Medical Sciences (SKIMS), Soura, Srinagar;
- (g) On 23 and 25, October, 2 AK series rifles, 1 gun, 2 pistols, 9 magazines, 2 grenades and 246 rounds of ammunition were recovered from the Lalded Hospital, Srinagar, and one nursing orderly was apprehended who was later identified as a self-styled Base Commander of one of terrorist outfits, Ikhwan-ul-Musalmeen;
- (h) On 7 October, 2 AK series rifles, 3 magazines and 7 rounds of ammunition were recovered from Ward No. 5 of SKIMS, where a few members of the staff were found to have connived to provide shelter to terrorists;
- (i) On October, 10 in a raid conducted in Medical Institute, Soura, no recovery was effected.
- (j) On 14 November, 3 AK series rifles with 3 magazines and 90 rounds of ammunition were recovered from Lalded Hospital.
- (k) On the same day a search was carried out in the Bone and Joint Hospital, Srinagar but no recoveries were effected.

15. All these details should give an idea of how the terrorists have not only created an environment of violence and fear in the State, but also of how they have blatantly misused medical institutions in this process. As for the specific allegations made in the report, the facts are shown in the enclosed statement. In the case of some allegations information is being collected and will be made available separately, at the earliest.

16. There is no doubt that continuing terrorist violence in the State has affected normal life and activity, including the medical and health sector. However, it is not as if the entire health net-work in the State or the Valley, has collapsed. The State Government has categorically stated that hospitals in the city of Srinagar, as well as in the rural areas continue to provide effective health services to the needy. The migration of a whole

community, as a result of terrorist brutalities, had resulted in the creation of over 100 vacancies in the posts of doctors and para-medical personnel in the Valley. In these circumstances, State Government recruited 78 doctors in March, 1992, and some adhoc appointments of Doctors and other para-medical staff have also been made, and further adhoc appointments are under consideration of the Government.

17. The report alleges that the immunisation programme has suffered seriously as a result of the "conflict", and has been frequently disrupted by crackdowns. It expresses the fear of certain "Doctors" about the spread of epidemics, and mentions sporadic cases of mumps having been documented. According to the State Health Secretary, while it is a fact that the unit immunisation programme has suffered due to the violence, but would be incorrect to say that immunisation work is not taking place and there are certainly no reports of spread of epidemics on account of lack of immunisation. Referring to the family welfare programme, the State Government has stated that the programme has suffered considerably because of opposition by the fundamentalist terrorist groups to methods of family planning as being anti-Islamic. Efforts are, however, being made to restore the programme to its original vigour.

18. The report has also alleged serious shortages of medical equipments and supplies. As for medical supplies, according to the State Government, the Principal of the Medical College, Srinagar, and the Director, Health Services, Kashmir had recently reviewed the position and the situation is reported by them to be reasonably satisfactory. Such difficulties as there might be due to budgetary limitations and rise in prices of drugs, etc., are not unique to Jammu & Kashmir. In the situation prevailing in that State, if necessary, additional funds will also be provided to augment the supplies.

19. As for the functioning of existing equipments like CAT Scan and X-Ray machines, and installation of new ones, it is a fact that difficulties have been experienced because Engineers from outside have been hesitant to go to Srinagar due to fear of terrorist violence. Efforts have been on to ensure that these difficulties can be surmounted and in the meanwhile, despite the odds, most of the equipments have been repaired and are in working order. As for the telephone services, the State Government has stated that they are quite satisfactory. The position of availability of Power, has at best of times been difficult in the area, but every effort is being made to maintain round the clock supplies to the hospitals. At the same time, a number of major projects are in various

stages of implementation for augmenting the Power generation capacity in the State as a part of normal developmental Plan programmes.

20. The report also refers to overcrowding of hospitals. This is true, but is neither a new phenomenon nor unique to the State. It is because of this that new hospitals have been set up over the years, and even now work is going on for the provision of additional bed-capacity. Work on a 300-bed hospital is well under-way in Badami Bagh, Srinagar. There are also plans to add to the capacity of the main SMKS Hospital in the current Plan.

21. Apart from the steps taken by the State Government to provide medical and health services to the people, the security forces deployed in the State have also been providing such services to the common people and in many cases even to the terrorists who may get injured in security force operations.

22. The Border Security Force has established M.I. Rooms in Rainawari, Alikadal, Chhattabal, Batmaloo and several other areas of Srinagar and the Valley. Over 29000 civilians have been provided medical help and treatment from such medical centres.

23. The Army has also launched a series of Civil Action Programmes in the Valley. In an ongoing programme, launched last month, five medical camps have been organised in which 2322 outdoor patients were treated for eye ailment, 477 cataract and other operations were performed, and 120 patients were given medical attention in a special dental camp. A copy of a press report titled "Army's successful civic action in the Valley" which appeared in a Kashmir Times issue in January, 1992 is enclosed. Also enclosed are copies of some photographs which show terrorists being treated in an Army Hospital. The press report, appearing over a year ago, would not only give an idea of the type of services that the forces have been providing by way of medical attention, but also of their attitude and approach in the matter.

24. Obviously no such evidence was either sought by the Asia Watch - P.H.R. team or their undisclosed sources are suspect. It may be mentioned that a senior doctor of the Government Medical College, Srinagar, who had been earlier quoted by another Human Rights Group regarding the alleged widespread use of torture by the security forces has stated in a communication to the State Government that "this whole matter is fallacious, arbitrary, unfair and based on unreasonableness. I request your goodself to treat the subject based on unfairness, misinformation, misrepre-sentation and impersonation by appropriate measures."

25. It is also revealing to hear the theory being propagated by a clandestine Radio operating from Pakistan occupied territory which states that the real purpose of 'Operation Goodwill' launched by the Army, was to distribute medicines among the Muslim masses which are injurious to health and will incapacitate the users, and appeals to people to frustrate this Operation. It was claimed in a news-item the same day (17, January, 1993) that a Pulwama-based group of Hizbul Mujahideen had actually blasted an Army medical camp connected with this Operation. Another statement of a terrorist group, quoted in a local daily Nida-e-Mushriq of 16 January, 1993 says that "the so-called operation good-will is a deadly weapon . . . and a conspiracy to crush Kashmiri people mentally . . . some conscienceless people in the garb of muslims are taking benefit of the operations. Jamiat deems it is necessary to kill such persons." Quite in line with this, in an incident on 10 September, 1992, the terrorists fired upon a BSF party engaged in flood relief operations to rescue marooned people. In this incident one BSF constable was killed and 3 wounded. However, this did not deter the BSF personnel who carried out extensive flood relief operations in various parts of the Valley.

26. Having said all this, it must be stated that curfew, which is a legal order of a prohibitory nature under section 144 of the Criminal Procedure Code, has had to be enforced on occasions to prevent the irresponsible acts of the terrorist groups which could lead to serious breaches of peace and order, and in spite of the best intentions and efforts there could be instances where even doctors may have experienced difficulties. But there is absolutely no evidence to suggest that this happens as a matter of course or deliberately, and that any serious disruption of medical services results from the enforcement of such necessary regulatory measures aimed at dealing with terrorist activities that seek to disrupt any and every form of normal life and activity of the citizens.

27. Inspite of all this, the Government has reiterated time and again that the prevalance of terrorist activities, at the cost of every norm of civilised and human behaviour, cannot constitute any justification for any form of "excesses" on the part of the security forces, even where their members are exposed to constant provocation and a lurking fear of death at any given instant. The very reason for which they are castigated is also the reason why they are constantly urged to maintain a superior discipline. Wherever there is transgression, action has been taken. By now, over the last two years, action has been taken against over 100 personnel of the security forces, and this has involved punishments including

imprisonment ranging from less than a month to seven years and various forms of departmental action including suspension pending enquiry in a number of cases. It may be mentioned here that in the case of Army and the Paramilitary forces, even the award of a reprimand or other seemingly minor departmental punishments which go into the service record can very seriously affect, and sometimes even kill the future prospects of advancement of the concerned officer in his service. Wherever allegations of excesses were made against the Security forces, in the course of their operations, police cases are also being registered. In a number of cases, where the police may have closed the matter or no case may have been registered, the concerned Security forces have taken suo-motu notice and initiated action against those who may have prima-facie appeared to be guilty of infringement or misconduct.

28. The sensitivity and the policy of the government would be evident from the response to the recent unfortunate incident at Sopore on 6th January, 1993 where, in an engagement with militants, 41 persons including 1 BSF personnel were reported to have been killed and a large number of houses/shops gutted. Apart from the suspension, pending enquiry, of 9 BSF personnel, including the Commandant and announcement of immediate relief for the victims and their families, a judicial enquiry by a sitting High Court Judge has also been ordered and investigation of the criminal case registered after the incident has been transferred to the Central Bureau of Investigation.

. . . .

14 May, 1993

EMBASSY OF INDIA
107 MASSACHUSETTS AVE., N.W.
WASHINGTON, D.C. 20008
(GENERAL)
TEL: (202) 939-7000
FAX: (202) 939-7027
(CONSULAR)
TEL: (202) 939-9850
FAX: (202) 797-4693

Comments on Asia Watch-PHR Report "Rape in Kashmir"

On May 9, Asia Watch-PHR have released a report "Rape in Kashmir: A Crime of War"

The methodology of the Report gives rise to serious doubts about its accuracy and impartiality. It is based on investigations conducted during a 7-day visit to Kashmir. Its findings can, therefore, be only as accurate as such a time frame would allow. The team did not, by choice, meet any Government official during its visit which further limits the objectivity of its findings. It did not give any indication of its intention to visit Kashmir and to that extent the exercise was conducted in a clandestine manner. The proclivity to unhesitatingly accept all allegations as true suggests the visit was utilised by interested parties to generate reports to further their political agenda.

Asia Watch's tendency to accept allegations as genuine is inexplicable considering that the report itself recognises the fear of militants among the population. It states that "most Kashmiris are reluctant to discuss abuses by militants out of fear of reprisal." It is the same fear and element of coercion used by militants which forces innocent civilians to make false allegations against security forces. Every allegation should, therefore, to be viewed against this background rather than be taken at face value.

It is encouraging to note that the report has at least acknowledged abuses committed by militants. Notwithstanding the difficulties Asia Watch may have had in obtaining details of such abuses, a glaring omission is the well documented case of a 19 year old girl Shahina of Handwara, who was kidnapped, criminally assaulted and tortured by various militant organisations including JKLF and Ikhwan-Ul-Musalmeen on suspicion of having sought the help of Border Security Force to identify two persons who had kidnapped her younger brother. Shahina was ultimately rescued by Border Security Force and the case came to light in early 1993. She has been interview by several major newspapers.

The report contains several sweeping generalisations about Government policy which are not supported by any detailed research or interviews but are based on value judgements, distortions of official statements and press reports. According to the report, for most Indian officials, rape is a rare but regrettable "excess". To the Government's knowledge, Asia Watch did not meet any official during the visit to Kashmir. The report states that the Administration in New Delhi has "essentially abrogated its responsibility to control its security forces". These are preposterous conclusions arrived at without any basis.

The Report tries to discern a "pattern of impunity" by Indian security forces in Kashmir where none exists. Actually the Report is only a recycling of allegations that have been made in the last three years and to which the Indian Government has already responded in detail. Unfortunately, many of those responses have been misinterpreted and twisted out of context. The Indian Government does not condone much less encourage human rights abuses by security forces. For example the statement that two of the alleged victims in the Shopian case were wives of terrorists is by no means an attempt to shirk responsibility. The Government's intention in bringing this fact to light was to caution Asia Watch about the possible motivations behind the allegations which would be to malign the security forces. It would be in the interest of Asia Watch's own credibility not to be used by groups which have an agenda which begins and ends with violence and terror. The Government's initiative to investigate the Kunan Poshpora case including by inviting the Press Council of India to investigate the matter is dismissed as a "Government campaign" to acquit the army of charges of human rights violations. This shows that Asia Watch proceeds from a fundamental distrust of all Government actions and statements.

And yet Asia Watch regularly calls for investigations to enquire into human rights abuses while simultaneously displaying an unwillingness, indeed an intolerance in accepting results of such investigations if they do not correspond to its own *a priori* views. The report questions the competence of Indian military courts, provisions of the Indian Evidence Act as well as the credentials of the Press Council of India -- practically, the credibility of every Indian institution.

Some cases cited by Asia Watch are factually wrong. Contrary to the assertion that security forces were never prosecuted in the Mubina Gani case, seven Border Security Force personnel have been suspended after a criminal case was registered and investigated.

The Report contains only one new allegation regarding the Jamir Qadeem case. This was not raised with the Indian Government earlier and efforts are now underway to ascertain the veracity of this allegation. In addition, there are references to some other cases of rape which Asia Watch claims to have documented. However, details such as even the names of alleged victims, location of the crime etc. are not provided and therefore it is not possible to comment on these allegations.

The Indian Government neither denies that human rights violations do occasionally occur nor rejects investigations by human rights groups. Indian human rights organisations are free to conduct investigations in all parts of the country including Punjab and Kashmir. In the case of international organisations, the Indian Government have held discussions with Amnesty International in 1992 for the first time in more than a decade and Asia Watch itself had visited Kashmir at least twice since 1990. Most recently, in March 1993, an ICRC delegation from Geneva held discussions with officials in New Delhi.

Indian security forces are under strict instructions to use the minimum force. But given the scale and sheer brutality of terrorist violence, some excesses by security forces do occur occasionally in combatting such violence. There are enough checks and balances in the Indian system to safeguard the rights of all people. All reported cases of human rights violations are dealt with firmly and those found guilty punished. In Kashmir more than 125 officers and men of the army and paramilitary forces have been prosecuted and proceeded against. In a number of cases where such enquiries are pending, security personnel have been placed under suspension. At the same time, a democratically elected Government is also mandated to act firmly against those who seek to subvert the rule of law and pursue an agenda through violence and terrorism. The question which needs to be addressed is whether terrorism is a legitimate means of political expression.

The Indian government has repeatedly stated its intention to initiate a political process in Kashmir. This is necessarily predicated on achieving a degree of normalcy at the ground. The climate of fear and terror unleashed by militant groups getting direct support from across the border is making the search for a democratic and political solution extremely difficult. Nevertheless, the political dialogue in Kashmir has begun even with those groups who continue to shoot at the security forces and indulge in other acts of violence.

Brief details on individual cases referred to in the Report are attached.

CLARIFICATIONS ON SPECIFIC CASES

(1) Mubina Gani case, May 1990:
The inquiry was held not by the police, but by a Staff Court of Inquiry. A criminal case was registered and investigated. Seven BSF personnel have been suspended.

(2) Jamir Qadeem case, June 1990:
This case has been raised for the first time by Asia Watch, and was not among the two allegations which Asia Watch had sent to the Indian government in advance of the publication of the report. Efforts are being made to ascertain the veracity of this allegation.

(3) Kunan Poshpora Case, February 1991:
This case was investigated not only by the government but by an independent and highly regarded body, the Press Council of India. The Divisional Commissioner of Kashmir, Wajahat Habibullah, after his inquiry into the allegation stated

> "While the veracity of complaint is thus highly doubtful, it still needs to be determined why such a complaint was made at all......I am of the opinion that the allegation of mass rape cannot be sustained" Another investigation at the level of Superintendent of Police concluded that the case was not fit to be prosecuted because of contradictions and gaps in the evidence.

The Press Council of India, in its report, stated:

> "It is held by some of those the Committee met that the mass rape story was an afterthought, retailed and orchestrated by the militants and their sympathisers and mentors to denigrate the Indian Army. It was the militants' revenge.... Kunan lies in a heavily militant-infested area along the main infiltration routes from POX (Pakistan occupied Kashmir) from where arms supplies, train personnel, ideological material and strategic doctrines flow. Kunan is vulnerable too. Unless far better evidence is forthcoming, the Kunan rape story stands totally unproven and completely untrue, a dirty trick to frame the army and get it to lay off Kunan Poshpura - which is precisely what it has done"

(4) Shopian Case, October 19,1992:
The case was enquired into by a senior officer of the army as well as by an officer of the level of Senior Superintendent of Police, M.M. Rafiqi, who concluded that the complaints and the evidence were both unreliable and the allegations could not be sustained. Two independent enquiries thus came to the same conclusion, exposing the efforts of militants to make false charges and terrorise or otherwise use innocent citizens to discredit the security forces.

(5) Haran Case, July 1992:
Details of this case have been provided to Amnesty International, an organisation which Asia Watch's report frequently quotes. At the time of the search operations, conducted by the army, no complaint of rape was made. A complaint had subsequently been filed before the Deputy Commissioner of the District and on enquiry, it was found that the house of the complainant had not even been searched. More details are being ascertained.

(6) Gurihakhar case, October 19,1992:
There was an exchange of fire between security forces and militants in which one army personnel was killed, two injured and a number of civilians died in cross fire. There was no report of any rape as alleged even when senior district officials visited the site after the incident. Asia Watch's comment is at best a sweeping generalisation without any basis in fact.

(7) The report refers to a few incidents to illustrate that "even when investigations are ordered, they do not result in prosecutions." Unfortunately, no details such as names of alleged victims, location of the incident etc. are given which would enable the Government to comment on these allegations.

(8) Killing of Kashmiri Human Rights Activists-1992 1993:
Asia Watch's keenness to provide instant judgement on the killings of Messrs. Wanchoo, Ashai and Guru and to weave a pattern into the killings and suggest Government complicity reveals the danger of reporting based on incomplete facts. As a footnote to the Report attempts to suggest, there could be more than meets the eye to these killings. Investigation of Mr. Wanchoo's death has clearly established the involvement of Jamait-Ul-Mujahideen, a pro-Pakistani militant group. Mr. Wanchoo, was an active member of the Kashmiri Hindu Forum and was perceived as a threat by this group which felt he was being used to give a secular colour to the anti-Government movement. In the case of Dr. Ashai, most of the reports that appeared in the local press (which Asia

Watch freely quotes in other instances) and enquiries made so far establish that -- there was an exchange of fire between security forces and militants following a grenade attack by the militants in that area around the time Dr. Ashai was driving past, that Dr. Ashai was not stopped at any para-military check point, and that he was in fact helped by CRPF personnel immediately into his car so that his daughter could drive him to the hospital. Dr. Guru's killing, it is widely believed, was the work of Hizb Ul Mujahideen, a pro-Pakistani fundamentalist group which has a running battle with the JKLF to which Dr. Guru was aligned.

Only 15 days before this incident, there were cases of kidnappings and killings of important personalities as a result of this rivalry.

(9) Migration of Hindus out of Kashmir Valley:

Figures quoted in the report as well as the insinuation that the migration was encouraged by Government officials fly in the face of established facts and rationality. 72,000 families consisting of Hindus, Sikhs and Muslims totalling nearly 300,000 have had to flee the Valley since the outbreak of militant violence there. Anyone who is familiar with the militancy in Kashmir would be aware of the radical ideology followed by some of the militant groups, who have no pretensions about their commitment to Islamic fanaticism. It would require ingenious logic to explain why the Indian Government should have encouraged such migration and force Hindus to live in refugee camps in different parts of the country. For centuries, not only has the Kashmiri Hindu community shared the Kashmir Valley with the majority Muslim population as Asia Watch notes, but for centuries Kashmir itself has been a part of India and Muslims and Hindus in India have peacefully co-existed.

The Human Rights Watch has issued its World Report for 1992 with a section on India. Some general comments are made with reference to the methodology and choice of issues included in the Report. Thereafter, government's findings with respect to some specific allegations are set out.

General

1. The Asia Watch team did not get in touch with any Officials during their visit to India in October 1992 to try to verify their assertions.

4. The Report does not take cognizance of the scale and dimension of the proxy war being fought on Indian territory as shown by the seizure by security forces of over 10,000 highly sophisticated weapons including over 7,000 rifles of the AK series, remote controlled explosive devices,

rockets, rocket launchers and communication systems in the last three years. Moreover, these weapons are only a fraction of the total quantities obtained by terrorists in Kashmir from across the border.

I. <u>Asia Watch</u>

Four students who were arrested during a search operation on October 14 in the Dal Gate area of Srinagar were shot dead that night and their bodies handed over to their families the next day. The security forces also broke up peaceful protests against these killings by beating, teargassing and shooting demonstrators;

<u>Government's findings</u>

The incident relates to a case of a joint operation by the Border Security Force and the Police. On October 14, 1992 when the party was approaching Dal Gate, militants opened fire which was returned by the security forces. During a search of the area, four bodies of terrorists who had been killed were found along with 3 AK 56 rifles with magazines and ammunition, a pistol with magazine and ammunition, two grenades and some documents and binoculars etc. The bodies of all the four terrorists were handed over to the Police. It would be clear from this that this was a targeted operation based on information and the persons who were killed can by no means be categorized as innocent students.

II. <u>Asia Watch</u>

On October 15, a man and woman were burned alive in Badasgam when Border Security Force troops locked them in a shop and torched it and ten other buildings after mistaking a sonic boom for a militant attack. An army investigator later confirmed that the troops' action was "unprovoked".

<u>Government's findings</u>

Three vehicles of the BSF were passing through the area of Badasgam when they heard two blasts which caused them to believe that they were being ambushed. They opened fire due to which a few shops got burnt. In the search, following the incident two bodies with bullet marks and 90% burns were found. Lt. General Zaki, Adviser to Governor, along with Inspector General, BSF Srinagar visited the place of occurrence and announced financial assistance to the families of the affected persons. In addition, a Special Court of Inquiry has been ordered to inquire into the incident and if anybody is found guilty of any excesses, action will be taken against him as per the law.

III. <u>Asia Watch</u>

On October 1, militants ambushed a patrol near the village of Battekut, killing one. In reprisal, the security forces rampaged through the village, killing ten villagers, raping four women and burning houses and grain stores.

<u>Government's findings</u>

The incident actually relates to a village called Bhaki Haker near Handwara in Kupwara District. When the army was engaged in cordon and search operations in the village it was fired upon by militants as a result of which one army personnel was killed and two injured. During exchange of fire the militants managed to disengage and escape. While escaping they were intercepted by another column of the army located outside the village. The militants discharged a heavy volume of fire including fire from rocket launchers. Due to the firing a thatched hut with paddy stocked outside caught fire. Before the fire could be contained with the help of fire tenders, which were rushed to the scene, 40 houses had been gutted. During the exchange of fire 10 civilians including three women also died. Senior District officials visited the site and an ex gratia relief of Rs.100000 to the next of kin of the deceased villagers and one month's free ration to those whose houses had been affected was immediately announced. During the search 1 AK 47 rifle was recovered from the area.

IV. <u>Asia Watch</u>

Eight women and an eleven-year-old girl were raped during a search operation by an army unit near Shopian on October 10.

<u>Government's findings</u>

Enquiries in the matter revealed that on October 10/11 the army contingent stationed near Chak-i-Saidpura, in the jurisdiction of Police Station Shopian, conducted search operations in the village on specific information that some militants were hiding there. The search operations were carried out from 0010 hours to 0145 hours during which 7 houses were searched in the presence of an elderly man. Each house was searched in the presence of male members and no female member was taken out of the house. The residents of the 7 houses identified and confirmed that the same 3 army persons had entered and searched each house and hence it is difficult to believe that the same persons could have indulged in acts of rape in different houses within a span of 1 hour and 35 minutes. Two of the women who have been alleged to haven been raped were wives of terrorists viz. Takub Hussain a Platoon Commander of Hizbul Mujahideen and Mohd. Yakub a Group Commander of the same militant group. It has also been observed that only four, including the above two women, out of the 9 women allegedly raped, had been medically examined. The reason for medical examination not having been got done in the remaining cases continues to be a mystery. As regards alleged rape of the 12 year old girl, Zia Toon it was found on enquiry that she was sleeping with her two sisters and her mother in a one room hut. During the enquiry she was not found to have any visible signs or marks of injury or any physical excesses nor did she display any sense of fear or anger and appeared to be oblivious of the alleged incident. The army carried out further search in the same village on October 12/13 and apprehended two militants along with one AK 47 rifle and one universal machinegun. Nevertheless, a case has been registered in Police Station Shopian under the relevant sections of the Law and has been transferred to the special investigating branch viz. the Crime Branch of the State for thorough investigation.